ALL THE WAY OUT OF BABYLON

RE-ORDERING THE CHURCH

Dennis R. Moel

Re-ordering the Church
By Dennis Moel

Printed in the United States of America

ISBN # 13:978-1493646012
ISBN # 10: 149364601X

All rights reserved solely by the author. The author guarantees all contents are original and do not infringe upon the legal rights of any other person or work. No part of this book may be reproduced in any form without the permission of the author. The views expressed in this book are not necessarily those of the publisher.

Unless otherwise indicated, *Bible* quotations are taken from the *King James Version, New King James Version, New International Version, New American Standard Version, Living Bible, New Living Translation, Revised Standard Version*, or the author's own free rendering.

All the Way out of Babylon
Re-ordering the Church

Foreword	4
Introduction	6
1. One Accord	11
2. Apostles and Elders	15
3. Apostolic Disorder	25
4. Coming out of Babylon	29
5. The Synagogue Factor	41
6. The Fate and the Destiny of Churches	55
7. The Sanhedrin	65
8. The Restoration of the Church	75
9. Re-establishing a Local Church	91
10. Confirming the Saints	109
11. Making Disciples	113
12. Rabbinic Discipleship in Jesus' Day	125
13. In Favor of Home Churches	133
14. Lay Hands Suddenly on No Man	139
15. Laying on of Hands	151
16. The Ministry of Melchizedek Today	159
17. The Basque Sheep Herder	181
18. Pastoral Counseling	187
19. Restoring the Ministry of Prophets	195
20. Going on to Perfection	205
21. Saviors	215
22. Doing the Lord's Work	225

ILLUSTRATIONS

The Altar, St. Peters, Rome	Front Cover
Russian Orthodox Church, Jerusalem	6
Ancient Babylon	23
Christ Church Cathedral	24
Mesmeah Yeshua Synagogue	36
Greater Bethel Apostolic Church	36
St. Peters	60
Laying on of Hands	98
Home Church, First Century	110
Home Church, Singapore	118
Shepherd and Sheep	169
Marriage Counseling	170
College of Cardinals	Back Cover

FOREWORD

My humble conviction is that this book, at this time in history, meets an urgent and important spiritual need in the church. In addition, it also responds to a set of personal beliefs I have adopted over the years from studying the Bible: The assurance that the church will be restored, the realization that the church is not there yet and the power of small group work. As far as I know, there are not many books dealing with the subject of the restoration of the church. In fact, this very idea is not very popular at all. However, I would like to suggest that, if we are only honest with ourselves, we need to acknowledge that, as far as spiritual effectiveness and growth are concerned, we are not yet where we ought to be. There is still much to be learned from the way the early church operated.

Regarding the power of small group work (discipleship, small group prayer meetings, etc.), this book helped me make the leap toward a wonderful discovery: the New Testament church was actually composed of small groups, home churches! Never did I pause enough to think about that. This insight actually put things under a very different light. It gives way to a whole different dynamic in church operation where every member becomes an active and important part of the larger "body", thus allowing them to rely on God's Spirit, exercise their spiritual abilities and become effective for the kingdom. These small groups also allow more intimacy and a deeper personal connection between members of the church. More care is therefore provided to individual saints who are more likely to grow into mature disciples. In fact, the term "disciple" is perhaps the most common New Testament term applied to individual Christians and it implies that we are to be learners, listening to our teachers and doing what they do until we become like them. We are to become like Christ, our model, both individually and as a group.

But how did we get out of that model? This is another issue the book seeks to solve. Besides the various influences affecting the early church, from Greek philosophy to Roman paganism and politics, Brother Moel suggests the heavy impact of Jewish synagogue worship and organization. This idea bears much weight when we consider that it comes from a Bible student with deep Jewish backgrounds. Moreover, it appears to be supported by the Bible, history and literary evidence.

How then do we move forward to restoration, "all the way out of Babylon"? We need, like Brother Moel, to seek God's patterns for the church in the Word and be willing to reject any human tradition that is not supported by Scripture. These patterns should help bring back correct church operation and leadership models. For that purpose, we need to entertain deep trust in God, knowing that his ways work. In spite of the reluctance we may feel, He will be protecting his church, ensuring that He is in control. Eventually, this work of restoration we have been studying about and longing for will be achieved by God and God Himself. It will be "not by might, nor by power, but by my spirit, saith the LORD of hosts." *Zechariah* 4:6

I thank the Lord for the insights He gave to Brother Dennis Moel, who undertook the challenging task of writing this book. As a personal friend of mine for years, I have had the opportunity to share with Brother Moel on a number of topics and I have enjoyed his understanding of the *Bible*, especially when it comes to Old Testament pictures. May the Lord keep blessing him and using him for the restoration of His Body! We all have a personal responsibility in this work for "the path of the just is as the shining light, that shineth more and more unto the perfect day." *Proverbs* 4:18

God bless your reading!

Paul-Émile César

Paul-Emile Cesar is a business and translation professional in Haiti, where he serves as a pastor under the oversight of Lemoine Masse and Alfred Daves.

ALL THE WAY OUT OF BABYLON

INTRODUCTION

Throughout the history of mankind religion has played a key role. There is no tribe that has not had its gods and their worship rituals. The ritual leaders have always been among the most important people in the society. These priests and shamans continuously have held great sway and influence in the daily, social life of the populace.

Not only have human beings had their religions, but they have also had religious centers, specific places where their gods might be worshipped. Religion required a worship center. Religion requires a worship center. Archeologists have been able to locate them in the ruins of most ancient civilizations.

How ancient is religion? Where might we find its origin? Could it be with Enoch, the seventh generation of Adam?
Genesis 5:22 And Enoch walked with God.

Hebrews 11:5 He had this testimony, that he pleased God.

This language had not been previously referred to anyone. Enoch taught his off-spring of his faith, which was faithfully passed on to Methusaleh to Lamech to Noah. After the flood God gave some specific instructions:
Genesis 9:4 But you shall not eat flesh with its life, that is, its blood.

Religion offers a code of conduct, and this was the first rule given. God made a covenant with Noah, the sign of which was the rainbow. It was but a short time till the worship of *Elohim*, the true God, was perverted by Nimrod, Noah's great-grandson, who
Genesis 10:8,9 began to be a mighty one on the earth. He was a mighty hunter before the Lord.

"Before the Lord" shows us that Nimrod's enterprise was religious. His movement culminated in a religious center.
Genesis 11:4 Come, let us build ourselves a city, and a tower whose top is in the heavens; let us make a name for ourselves, lest we be scattered abroad over the face of the whole earth.

That God was displeased with Babel, its tower, and its religion is evidenced that He confused their language and scattered them abroad. (We might note that the word "Babel" is a play on the word "Baal.") Religion did not end at Babel, for men took their particular version wherever they migrated. And, the custom of building towers and initiating priests to officiate in them spread, as

well. This was an alternative religion to the worship of the true God, and its origin was in rebellion. Asshur carried Babylonianism north to his new city of Ninevah, where the cult worship was enthusiastically evangelized to the world. Of perverted Ninevah, the prophet declared:
> *Nahum 3:4 ...the multitude of the whoredoms of the well-favored harlot, the mistress of witchcrafts, who sells nations through her whoredoms, and families through her witchcrafts.*

God spoke to Abram, who heard Him and obeyed Him and faithfully translocated away from his pagan surroundings.
> *Genesis 12:7-9 Then the Lord appeared to Abram and said, "To your descendants I will give this land." And there **he built an altar** to the Lord, who had appeared to him. And he moved from there to the mountain east of **Bethel**, and he pitched his tent with Bethel on the west and Ai on the east; there he built an altar to the Lord and <u>called on the Name of the Lord</u>.*

When Jacob, his grandson, spent a night there, the Lord also appeared to him. Jacob called the place: *Beth-el*, the House of God.
> *Genesis 28:16-18 Then Jacob awoke from his sleep and said, "Surely the Lord is in this place, and I did not know it." And he was afraid and said, "How awesome is this place! This is none other than the house of God, and this is the gate of heaven!" Then Jacob rose early in the morning, and took the stone that he had put at his head, set it up as **a pillar**, and poured oil on top of it. And he called the name of that place <u>Bethel</u>.*

Both Abram and Jacob erected shrines, memorials to their experiences with the Lord.

Later on, after the Israelites had left the bondage of Egypt, God instructed them on building a tent in the desert, a place where some Presence of God might reside. In the reign of King Solomon, a permanent temple was erected, and the Presence dwelt in it. Religion had to have a particular site for God to dwell.

Unfortunately, the Israelites were none too faithful, but blended false religion into their worship, for which they were punished by being expelled from their country and carried away captive. The Temple was destroyed, but God gave them reprieve seventy years later, and they constructed a second Temple.

The most marvelous thing occurred five hundred years later in Jerusalem, the grandest thing that ever happened: the holy spirit of God fell on those who were believing in Jesus of Nazareth. The evidence was that when the spirit entered into them, they began speaking in another language, the utterance of which was God-inspired and unintelligible but to Him. For the next two thousand years believers in Jesus Christ have been receiving the indwelling of God's spirit. Now, God had entered <u>into</u> the believers, who themselves became a habitation of God. In short, they became temples, themselves. No longer did men have to construct grand edifices in which they worshipped God. Individuals now housed God, Himself; He became ever-present, as near as their breath.

Thousands of Jews received this spiritual experience, and subsequently it began happening to non-Jews, too, who likewise came to believe on Yeshua-Jesus.

However, there were those Jews who came to Yeshua-Jesus who were very religious, steeped in the old ways of worshipping Yehovah. They were able to completely comprehend that a new phase of the Kingdom of God had been inaugurated. They were staunch in their belief that only Jews could receive this new salvation, that one must first become a Jew to enter into God. In particular, they insisted that the rite of circumcision must be administered to gentile converts, and that they must observe the Jewish Sabbath.

Further, the practice of the housing of the Church in synagogue-like buildings crept into the early Church. As we have discussed in more detail in Chapter 4, Emperor Constantine impelled the Church into newly-built buildings and also into vacated old pagan temples. Over the centuries Christian churches have become very elaborate and utilitarian, meeting the needs and comfort of the people. Sadly, housing the Church of God in buildings has had the effect of formalizing meetings and diminishing the free flow and exercise of the holy spirit.

However, this has not altered the Plan of God, which still holds sway:

> *Hebrews 9:11 So Christ has now become the High Priest over all the good things that have come. He has entered that great, perfect sanctuary in heaven, **not made by human hands** and not part of this created world.*

That the beautiful Church of God has declined to a system of formality, religiosity, custom, tradition, ritual and routine is what the Almighty has been correcting little-by-little since Martin Luther and the Protestant Reformation. It is the purpose of this work to expose the apostate teachings and rules to which God's Church has become accustomed, and to encourage the reader to be liberated from the bondage of Babylon.

The greatest Move of God ever is just before us, the culmination of which will be the utter destruction of Babylonian practices forever. I believe that the God of Heaven has put it on my heart to prod you toward the complete restoration of Light in the Great and Holy Congregation. Be careful before going further with this book, because God will surely hold you personally accountable for any truths revealed herein. [I pray the Holy One will reveal to me the errors I may have made in this book.] It is a danger to know what the truth is, but yet to continue to compromise with paganism. **It is time to cease trying to perfect Babylon**.

How can you declare to others to come out of Babylon, when you are still dawdling in it, yourself? "Religion" requires a worship center. Religion requires a worship center. But, true worshippers of God worship Him in the spirit and in truth. They are God's building. That's all He requires.

Dennis R. Moel
Louisville, Kentucky
August 16, 2010

9   All the Way out of Babylon

The author Dennis R. Moel on the Mount of Olives; gold domes of the Russian Orthodox Church

*Isaiah 13:19 And Babylon, the glory of kingdoms, the **beauty** of the Chaldeans' pride,
will be as when God overthrew Sodom and Gomorrah.*

10 All the Way out of Babylon

*Psalm 133:1 Behold, how good and how pleasant it is for brethren to dwell together in **unity**!*

Chapter 1. One Accord

Jesus said:
John 6:38 I have come down from heaven, not to do My own will, but the Will of Him who sent Me.

Palms 40:8 I delight to do Your will, O my God.

One could say many things of the relationship of God the Father and His Son. But, one thing that would stand near the top of the list is that they always agree. They are in such unity that Jesus could even say:
*John 10:30 I and My Father are **one**.*

*John 17:11 Holy Father, keep through Your name those whom You have given Me, that they may be **one** as We are.*

Jesus prayed to God that His followers could be in unity as They were. One might pass over that statement without noticing the import of it. When you stop and consider that we could be in unity and in agreement at all times, Jesus' desire for us begins to sound like its fulfillment might be impossible.

Actually, that is the test! We, who are so very different in temperaments, and goals, and moods, and likes and dislikes and personalities, how can we be in unity? How can we even get along? I say, that's the test! Can it be done at all?

We have it on record that at one time this was true of the Believers. Before the Day of Pentecost there were one hundred twenty gathered in "the upper room."
*Acts 1:14 These all continued with **one accord** in prayer and supplication, with the women and Mary the mother of Jesus, and with His brothers.*

"With one accord" denotes the entire harmony of their views and feelings. This was a dangerous time; their leader had been killed; they were in peril. Yet, there were no schisms, no divided interests, no discordant purposes. They were knit by a bond stronger than death. They were together in holy love, and that there were no quarrels or friction among them. They continued that way.
*Acts 2:1 When the Day of Pentecost had fully come, they were all with **one accord** in one place.*

They were of such unity that they thoroughly impressed three thousand that day. And every day thereafter they still impressed everyone.
*Acts 2:46,47 So continuing daily with **one accord** in the temple, and breaking bread from house to house, they ate their food with gladness and simplicity of heart, praising God and having favor with all the people. And the Lord added to the church daily those who were being saved.*

They were a true picture of genuine Christian fellowship. They were not perplexed or anxious. Out in the open in the courtyard of the Temple where all their enemies could see and hear, they were untouched. Of all the miracles they performed, all the testimonies they gave of the risen Christ, nothing was more impressive than their bond of love.

Once, Peter had been arrested. What did they do? They gather together to pray:
Acts 4:27-33 "For truly against Your holy Servant Jesus, whom You anointed, both Herod and Pontius Pilate, with the Gentiles and the people of Israel, were gathered together to do whatever Your hand and Your purpose determined before to be done. Now, Lord, look on their threats, and grant to Your servants that with all boldness they may speak Your word, by stretching out Your hand to heal, and that signs and wonders may be done through the name of Your holy Servant Jesus." And when they had prayed, the place where they were assembled together was shaken; and they were all filled with the holy spirit, and they spoke the Word of God *with boldness. Now the multitude of those who believed were of* **one heart and one soul***; neither did anyone say that any of the things he possessed was his own, but they had all things in common.*

Think of it! They were not concerned of luxurious living or aspiring after the vain objects of the people of the world. What they possessed, they knew was really God's, theirs but for a season.

They were in a state of the most perfect friendship and affection. Then five thousand more were added to their ranks, and they all appeared to be but one heart and one soul; so perfectly did they agree in all their views, religious opinions, and holy affections.

There was no kind of difference or dissension among them.

What could one state of friends that would be more striking than to say: "They have one soul?" There could be no greater demonstration of union and love than to say of more than five thousand suddenly drawn together that they had one soul! And this union they demonstrated in every way possible--in their conduct, in their prayers, and in their property. What might have been the picture of the church, if the union had continued to the present time?!!!

We ought to point out that those believers were Jews, people who notoriously can never agree. Someone said that if there were two Jews in a room, they would have three opinions. And, these people had been of different sects among the Jews, before their conversions; they also once had friction upon civil matters; but now these were all forgotten and laid aside, and they were unanimous in the faith of Christ, and, being all joined to the Lord, they were joined to one another in holy love. This was the blessed fruit of Christ's dying-precept to his disciples, to love one another, and his dying prayer for them, that they all might be "one." We have reason to think they divided themselves into several congregations, or worshipping assemblies, according as their dwellings were, under their respective ministers; and yet this occasioned no jealousy or uneasiness; for they were all of one heart, and one soul, notwithstanding; and loved those of other flocks as truly as those of their own. Thus it was then, and, if we faint not, we may see it so again, when the spirit shall be poured out upon us from on high.

One cannot comprehend the heavenly power and authority attendant upon a folk so unified. It was not even possible to get away with a lie in such an environment, as did Ananias and his wife Sapphira, who lied about the amount of money they had made on the sale of property. First he, then she fell dead before Peter.

*Acts 5:10-13 Then immediately she fell down at his feet and breathed her last. And the young men came in and found her dead, and carrying her out, buried her by her husband. So, great fear came upon all the church and upon all who heard these things. And through the hands of the apostles many signs and wonders were done among the people. And they were all with **one accord** in Solomon's Porch.*

The miracles they wrought proved their divine mission. There were not a few, but many, of divers kinds and often repeated; there were signs and wonders, such wonders as were confessedly signs of a divine presence and power. They were not done "in a corner."

These miracles proved their divine mission. Many miracles, oft repeated, signs and wonders, undoubtedly due to the divine Presence and Power, were performed. These sometimes happened in quite public places, such as Solomon's Porch in the Temple courtyard. The rulers of the people had no choice but to permit their congregating there. This all happened that the Good News might spread the more. Even many of the priests converted to Yeshua, the Christ, which was amazing in its own right, since they had previously believed there was no messiah at all.

The saints were in one accord; they were unanimous in what they preached, how they worshipped, what they taught. There was no discontent or murmuring about the death of Ananias and Sapphira, as there had been against Moses and Aaron about the death of Korah and his company:

Numbers 16:41 You have killed the people of the Lord.

I think no one said a word against the twelve. (Moses would have been most impressed.)

But, that was a special time; it was like a honeymoon, if you please. The farther one got away from Calvary in both time and geography, the people's humanity began to intrude. The followers of Yeshua were, after all, just people. They believed in Christ, but they discovered that they still possessed their old opinions and natures, too.

Not that God has been dismayed; He was prepared for this from the beginning. What a task Paul had in dealing with all those different nationalities and backgrounds! I would like for you to notice, after all was said and done, however, what the bottom line was for God's Church:

*Romans 15:5,6 Now may the God of patience and comfort grant you to be **like-minded** toward one another, according to Christ Jesus, that you may with **one mind and one mouth** glorify the God and Father of our Lord Jesus Christ.*

*2 Corinthians 13:11 Finally, brethren, farewell. Be perfect, be of good comfort, be of **one mind**, live in peace; and the God of love and peace shall be with you.*

Philippians 1:27,28 Only let your conduct be worthy of the Gospel of Christ, so that whether I come and see you or am absent, I may hear of your affairs, that you stand fast in one *spirit, with **one mind** striving together for the faith of the gospel.*

*Philippians 2:2 Fulfill my joy, that ye be **likeminded**, having the same love, being of **one accord, of one mind**.*

The apostle Peter expressed those same sentiments:
*1 Peter 3:8,9 **Finally**, all of you be of **one mind**, having compassion for one another; love as brothers, be tenderhearted, be courteous; not returning evil for evil or reviling for reviling, but on the contrary blessing, knowing that you were called to this, that you may inherit a blessing.*

Where did the saints get such a doctrine of unity? Why, it came from none other than Jesus, Himself:
*Matthew 18.19 Again I say to you that **if two of you agree** on earth concerning anything that they ask, it will be done for them by My Father in heaven.*

It has been the sad history of the Church of Jesus for the saints to get embroiled in controversy and strife and bickering. It is not possible to number all the Christian churches that have split; I almost think we must have invented the sword "split." How repugnant to God that must be!

God has always loved unity; He has always blessed it magnificently. For example, there are all kinds of analogies and sermons to be preached about the unity that existed the day Solomon's Temple was dedicated.
*2 Chronicles 5:13-14 It came to pass, when the trumpeters and singers **were as one**, to make one sound to be heard in praising and thanking the Lord, and when they lifted up their voice with the trumpets and cymbals and instruments of music, and praised the Lord, saying: "For He is good, For His mercy endures forever," that the House, the House of the Lord, was filled with a cloud, so that the priests could not continue ministering because of the cloud; for the glory of the Lord filled the House of God.*

God honors unity. I look forward to something like this following to happen again. There was a time when King Hezekiah invited the other tribes of Israel to move to Jerusalem so that they might fully serve God.
*2 Chronicles 30:12 The Hand of God was on Judah to give them **singleness of heart** to obey the command of the king and the leaders, at the Word of the Lord.*

With the Church today divided and tattered, we might repeat Paul's exhortation:
*Ephesians 4:1-3 I beseech you to walk worthy of the calling with which you were called, with all lowliness and gentleness, with longsuffering, bearing with one another in love, endeavoring to keep the **unity of the spirit** in the bond of peace*

How am I doing in my relationships with others? Do I clash with my brother, parents, child, wife, teacher, anyone? I might not be judged worthy of eternal life when God requires love and unity. Actually, nothing less will do. Unity!
Psalm 133:3 This is where the Lord has commanded the blessing, even life for evermore.

Is it possible for such unity to be restored to Jesus' holy congregation? How could it happen? What changes would have to be made? Who would instigate it?

Surely our fathers have inherited lies!
Jeremiah 16:19

Chapter 2. Apostles and Elders

It has certainly been our desire and goal to see the restoration of the Church of Jesus Christ at the conclusion of the Gentile Age. We look forward to the full operation and manifestation of the holy spirit in the Body of Christ, especially miracles and healings.

We would, however, be foolish to think that it is merely a matter of waiting for God's timing for all this to unfold. It would be absurd to think that there is nothing on our part that needs changing. One definition of insanity might be: doing something the same way over and over, and expecting different results.

It is my point that there are, indeed, some things that we might change, perhaps need to change, and one of those things might involve church order. I have <u>begun</u> a list of thoughts and ideas which, if employed, could make a difference in our assemblies and in the lives of the saints.

You might get a notion, when considering the following, that I am being critical of the way things are right now, that I'm reproving different ones and certain places for being incorrect here and there. I am not. I have had no particular person or place in my mind at any time. Yet, I'm sure that all of us and all of our assemblies fall short here and there on this point and that point. Some of us are strong in one area and weak in another.

Also, what follows is not meant to become law. Nor is it meant to become a handbook of regulations for the "normal" Christian Church.[*1] As a matter of fact, I expect to see great variations between individuals and localities. And what may be God's Way here may not be over there.

Actually, don't you think that was the case in the early church? For example, what happened to those three thousand who received the holy ghost on the Day of Pentecost? We see that many of them were visitors to Jerusalem who heard the praises of God in their native tongues. They did not remain in the city and became part of that glorious church there, but rather, after Pentecost they returned to their homes, families, and jobs in their native countries.

Those folks got the holy ghost and went back home to Asia and Crete (*Titus* 1:5) and Cappadocia and Bithynia and Parthia. If so, are we to imagine that they went back home and said nothing about what happened in their lives? Why, no. I imagine that they could hardly contain themselves. I suspect that many more people were touched by their testimonies. I suspect that there were groups of "new believers" in the synagogues everywhere. If that be so, do you think that these scattered groups somehow came into "apostolic order," or do you think that they were serving their Lord and Savior in a variety of ways that might <u>not</u> have been perfect order? Perhaps they came to Jerusalem for the holidays, met with the elders, and received some guidance for the works back home. If there were these scattered believers, there is nothing in the *scriptures* that says the apostles went to them. All we know about in those earliest years after Christ regards only the church established in Jerusalem.

After the persecution concerning Stephen, the Jerusalem assembly was put in disarray, and the saints were scattered everywhere. We know for sure that the church in Antioch, Syria began precisely in this way and at that time. Probably there were others.

And probably, these works were apart from the local synagogues. And probably, these works included non-Jews. Consider the prophets and teachers in the Antioch assembly besides Barnabas and Saul, who were Jews. There was one named Manaen, who was raised in Herod's home. His name appears to not be Jewish. Lucius of Syrene has a Roman name. And lastly, Simeon, who was also called Niger, does have a Jewish name, and seems to have been a Negro. Just from this handful of men, we could imagine that the Antioch church was a mish-mash of people.

I am suggesting that many assemblies started in a variety of ways, just as our assemblies in these last days began. I am suggesting that those assemblies, regardless of their beginnings, strove to come into "divine order." Is it possible that eventually apostles came here and there and established order? Did these Jewish saints visit Peter in Jerusalem during the early days? Peter seems to have felt responsible for them; he wrote to them.

> *1 Peter 1:1 Peter, an apostle of Jesus Christ, to those* [Jewish believers] *who reside as aliens, scattered throughout Pontus, Galatia, Cappadocia, Asia, and Bithynia, who are chosen* (NASU).

Regardless of how the Antioch, Syria church began, there is no doubt (*Acts* 13:1-4 and *Acts* 14:26-28) that it became well-ordered.

The church in Rome was another story. Not only did it likely not begin apostolically, but it had a variety of people, including saints from all parts of the Empire of various nationalities, local slaves and run-away slaves, royalty, and paupers. We must conclude from Paul's letter to them, somehow they had come into God's order.

Over all, there was likely much variation between assemblies in the early days of the church. I suspect that in these last days you will not be able to put all the churches into the same mold, either. And this will be pleasing to God, and it will be divine order.

I would like to make a few comments regarding how much we know about the *Biblical* apostles. Truly, only about Paul do we know a great deal. *Scripture* tells us a little about Peter and John. Some of the things we've heard about them in "tradition" are plausible. We are also told that Thomas went to India and established many churches there. Then he went with Thaddeus and Bartholomew to Assyria. James, John's brother, was killed early on. Of the rest, we know almost nothing. But, you can be sure that they were actively working, moving around, at the behest of the holy ghost. We wish we knew more so that we could know more about God's order.

There is one person who knows exactly how the Body operated back then: the Head of the Body. What we have written in this book is just a scratch on the surface of what we need to know. I say: there is no choice left to but to devote ourselves to corporate pray and fasting, that we might show Him how sincere we are to know what we need to know. Fast and pray! Pray and fast!

Another point I would have you consider is the situation and circumstance of a local church after its apostle has passed on. It is given that after an apostle (or a pair of apostles) establish a local church in a city, that it is established, and that **no other apostle** may come to that place and establish another work. Once the work is established, that's the work of God in that city. Anything else that happens there must be under the auspices of that church. After the founding apostle(s) has died, no other man can be the apostle of that church. That church can still be in apostolic order, because elders were ordained from the start. Years later, new apostles, prophets, teachers, and evangelists may minister to that church, but none of them can become "its apostle."

Had it not been for the "falling away," probably there would be old assemblies in existence today that could trace their line back to the ancient beginning of that work.

It is curious to me that Jesus actually allowed his church to fall away. Certainly, this didn't <u>have</u> to happen. But, such was fore-ordained:
2 Thessalonians 2:3 That day shall not come, except there come a falling away first.

Acts 20:29,30 For I know this, that after my departing shall grievous wolves enter in among you, not sparing the flock. Also of your own selves shall men arise, speaking perverse things, to draw away disciples after them.

It seems that the "perfect church" is an elusive thing, doesn't it? And when you consider that the church <u>must</u> have its "vessels of dishonor," its Ananiases and Sapphiras, I should not imagine the perfect church doesn't and will not exist in this age.

It was previously said that it would be foolish to expect different results when we keep doing things the same comfortable way we've always done them. If we are to go on to that place we believe God has ordained for the Body of Christ, we will have to bust out of our warm, dark, velvet cocoons of yesterday. Truly, many things in our pasts have **not** been done according to *Scripture*. However, we couldn't say, "God wasn't in them," could we? He was. This is part of the great variety of which I have been speaking. On the other hand, we ought not expect God to continue to bless, continue to honor what has been revealed to us as "out-of-order." He may have winked at our ignorance, but He does have <u>His</u> Way. I want that, don't you?

Following are a collection of some guidelines that are intended to direct us to greater and greater divine order.

1. Although some elders in a local church may submit to another elder in spiritual matters, all elders in a local assembly are equal <u>with regard to governance</u>.

2. Elders' decisions should (and will) be unanimous, since they are each receiving their directions from the Head.
Proverbs 11:14 Where no counsel is, the people fall: but in the multitude of counselors there is safety.

3. Elders not only administrate, but they teach and counsel.
*Acts 20:28 Take heed therefore unto yourselves, and to all the flock, over the which the holy ghost has made you **overseers**, to **feed** the church of God...*

*Titus 1:9 Holding fast the faithful word as he has been taught, that he may be able by sound doctrine both to **exhort** and to **convince** the gainsayers.*

*1 Peter 5:2 **Feed** the flock of God which is among you, taking the **oversight** thereof, not by constraint, but willingly; not for filthy lucre, but of a ready mind.*

4. The <u>local</u> church sends out apostles.
Acts 13:3 And when they had fasted and prayed, and laid their hands on

*them, they **sent** them away.*

5. Apostles are to start new works.

6. Apostles are <u>not</u> to settle down in a work they have established; ***they are travelers, not settlers.***
   *Acts 13:4-6 So they, being **sent** forth by the holy ghost, departed unto Seleucia; and from thence they sailed to Cyprus. And when they were at Salamis, they preached the Word of God in the synagogues of the Jews: and they had also John to their minister. And when they had gone through the isle unto Paphos...*

7. Apostles are to ordain elders, who are the ones who will care for a work.
   *Acts 14:21-23 And when they had preached the gospel to that city, and had taught many, they returned again to Lystra, and to Iconium, and Antioch (not Antioch of Syria, but Antioch of Pisidia), **confirming** the souls of the disciples, and **exhorting** them to continue in the faith, and that we must through much tribulation enter into the kingdom of God. And when they had **ordained** them **elders** in every church, and had prayed with fasting, they **commended** them to the Lord, on whom they believed.*

8. Apostles are members <u>only</u> of the church from which they were sent; but they function there, <u>not</u> as apostles, but in the capacity they always have had there. E.g., Jesus was the apostle of the Jerusalem church. Peter and the eleven <u>were elders</u> in Jerusalem, but functioning <u>everywhere else</u> apostolically. Peter and John noted that they were "elders."
   1 Peter 5:1 The elders which are among you I exhort, who am also an elder

   2 John 1 The elder unto the elect lady...

9. There are <u>no</u> apostles in the local church (except a founding apostle).

10. It is the elders who govern the local church.

11. The word "elder" is virtually the same as: pastor, shepherd, bishop, over-seer, presbyter.

12. There are **many** shepherds or pastors in a local church, but few prophets, teachers, and evangelists.

13. It is not scriptural, not practical, not efficient, for one pastor to minister to scores or even hundreds of people. Jesus, himself, inves<u>ted</u> himself in only twelve.

14. Shepherds **do not** have authority beyond the boundary of the local church. Ministers can only have authority in **one** church. There is no such thing as a pope or an arch-bishop. **Trans-local supremacy is unknown in *Scripture*.**

15. No local church has authority over a local church in another city.

16. Ministers may visit other local churches and home churches; but it is the local elders' business to convene any meeting with them. Elders are not obligated to convene a meeting, even with an apostle, that is, a non-founding apostle.

17. Apostles are "sent ones," never volunteers, never self-appointed, always by divine commission.

18. The *Bible* does not recognize the labors of most modern missionaries [but that is the

best we have today].

19. Apostleship is based on "commission" (calling), not "giftedness."

20. "Apostle" is an office, not a gift.
   1 Timothy 2:7 Whereunto I am ordained a preacher, and an apostle...

21. Likewise the prophet, evangelist, teacher, and pastor are offices, not gifts. **They** are the **gifts from God to the church**.
   *Ephesians 4:11,12 And **He gave** some, apostles; and some, prophets; and some, evangelists; and some, pastors and teachers: for the perfecting of the saints, for the work of the ministry, for the edifying of the body of Christ...*

22. If the Lord makes pastors today, why would He not also make the other offices?

23. Workers cannot "go out" on-their-own; **they must be sent**. Directions are from the Head. They are never to be independent from the rest of the other members.

24. A personal "call" requires confirmation of the representative members.

25. "Sending out" is preceded by prayer, fastings, and the laying-on of hands.

26. The members differ from one another, but share one Life.

27. Prophets and teachers occasionally meet together, apart from the rest of the church.
   *Acts 13:1,2 Now there were in the church that was at Antioch certain **prophets** and **teachers**...As they ministered to the Lord, and fasted, the holy ghost said...*

28. All the fruit of an apostle's work is handed over to the elders. Apostles exercise no authority in local affairs. *If* the founder stays permanently, the saints and the work will NOT mature.

29. All the members are to be workers, ministering to one another. None are devoted exclusively to secular affairs.
   1 Corinthians 12:21-24 And the eye cannot say unto the hand, I have no need of you: nor again the head to the feet, I have no need of you. Nay, much more those members of the body, which seem to be more feeble, are necessary: And those members of the body, which we think to be less honorable, upon these we bestow more abundant honor; and our uncomely parts have more abundant comeliness. For our comely parts have no need: but God has tempered the body together, having given more abundant honor to that part which lacked...

30. Elders are models, not masters.
   1 Peter 5:3 Neither as being lords over God's heritage, but being ensamples to the flock.

31. Men from the local flock, NOT outsiders, are to be pastors.
   1 Peter 5:2 Feed the flock of God which is among you.

32. Elders must make themselves available to intimately minister to the saints most of the time, especially elders who are not secularly employed.

33. One elder cannot be responsible for large numbers of people, perhaps less than thirty including 1) adult men (some of whom are being groomed for eldership for the time the group grows larger), 2) their wives and children, 3) singles, and 4) the

elderly.

34. A local church is <u>indivisible</u>, even though it may meet in different places.

35. <u>If a "truth" becomes the ground of fellowship, it becomes a sect.</u> The Lord has seen fit that all of us believe some things differently from one another to discover, if we **will** stay together in charity.

36. Other apostles may, over a period of time, visit a particular city, but all <u>their</u> work is contributed to the original local church.

37. Finances:
a. Faith is the most important factor in God's service.

b. In spiritual work there is need for an <u>unsettled</u> income.

c. If we are supported by men, our work will be controlled by men.

d. If a worker cannot look to the Lord alone for the meeting of his daily wants, then he is not qualified to be engaged in His work.

e. Preachers may receive gifts, but no stipulations are to be made with the gift.

f. If we are the laborers of God, then we must look to none other but Him, though He may meet our needs through our fellowmen.
Luke 10:7 The laborer is worthy of his hire.

1 Corinthians 9:11,14 If we have sown unto you spiritual things, is it a great thing if we shall reap your carnal things?...Even so has the Lord ordained that they which preach the gospel should live of the gospel.

g. Although absolutely independent of men regarding finances, ministers must preserve humility and willingness to accept advice from members of the Body (who are in close contact with the Head), expecting confirmation through them of His leading.

h. Ministers may not accept support from gentiles.
3 John 7 For His Name's sake they went forth, taking nothing of the gentiles.

i. Ministers may not accept support from gentiles unless ordered by God.
Acts 28:7,10 Publius...received us, and lodged us three days courteously...When we departed, they laded us with such things as were necessary.

j. Money collected by churches is for: I) the poor saints;
Romans 15:26 For it hath pleased them of Macedonia and Achaia to make a certain contribution for the poor saints which are at Jerusalem.

II) elders who have given up their ordinary income to devote themselves to the interests of the church; and III) apostles, prophets, evangelists, and teachers (who should be sustained equally as well as pastors).
1 Timothy 5:17,18 Let the elders that rule well be counted worthy of double honor, especially they who labor in the word and doctrine. For the scripture says, "You shall not muzzle the ox that treads out the corn." And, "The laborer is worthy of his reward."

k. Workers should be careful to disclose their needs to none but God. E.g.: Paul did not "burden" the Corinthians. Yet, the Macedonians contributed to him generously.
2 Corinthians 11:8,9 I robbed other

churches, taking wages of them, to do you service. And when I was present with you, and wanted, I was chargeable to no man: for that which was lacking to me, the brethren which came from Macedonia supplied: and in all things I have kept myself from being burdensome unto you, and so will I keep myself.

Philippians 4:15,18   Now you Philippians know also, that in the beginning of the gospel, when I departed from Macedonia, no church communicated with me as concerning giving and receiving, but you only...But I have all, and abound: I am full, having received of Epaphroditus the things which were sent from you, an odor of a sweet smell, a sacrifice acceptable, well-pleasing to God.

2 Thessalonians 3:8 Neither did we eat any man's bread for naught; but wrought with labor and travail night and day, that we might not be chargeable to any of you.

l. The elders should receive an offering for visiting ministers (ahead of time, when possible) that the people should know they have not partaken of the *Word* without paying (*1 Timothy* 5:18).

m. To profess trust in God and then to disclose one's needs to provoke to pity, is a shameful thing.

n. Ministers must bear the burden of their own needs, plus that of the work. If God has called them, it is entirely His affair.

o. A worker may encourage the saints to remember the needs of all other ministers except his own.

p. By pushing for something in the church to happen, including financing, we prevent the holy spirit from hindering us where it will.

38. Scripture does not mention any church where a singular minister controlled its affairs, that is, not only one minister in the church.
   Philippians 1:1 To all the saints in Christ Jesus which are at Philippi, with the bishops (plural) and deacons.

   Titus 1:5,7 For this cause left I you in Crete, that you should set in order the things that are wanting, and ordain elders (plural) in every city, as I had appointed you...For a bishop must be blameless, as the steward of God

   Acts 20:28 Take heed therefore unto yourselves (elders), and to all the flock, over the which the holy ghost has made you overseers, to feed the church of God, which He has purchased with His own blood.

39. Deacons, under the oversight of the elders, deal exclusively with the business side of things, including most handling of money. Deacons' works may be ongoing OR for only one event. They are ordained for their job with the laying on of hands.
   *Acts 6:3,6 Wherefore, brethren, look out among you seven men of honest report, full of the holy ghost and wisdom, whom we may appoint over this business...whom they set before the apostles: and when they had prayed, they **laid their hands** on them.*

40. "Going to church," "having church," "going into the sanctuary," and "having services" are **not** scriptural expressions. They take their origin from "synagogue" worship. These Judaistic things crept into

the church, and will be expunged.

41. The church is composed of the living believers. It is NOT a building.
Acts 5:11 And great fear came upon all the church

Matthew 18:17 And if he shall neglect to hear them, tell it unto the church: but if he neglect to hear the church, let him be unto you as an heathen man and a publican.

42. It is *Judaism*, not *Christianity*, which teaches that there must be sanctified places for divine worship.

43. *New-Testament* believers assembled in a great variety of places and had **no** official meeting-place. They made use of any building, amphitheater, or open place that suited their needs.

44. There is something of a home-atmosphere about the "upper room," where the gatherings of God's children are "family" affairs.

45. The early church met often in private homes.

*Acts 20:20 I (Paul) have taught you publicly, and from **house to house**,*

*Romans 16:5 Likewise greet the church that is in their **house**.*

*Romans 16:10 Salute them which are of Aristobulus' **household**.*

*1 Corinthians 16:19 Aquila and Priscilla salute you much in the Lord, with the church that is in their **house**.*

*Colossians 4:15 Salute the brethren which are in Laodicea, and Nymphas, and the church which is in his **house**.*

*Philemon 2 ...And to our beloved Apphia, and Archippus our fellow-soldier, and to the church in your **house**.*

You will find a more extensive list of verses like these on Page 123.

46. Upon occasion the elders may summon a meeting of all the assemblies in the city, in a rented facility, or their own, if they have such means.
1 Corinthians 14:23 If therefore the whole church be come together into one place...

47. Most individuals are freer to participate and manifest spiritual gifts in a smaller building and with a small number of people.

48. Grand edifices with lofty spires speak of the "world" and the "flesh" rather than of the spirit.

49. Enormous amounts of money are spent by Christians for church buildings, rather than upon the work and the ministers. Disputes often arise when the church owns property.

50. There is no mention that the cause of the early churches' meeting-in-homes had something to do with persecution.
*Acts 2:46,47 And they, continuing daily with one accord in the temple, and breaking bread from house to house, did eat their meat with gladness and singleness of heart, praising God, and **having favor with all the people**. And the Lord added to the church daily such as should be saved.*

51. Assembling is absolutely essential. Do not forsake it (*Hebrews* 10:25).

52. "Home churches" are not only for the purpose of meeting, but become an extended family all week long, with the members caring for one another. Too-much-assembling takes up the time the members need to minister to one another and to their families.

53. When the church grows too large for the house, it divides; a new elder/shepherd takes a portion of the saints to another location.

54. Some meetings are convened for the specific purpose of prayer.
> *Acts 4:31 And when they had prayed, the place was shaken where they were assembled together...*
>
> *Acts 12:5 Peter therefore was kept in prison: but prayer was made without ceasing of the church unto God for him.*

55. Some meetings are convened for the specific purpose of reading.
> *Colossians 4:16 And when this epistle is **read** among you, cause that it be **read** also in the church of the Laodiceans; and that you likewise **read** the epistle from Laodicea.*
>
> *1 Thessalonians 5:27 I charge you by the Lord that this epistle be **read** unto all the holy brethren.*
>
> *Acts 15:30,31 So when they were dismissed, they came to Antioch: and when they had gathered the multitude together, they delivered the epistle: Which when they had **read**, they rejoiced for the consolation.*

56. Some meetings are for eating a meal together.
> *Acts 20:7 When the disciples came together to **break bread**...*
>
> *1 Corinthians 11:33 Wherefore, my brethren, when you come together to eat, tarry one for another.*

57. The most common meeting is for the exercising of spiritual gifts. Every member comes spiritually prepared to contribute and to be used by the spirit. It is a great blessing when Heaven speaks to the church, and each utterance is to be specifically considered, reconsidered, discussed, and honored with the great importance deserved, or to be otherwise declared "not in order" by the ministry.
> *1 Corinthians 14:26 How is it then, brethren? When you come together, every one of you 1) has a psalm, 2) has a doctrine, 3) has a tongue, 4) has a revelation, 5) has an interpretation. Let all things be done unto edifying.*

58. Some meetings have a combination of the above purposes.

59. Most meetings these days consist of a preacher speaking to people seated in rows of pews, but this was unknown in the early church, except when convened to hear a message from visiting ministers, included apostles, prophets, evangelists, and teachers.

60. To have the saints passively sitting in church meetings most of the time, rather than dependently leaning upon the holy ghost, spells spiritual death. William Sowders once said:
> "It will be a sad day when the Pentecostal churches learn to have church without the holy ghost."

61. In regular church meetings there is no apostle present, and **each person** bears the responsibility to share what he has received from the Lord, including spiritual gifts as in

1 Corinthians 14. The local (and visiting) prophets take the lead, along with evangelists and teachers.

62. Other then manifesting spiritual gifts, shepherd/pastors do NOT speak in meetings unless there is a need to attend to business matters of the church.

63. There is NOT to be just one shepherd-pastor in a local church.

64. The major responsibility for visiting the sick lies with the saints in their own group, not the entire church, nor the other elders, unless they are called upon for prayer.
> *Matthew 25:36 I was sick, and you visited me: I was in prison, and you came unto me.*
>
> *James 5:14 Is any sick among you? let him call for the elders of the church; and let them pray over him, anointing him with oil in the name of the Lord.*

We have begun here a list of changes that might be considered in completely coming out of Babylon. Is this list complete? No. Then, how will ever know what to do differently?

By prayer and fasting, it is the holy spirit that must reveal to us all that is lacking in our understanding of the church and its order.

I have been asked, "Where do you get your facts for all this data?" "Where are your footnotes?" "Who told you all this stuff?" I know Who told me! Now, I'll ask you a question: Who told you how to have church like you do?

*1 This chapter is not based on the works of Watchman Nee, whom we do admire.

Chapter 3. Apostolic Disorder

The word "apostle" means "sent one." Many men in Christian-Church history have "gone" without having been "sent." This is the first "dis-order;" there are more. If a man is an apostle, then he is to do the work of an apostle. An apostle is to plant and establish a work. Then he is to go to the next place and plant and establish a work. Go, plant, establish. Go again. When an apostle starts a work and then stays there, he is establishing HIMSELF, not the church. Some call that "feathering the nest." But, an apostle is not to sit upon the nest. He builds the nest, and then leaves, after having first established elders.

In launching a work, the apostle is to step aside, observing whom the holy ghost is raising up to eldership. When the apostle builds his "own" nest, he quenches the operation of the spirit to raise up elders. Thus, ministerial callings might be working in several brethren, but are not allowed to manifest to the fullest. These brethren are apt to feel frustrated, quenched, dwarfed, and unfulfilled. Feeling this calling, they get itchy to preach. So they leave their assembly (like a finger departing the body) and try to take over an established work or start a new one. But now, they are out of order. Their calling is likely not apostolic. They are perhaps a pastor/shepherd or a teacher or an "exhorter" (*Romans* 12:8). They should have stayed home.

Furthermore, many who are called to the ministry become exalted in their calling (like Diotrophes).
> *3 John 9-11 Diotrephes, who loves to have the preeminence...Neither does he himself receive the brethren, and forbids them that would, and casts them out of the church.*

Could this happen in a modern church? Do you see the spirit of Diotrephes was very unlike the Nazarene?

Being called to a ministerial office is not a promotion in the kingdom. It is not. It is just a calling. <u>The highest you can be is "an overcoming saint."</u>……Some men get so exalted they cannot see the saint's feet, which they are supposed to "watch" and wash. God resists the proud and gives grace to the humble. This is a "mystery," but...those that have the rule," must be humble. This is a <u>humbling call</u> and a <u>humble calling</u>. To minister is to serve. From where does one serve? He ministers at the saint's feet. He is to "wash" their feet, that is, he is to minister and counsel them as they go through life in this present world.

A minister may like a church "platform" or dais. He likes that three-foot elevation above the congregation; he wants the saints to know his position. He wants them to "see" his authority. Firstly, this, being a spiritual kingdom, the evidence is not to be in things which are seen. If it takes a three-foot platform to confirm his clout, he is in bad shape. And then, more importantly, such an exalted attitude has no place in the body of Christ. This is "being a lord over God's heritage." There is but one Lord. Amen. The bishop/shepherd must rule,…..but not as a lord. On the other hand, there are those groups who unknowingly adhere to the doctrine of the Nicolaitanes, where the "lay people" "rule." And this is even worse. Some see this doctrine as lording over the people. I see it just the opposite, as the people ruling the church, which may include electing their minister.

Let's see; how many "disorders" have we listed so far?

So the body is not to have a great big head and a little torso or visa versa. No. The whole body must be fitly joined together. And, it must be proportionate. And, it must have every part contributing. This is a healthy body. This is a strong body. Even the uncomely parts have more abundant comeliness. We appreciate the ministry, and want it to be greater. Of course, when it is in better order, it will be greater. But, today it flounders in the Babylonian disorder influenced by Constantine and Luther. Until the Church is willing to step out of the box of tradition in which it now dwells, it will be powerless, ineffective, and inept, AND in "apostolic disorder."

In this day of the rise of so many "mega-churches," one might question that they have weakness. I think some of those big churches may be giving some good teaching to their people, but they have no message that befits the following examples of God's *Word*:

Titus 2:11,12 For the grace of God that brings salvation has appeared to all men, teaching us that, denying ungodliness and worldly lusts, we should live soberly, righteously, and godly in the present age.

Romans 8:13 For if you live according to the flesh you will die; but if by the spirit you put to death the deeds of the body, you will live.

2 Corinthians 7:1 Therefore, having these promises, beloved, let us cleanse ourselves from all filthiness of the flesh and spirit, perfecting holiness in the fear of God.

Most likely, if they preached this in the mega-church, they would no longer be "mega." Whether by ignorance or deliberate omission of this message of "over-coming," they are in "disorder." They have the big crowd, but they do not manifest the big power of the spirit. But, on the other hand, who does????

The earliest church in Jerusalem was "mega" WITH power. Deacons took care of the natural affairs of the congregations; prophets and evangelists preached; teachers taught; the shepherds counseled; apostles were "sent" out. The members lived in harmony. The Church was IN apostolic order. AND (listen to this!) AND there were signs and wonders and miracles attesting to their order. You may have some semblance of order in your congregation, but, might you still yet have some apostolic disorder?

Here are a few quick suggestions: let's get rid of our synagogue real estate; let's get rid of professional music and let the harpers harp with their voices; cease play-acting, performance-preaching, and simply speak by personal example; cease pretending there is yet divine power in the prayer-lines. When you step out of the box, you may discover that God was not in it; He had left, and you didn't even know it. How sad! Churches without spirit!

We have but scant knowledge from the Epistles and *Acts* of exactly how the saints operated in the first century. We're grateful they had to address a few problems that give us some hints. But, mostly we are going to have to depend upon divine inspiration to get this house totally rebuilt. When they built the second Temple in Jerusalem, they could not discern Ezekiel's "innovations," so they fell back on their own best ideas. We shall need fresh insight.

There will be churches in the latter day which will have apostolic order. By much prayer, study, and fasting they will find the keys to unlock our prison doors of Babylonious tradition and rediscover the glorious Church of Jesus Christ.

Photograph in Ancient Babylon

Christ Church Cathedral, Episcopalian, Louisville, Kentucky

Chapter 4. Coming out of Babylon

Surely our fathers have inherited lies! Jeremiah 16:19

Since Pentecost, in every age there have been a few true worshippers of Jesus Christ. These refused to believe that the institutional church was a "development" of the church, but a "departure" from it. They were persecuted by those who loved the pagan traditions of Rome and her daughters. The Church will never be able to tell others to come out of Babylon until she has come out of it herself.

I recently heard of a book by Frank Viola entitled, *Pagan Christianity*. I purchased a copy, and I liked most everything in it. What follows are some of my thoughts and experiences. I lifted some sentences right out of this book. For example:
> Church today is held together by religious programs.
> Rather than being spirit-led, we are music leader-led or pastor-led.
> The church has neither biblical nor historical right to function as it does.

But, most of all, we need the guidance of the spirit of God in the most serious way. When you read the epistles, you will find problems in the early church being dealt with. We are grateful for their mistakes, because it gives us some information about "church." But, what about the many things they did right? They didn't need correction; they are <u>not</u> in the *Book*. What did they do right? That is why we need the guidance of the spirit so desperately.

Much of what <u>we</u> do in religion has no precedent in *scripture*. Believers for almost two thousand years have been carried along with the tide.

The Calf Path

Once upon a time there was a calf who wondered home through the woods going this way and that way. The next day a dog followed that same path through the woods. The day after that, an old bellwether led her fellow sheep along that calf path. The next day a group of hunters trod the path. Although the path was none too straight, no matter, people began to use that path, too. No one stopped to ask why the path was not in a straight line; they just took it. Eventually a town grew up along the old calf path. The town became a large city, and, you guessed it, that old calf path developed into the main street of that metropolis. Everyone cursed the course of the street and all its inconveniences, but no one remembered that it had its beginnings many, many years ago by a wondering calf.

Do you reckon that a lot of the things that we do began similarly?

Some Facts

Christianity is the world's first non-temple-based religion; *It* teaches that "people" are the temple.
> *1 Corinthians 3:16 your are the **temple** of the living God*

> *Ephesians 2:21 (we) are the **building** fitly framed together – a holy Temple of God*

See *1 Timothy* 3:15 and *Hebrews* 3:6.

In the first century *ekklesia*, which is used 114 times in the *Bible*, meant "assembly," not a place.

In 190 AD, Clement of Alexandria was the first to use the expression: "go to church."

Emperor Constantine, 285-337 AD, empowered the Church to hold property. Previously the church met in houses or rented commercial buildings:
> *Acts 19:9 But when some were becoming hardened and disobedient, speaking evil of the Way...Paul withdrew from (the synangogue)...and took away the disciples, reasoning daily in the school of Tyrannus.*

For three months, Paul had reasoned and persuaded in the synagogue. Some believed; some were "hardened." Paul never had a Christian assembly in a synagogue thereafter. In the school of Tyrannus and elsewhere miracles tremendously amplified Paul's messages Including Paul's sequestered years in Rome, his ministry lasted less than thirty years. Afterward, his works all declined and apostatized.

In the year 321 AD Sunday became a legal holiday. In 327 AD Constantine began building churches; he also began converting pagan Temples into churches at public expense. He named them after saints.

A Roman *basilica* was a raised platform, which became part of church structure. From the platform the Roman Catholic clergy ministered. The same structure in the Jewish synagogue is called the *bema*.

The Bible-stand in the synagogue is called the *lu-akh'*. In the pagan Roman temple there was the *ambo*; in the year 240 AD in the Latin churches it was called the *pulpitum*. It had no place in the earlier churches, nor did the platform.

In the synagogue and also in the pagan temples there were special seats on the platform. Jesus lamented that the Jews strove for positional seats. The Bishop's chair (the *cathedra*) grew more and more important in the Church. The expression "*Ex cathedra*" means "from the throne" and refers to any statement made by the Pope or other Church official. The word "cathedral has the same origin.

I will devote little more time to much of the pagan garbage which came into the church over the centuries, because the Reformation undid some of it, and later movements saw the light on other paganisms. There is a difference between "Babylonian" and "Babylonious," (similar to "Babylonish") as I am using these two words. "Babylonian" refers mostly to the doctrinal errors that have corrupted our faith; "Babylonious" refers to the buildings, the traditions, the governance, and the order that we have and practice, which also have their origins in pagan religion.

But, while the Protestant Reformation rid the church of some Babylonian things, it added some Babylonious things. One thing was the "altar rail," which surrounded the platform. This was done to enhance the appearance of the clergy. The platform seats in Protestant churches began to be known as "Chairs for the elders."

Although church buildings were not part of the early church, we could not think of having church today without them. The value of church buildings in the United States today is $230 billion, with an annual income of $60 billion with debt-service and maintenance at $12 billion, all of which otherwise could be spent on ministry or charity.

Jesus' Church began in Palestine as the Body of Christ; she moved to Greece and became a philosophy; she moved to Rome and became an institution; she moved to Europe and became a culture, she moved to America and became a business.

You think not that the church has become a business! Look at the church's books; look at the payroll deductions for social security and income tax; look at the staff; observe that the church has a "tax-exempt number," which means she is government supported and sponsored; note the real estate she owns.

The church in Thessalonika (*Acts* 17:6) turned the world upside down, WITHOUT a building.

What shall we call a church like they had in 50 AD? Viola calls it an "organic church," which supports the ministry and the church, but, most likely, not a building.

Can we defy this church-building tradition? Can we imagine a church being building-less.

Babylonious Services

One of things that has developed in the church through the centuries is the "service." The Temple in Jerusalem had "services," two every day, as a matter of fact, one in the morning and one in the evening, plus additional services on the holy days. These services and all their rituals were designed by the Almighty God as pictures of His coming Christ. They are powerful pictures to us of how sacrificial Christian-living ought to be.

When the first Temple was destroyed, the synagogue was invented in the Babylonian Captivity. The synagogue borrowed the word "services" for its meetings. When the Jews returned to the Promised Land they brought the synagogue concept with them and all its trappings. Little of the synagogue had a place in the early Christian Church. However, when the church began to apostatize, some "Jewish things" crept into church customs. Going through the "Wilderness," the Church was filtered through Rome until few ultimately knew what was legitimate and what was Babylonious or Jewish. So the Reformation did its best to weed out the worst Romish abuses and yet strove to not lose the "appearance" of "church."

One important word in the church is "liturgy," a prescribed form for public religious worship. Of course paganism had it. So did the synagogue. If you want to know what tradition is, just look at the Jews: two thousand five hundred years have gone by since synagogues began, and they have almost the same services week after week, year after year that they had in Babylon.
Definition: Liturgy

1. A body of rites prescribed for public worship
2. A customary repertoire of ideas, phrases, or observances
3. A prescribed form or set of forms for religious worship

"Liturgy is like a strong tree whose beauty is derived from the continuous renewal of it leaves, but whose strength comes from the old trunk, with solid roots in the ground:" Pope Paul VI.

Following is the typical calf-path church service liturgy as laid out by Luther and Calvin: call to worship; opening prayer, scripture-reading; singing psalms; pre-sermon prayer; sermon; communion.

The Puritans modified that order: three songs; scripture reading; choir music; unison prayers; pastoral prayer; sermon; offering; benediction.

There are many drawbacks in having church services: they hinder personal spiritual development; they encourage passivity by the saints; they limit the functioning of the holy spirit; they imply that "attending church" is the key to a victorious Christian life: one is led to believe that by his attendance he is fulfilling his service to God.

Sitting through a ritual service does not transform the saints. Preaching-from-the-pulpit-to-the-pew WILL NOT make disciples. (They are to be made in day-to-day, continual, faithful shepherd-sheep relationship.)

In the early church they grew by functioning: testifying, exercising the spiritual gifts, and serving, not passively watching and listening.

Clement of Alexandria lamented how sermons effected so little change in Christians. Preaching from the pulpit to the pew does not make disciples; it makes an audience.

Sermon-preaching harms the church: it makes the preacher the virtuoso performer of a "regular" gathering of the church; it hampers congregational participation; it turns the church into a preaching station; it degenerates the congregation into a group of muted spectators watching a performance; it makes the saints into a docile priesthood; it stalemates spiritual growth; it suffocates mutual ministry; it smothers individual participation.

Paul wanted ALL the church members to be functioning, not just sitting.

*Hebrews 10:24-25 And let us consider one another to **provoke** unto love and to good works: Not forsaking the assembling of ourselves together, as the manner of some is; but **exhorting one another**: and so much the more, as ye see the day approaching.*

*Ephesians 4:12, 16 perfecting of the saints, **for the work of the ministry**, for the edifying of the body of Christ...From whom the whole body fitly joined together and compacted by that which **every joint supplies**, according to the effectual working in the measure of **every part**, makes increase of the body unto the edifying of itself in love.*

Paul envisioned ALL the members of the church ministering, functioning, serving their families, and exercising their spirituality. He thought every joint should be working.

If God's people are properly equipped, they can have meetings that have no leader but Jesus Christ, who is the Head.

The *New Testament* knows nothing of a "worship service" or a "song service."

The saints cannot "go" to church. They ARE the church. "Going to church" is Babylonious.

The early church met for the purpose of displaying Jesus Christ through the every-member-functioning of the body. The goals were to make Christ visible and to edify the whole church. There is nothing that we do today which is like this.

When the church meets, the members are ALL to manifest the spiritual gifts. It is critical that each member "exercise" in the spirit. They will later on need the benefit of this exercise in their every-day lives and even in crisis situations.

It seems to me in *Acts* that the church was community all week, functioning, helping, led by the spirit, manifesting the spirit.

With the passing of the original traveling apostles, church leadership began to formalize. Without the monitoring of the leaders, the church began to drift toward organizational patterns. By 107 AD Ignatius pushed for the one-bishop-per-church rule. Instead of having multiple pastor/shepherds in each city, he wanted only one.

Clement of Rome in 100 AD was the first to use the word *laity*. Tertullian was the first to the use the word "*clergy.*"

By the fourth century a graded hierarchy dominated the Christian faith. Certain churches began to exercise authority over other churches. Cyprian, like Tertullian and Hippolytus, around 200 AD began to use the *Old-Testament* language regarding the "priests" to apply to the clergy. "Sacerdotalism"—the belief that there exists a divinely appointed person to mediate between God and the people—originated with Cyprian. He maintained that the priests offered the Eucharist (the holy sacrifice) and that they were sacrosanct (holy themselves). Cyprian advanced the notion that when the priest served the Eucharist, he was offering up the death of Christ. He must be credited with promoting the increased dependence of the laity upon the clergy.

The hierarchical structure of the ministry emerged in Egypt, Babylon, and Persia, and was carried over to Greece and to Rome. The Persians made two outstanding contributions to the ancient world: The organization of their empire and of their religion. The system of imperial administration was inherited by Alexander the Great, then Rome, and lastly modern Europe. Later, Pope Gregory shaped the ministry of the entire church after Roman law, thus the pagan structure of the Christian Church.

Please compare with Jesus' Church:
*Matthew 23:10,11 Neither be called masters: for One is your Master, even Christ. But he that is greatest among you shall be **your servant**.*

*Mark 10:42-44 You know that they which are accounted to rule over the Gentiles exercise lordship over them; and their great ones exercise authority upon them. But, so shall it **not** be among you: but whosoever will be great among you, shall be your minister: And whosoever of you will be the chiefest, shall be servant of all.*

Ministers are not "dignitaries." Do you impose "lordship" over your church? Do you have departments in your church? Jesus did not impose any fixed organizational patterns for New Israel.

God takes the lowest members of the body, raises them up to the ministry, and then expects the rest to honor their servants. Oh, this is so different from Babylon, isn't it?

The Pastor

Constantine gave much authority to the clergy, even more power than Roman

the first time, the clergy
...rial pay in annual ...
...he government. In 313 ...
... them from paying taxes.
...rics," and endowed them
... vileges as government
...cials, making them part of the favored class. They began to dress in robes and to groom differently. In all this, the differences between the church and the world began to vanish. It was advanced that the priests were high above the laity.

In the sixteenth century the Reformers rejected apostolic succession, encouraged the clergy to marry, revised the liturgy giving the congregation more participation, abolished the office of bishop, and reduced the priest back to a presbyter. Their cry was "the priesthood of all believers." However, while promoting the individual Christian's role as a priest, they did not recover the priesthood to all believers collectively. However, the Anabaptists did practice that, which is one reason they were persecuted by both Catholics and Protestants.

In 1520 Martin Luther wrote, *A Prelude on the Babylonian Captivity of the Church*. He called Pope Leo X "the leader of the Kingdom of the Anti-Christ." He referred to "the pagan servitude of the Church."

However, the Reformation still affirmed the clergy-laity split. Luther held that the ministry had to be specially trained to preach, baptize, and to serve communion, and he rejected the Anabaptist belief that it was every Christian's duty to minister, which he said came from "the pit of hell" and that those who were guilty of it should be put to death (and many Anabaptists were killed).

In the seventeenth century the Puritans like John Owen and Thomas Goodwin focused all authority on the pastor, who had been given "the power of the keys" and alone could preach, administer the sacraments, read the *scripture* publicly, and be trained in *Greek* and *Hebrew*.

John Calvin did not like using the word "priest" for the clergy, but preferred the *Latin* word for "shepherd," *pas-tor*. He believed he was restoring the *episcopos* (bishop) in the person of the *pas-tor*. He stated that "the pastoral office is necessary to preserve the church on earth in a greater way than the sun, food, and drink are necessary to nourish and sustain the present life." Luther also adopted the Babylonious terms "preacher" and "*pas-tor*." So did Zwingli.

Luther commented, "We are ALL priests insofar as we are Christians, but those whom we call priests are ministers selected from our midst to act in our name, and their priesthood is our ministry." Unlike the Catholics, he rejected a sacrificing priesthood, but he yet felt that the sharing of God's *Word* belonged to a special order (which is simply sacerdotalism).

Luther felt the church was to be a preaching station. "The church should never assemble unless God's *Word* is preached and prayer is made." The people gather to listen. He called the church building a *mund-haus*, that is, a "mouth house." He said, "The ears are the only organs of a Christian."

It is my belief that "preaching" in the church is to be done by those who hold the offices of prophet and evangelist. Then what does the shepherd/pastor do? He ministers to the sheep; he probes their wool; he checks them out for burrs and fever; he counsels them. A great deal of Paul's instructions to Timothy and to Titus dealt with caring for the sheep. There is naught said about "pastoral preaching." **Shepherd/pastors do not preach**, but prophets and evangelists do. If you like to preach, then maybe you are a prophet or an evangelist.

In addition to the pastoral roles of preaching and serving communion, John Calvin added a third element, providing care and healing to the congregation, that is, "the cure of souls." In the pastor's role as "*curate*," the pastor was required to visit the congregants, the sick, and those in prison. The church often came to be referred to as the preacher's church. Even we today refer to a church as Brother So-and-So's church.

But, remember that after Pentecost, those serving-functions fell upon the shoulders of the entire assembly. I do believe that this will be one of the most difficult things to restore to the true church. The New-Testament word *diakonos* means "servant" or "minister," but has become distorted to mean a professionalized ministry.

This has resulted in the pastor becoming the one huge member of the congregation, the only huge member, with the possible exception of the piano player/song leader. Everyone else has been relegated to being a tiny ear, a theater spectator watching a weekly performance, a mute onlooker proficient in taking sermon notes and passing an offering plate. The huge position of the "pastor" has damaged the following scriptures:

*1 Corinthians 12:11 But one and the same spirit works all these things, distributing to **each one** individually as he wills.*

*1 Corinthinians 7:17 But as God hath distributed to **every man**.*

*Ephesians 4:7 But unto **every one** of us is given grace according to the measure of the gift of Christ.*

*1 Peter 2:9,10 But **you** are a chosen generation, a royal priesthood, a holy nation, His own special people, that you may proclaim the praises of Him who called you out of darkness into His marvelous light.*

The huge Babylonious office of the "pastor" damages body life. Paul and Barnabas demonstrated the importance of "church-planters" not staying long-term in any one church. Why did they not stay permanently? It was their mission to continue establishing new works, but they also wanted the church to learn to function under the headship of Christ. They did not want the members looking to them, but to the holy spirit. They wanted the members to exercise their own gifts.

(By the way, I prefer to no longer use the Catholic/*Latin* word *pas-tor*, but the *English* word "shepherd.") Our pastor/shepherds are over-worked performers of many roles, some of them outside of their giftedness. By doing so much, they do not permit the other members of the body who possess these gifts and talents from using them. I have observed that rather than functioning as shepherds, many pastors today look more like work-horses. If you ask some of our pastors, "How are you doing?" They might answer: "frazzled" and "drained."

(I urge members of Hispanic assemblies to view their *pastores* in the humble sense which Paul employed, rather than the sacerdotal Romish priest.)

Music

In Bohemia, John Huss (1372-1415) re-introduced congregational singing to the Church. Additionally he employed the organ and other musical instruments, which had not been used until recently. Luther encouraged congregational singing during specifically appointed times in the church service. Congregational singing reached its peak in England with the Wesleyan revival.

The first church in the United States to employ an organ was Trinity Church in New York in 1704. Within fifty years choirs began to flourish. They were assigned special seats to show their special status. The organ and choir were moved from the chancel (platform) to the rear of the church, but by the twentieth century they were back on the platform, now wearing ecclesiastical robes.

More recently the "worship team" has replaced the choir; amplified guitars and keyboards have been added to the special vocalists, with words projected on a screen. Hymnals are rarely used in charismatic churches. The lead-in music to the services is often selected to correspond to the upcoming sermon. Question: could this pre-planned music and sermon be spirit-led?

More Remarks

When the autonomous nature of every church is preserved, the spreading of error is more likely to be localized. When each church is autonomous, it is difficult for an ambitious false teacher to seize control of unrelated congregations, because "pastors" do not have trans-local authority.

Also, we have seen situations where a very good preacher will begin to steal sheep from another church, reasoning: "Those poor souls are starving to death for lack of teaching," says he. But, I believe that God knew what he was doing when he baptized each one of us into the church where He wanted us to be. He has moved people great distances to put them where He wanted them. While God does not want us to be locked into untenable situations (the multitude of possible peculiar aberrations of which are too outrageous to contemplate), I believe the day of playing "musical pastors" and "musical churches" is over. The saints need to bloom where they have been planted.

We Christians have made (as acceptable and normative) practices that the *New Testament* neither teaches nor exemplifies. On the other hand, we have abandoned church practices that had been acceptable and normal in the early days of the Church.

Organizing-church-institutions have been a calf path, worldly, Babylonious adaptations.

Other Offices of the Ministry

As it was in the early days, so it ought to be today, that local congregations send out ministers (*apostolos*) to found new works. Apostles operate under the authority of their local church. Not only do they begin new works, but they may also visit existing works, which they did not found and recommend corrections and changes that the local elders may enact. They may preach and exhort the local church. Then, they move on. We shall later speak of this in more detail.

When apostles found a new work, they remain only briefly, and then they continue on to another place. They NEVER remain to enjoy the fruits of their labor. They are forever on the go. Dedicated they are!

Most church-founders these days remain there till they die.

Prophets, teachers, and evangelists ought to be ordained after prayer, fasting, and the laying-on of hands. They may minister in the local church, working in the home groups and in "altogether meetings." They may also be led by the spirit to minister in other cities. All churches on the "vine" should accept visiting ministers and render unto them due honor. Prophets, teachers, evangelists, as well as apostles are mobile.

However, the shepherd-pastor-elder-bishop-overseer-presbyter does not generally minister trans-locally. He only cares for a small number of saints locally. "Shepherds" are the most-numerous office of the ministry. There may be many of them in the local church.

Judaization of the "falling church" eliminated all the offices of the ministry except for the one rabbi-like preacher, because those offices: apostles, prophets, teacher, and evangelists, had no corresponding officials in the synagogue. Removing multiple ministers was a travesty from which the church has not yet recovered.

An Example

I have been in many house meetings. Once, I recall, we were meeting in someone's large living room. A neighbor couple was invited by the hosts to see and experience what the hosts were involved in. They were drawn by the love and clean life-style of the hosts. A skeptical man was also a guest. As we were sitting around quietly chatting in small groups, someone began singing a song, and we all joined in. The spirit of God was immediately present. Someone else a moment later started another song. This was followed by a message in tongues. We waited a while for the interpretation to come, but it was worth having waited. Another fitting song followed which was very intense and convicting and moving. After a short silence, the shepherd of the group began to speak. His lesson was an affirmation of the previous interpretation of tongues. There were interspersed in his talk a few comments by others and a question of clarification. The lesson was followed by several brief testimonies. There was, after a while, an obvious theme for the meeting. Probably every member had contributed something in the course of the evening. The skeptic was simply overwhelmed and began to weep. A couple of days later he got saved and received the gift of the holy ghost. Also, it was not long before the interested neighbors were part of the group.

Another Example

Every meeting of the saints is "**unprecedented**." This is because there is infinite variety that the holy ghost provides. One time an American Baptist preacher and his wife were invited. As they sat in the family room, the meeting began with a few cordial remarks about and to the guests. Someone started a lively song, and everyone was clapping and singing and rejoicing. The room erupted with joyful and loud praises. Someone started another song, which was followed by a few thoughtful moments. Then one sister spoke in tongues, which someone else followed with the interpretation. There were a few more uplifting songs. The guest pastor was then asked to speak. He said that he was very impressed by the love he had felt from everyone. His wife concurred. He then said that he could not understand what that young lady had said, but that he felt it was from God. Imagine that, a Baptist pastor, who didn't believe in tongues, heard a message in tongues and simply thought he could not make out what she had said, but he knew it was divine. After he spoke a good while, and all patiently and thoughtfully listened, the shepherd questioned the church on what were some significant things the guest had said, and he then really knew that they had paid attention.

Regarding the tongues and interpretation in that meeting, they occurred in a moment of quietness. My thought is that if Heaven speaks to us in a "still, small voice," we will never be able to hear in a noisy atmosphere. These is time for a joyful noise, and there is a time for holy quiet. It is exceedingly important that the saints learn to hear "the Voice," and the home church is a laboratory for this. [Please see Chapter 12 on "Home Churches."]

Another Example

After we had eaten some refreshments which a couple of the members had brought, we gathered in the family room with overflow seats on the adjoining sun porch and dining room. Several different saints began songs accompanied by guitar. Others songs were *a capello*. This group was getting large, and it had a second shepherd who several months later took half the people and formed another home group. He gave a lengthy and detailed lesson on "eternal judgment," vividly setting forth the scenes, the purposes, and the principles of God's several great eternal judgments. This provoked much discussion. This was followed by prayer for a couple of needy members of the group. The meeting ended with a song, *Victory in Jesus*.

Other Examples

Some meetings included meals together. Some meetings were exclusively meals, usually with some contribution from each of the sisters. Single men were assigned things like drinks and dinnerware. Sometimes the women gathered during the week and cleaned one of the member's homes. This usually included lunch. Sometimes the men in the group took an over-night retreat, which included some fun and some time for serious instruction in "life." Once, a sister was hospitalized, and a private room was granted to her home group to meet right there in the hospital. The body of Christ can assemble just about anywhere and get in touch with heaven.

A few years ago an assembly was selling its building and began searching for a new one. I pleaded with the pastor to raise up many shepherds, to meet in homes, and to not buy another building. He told the church what I had been saying, but he concluded that the congregation still needed a central meeting place.

Some have said that this is a different day, a different age than the early church. They say that customs and culture are no longer like the early days. However, I say that they are just making excuses so they don't have to make amends. They are content with the "calf path."

I believe that God is shaking the earth, the sea, and the dry land these days. Do you think heaven will not be shaken, too? Do you think the early church was not shaken? Well, it was. Saul of Tarsus provided some of it, himself. It is too horrible to think of what is accomplished in shakings, but suffice it to say that God needs to do it. And further, we will have to go through it.

If we do not soon return to our pure roots, we saints will be ill-equipped to weather the storms. We shall also fail in our manifest destiny to build the "garner" and to be God's brilliant beacon of light at the end of the age.

May I urge you to more than ever be "given to prayer, often in fasting, buried in the *Bible*." Those who seek Him <u>will</u> find Him. There is a great deal yet to be revealed to us by the Head; in this chapter we have just scratched the surface. Be not content with our Babylonish traditions. But, only change when the spirit leads. God wants us to be different, and He <u>will</u> direct us.

Without heeding these warning words, the spirit will continue to dry up in your services.

Paul quoted God:
Hebrews 8:5 See that you make all things according to the pattern.

If you don't build the church "according to pattern," it won't work. Let's seek the pattern! I have been accused of trying to destroy the foundation which has been established. Personal authority of strong preachers is threatened. However, that is what Yeshua wanted to avoid! AND, But, it was we, ourselves, who instituted our traditions, not the pattern, not from Jesus and the apostles. We made the pattern. There is more new wine coming, which the old bottles we are using cannot hold. It was new wine in the early church, but a lot of it spilled out or got tainted along the way. When God withdraws His Presence, He may be provoking us to make changes quickly while we have time. How long aught we to wait to change? How long shall we yet remain in Babylon's bonds?

Revelation 18:4 And I heard another voice from heaven, saying, "Come out of her, My people, that you be not partakers of her sins, and that you receive not of her plagues.

Isaiah 52:2 Shake yourself from the dust, arise; Sit down, O Jerusalem! Loose yourself from the bonds of your neck, O captive daughter of Zion!

It is apparent that we are able to continue to function in church as we always have, employing the traditions handed down to us from the synagogue, Constantine, and Luther. But, we are witnessing something very telling, if anyone will stop and observe: the spirit of God is not being manifested much anymore when the preachers preach. God has withdrawn His Presence. In many places they work up fleshly demonstrations. But, there is nothing in this world like the true witness from Heaven. There is such a thrill in the assembly when Heaven is touched.

I suppose tradition will be able to carry us on for a long while longer, and we'll still be thinking that we are setting the world on fire. But, the reality is that God has turned the corner,......and <u>we</u> have not; we've not yet come all the way out of Babylon.

That which you <u>suppose</u> you know is that which prevents you from progressing.

40 All the Way out of Babylon

Musmeah Yeshua [Bringing Forth Salvation] Synagogue, Rangoon, Myanmar (Burma)

Temple Adath Israel, Louisville, Kentucky became Greater Bethel Apostolic Church

Acts 2:1,2 When the Day of Pentecost had fully come, they were all with one accord in one place.

Chapter 5. The Synagogue Factor
In The Fall Of The Church

It was being taught in some of the churches around 50 AD that the second coming of Jesus had already occurred and that the bride of Christ had already been caught away, which teaching was overthrowing the faith of some of the saints. It was also sowing confusion in the congregations, especially since Paul had specifically instructed them otherwise. He felt it necessary to reiterate this in a letter to the Macedonian churches. He urged them

2 Thessalonians 2:2 not to become easily unsettled or alarmed by some prophecy, report or letter supposed to have come from us, saying that the day of the Lord has already come (NIV).

He further exhorted:
*v3 Let no man deceive you by any means: for that day shall not come, except there come a **falling away** first, and that man of sin be revealed, the son of perdition.*

(Aside from the *KJV*, most other translations render the word *apostasia* as "rebellion," but we think "falling away" is an appropriate rendering.)

Paul was saying that the day of the second coming would not occur until two things happened first:
1) that the church would fall away, that is apostatize (The *Greek* word used here is *a-post'-a-si'-a*); and
2) that the "man of sin" be made known.

Paul even reminded the church:

v5 Don't you remember that when I was with you I used to tell you these things?

Upon point #2 above we shall make no comment in this article, but the first item is one of our topics of discussion. When considering this "falling away" I had several thoughts and questions come to mind:
1) Paul knew the church was going to apostatize;
2) Was it necessary for Jesus' church to fall away?;
3) Couldn't Jesus have prevented this from happening?;
4) It was fore-ordained that the church would fall;
5) Why did it happen?; and
6) What divine purpose was to be accomplished by this apostasy?

With regard to Paul's foresight concerning the falling away we have much evidence. Paul told Timothy about it.
1 Timothy 4:1 Now the spirit speaks expressly, that in the latter times some shall depart from the faith, giving heed to seducing spirits, and doctrines of devils...

The holy spirit had spoken, perhaps in many different church meetings around the world by interpretation of tongues and by prophecy that these things would occur.
2 Timothy 4:3,4 For the time will come when they will not endure sound doctrine; but after their own lusts shall they heap to themselves teachers, having itching ears; And

they shall turn away their ears from the truth, and shall be turned unto fables.

Acts 20:29,30 For I know this, that after my departing shall grievous wolves enter in among you, not sparing the flock. Also of your own selves shall men arise, speaking perverse things, to draw away disciples after them.

Peter also predicted the same apostasy:
2 Peter 2:1,2 But there were false prophets also among the people, even as there shall be false teachers among you, who secretly shall bring in damnable heresies, even denying the Lord that bought them, and bring upon themselves swift destruction. And many shall follow their pernicious ways; by reason of whom the way of truth shall be evil spoken of.

John too, was aware:
1 John 2:18,19 Little children, it is the last time: and as you have heard that antichrist shall come, even now are there many antichrists; whereby we know that it is the last time. They went out from us, but they were not of us; for if they had been of us, they would no doubt have continued with us: but they went out, that they might be made manifest that they were not all of us.

The epistle of Jude deals with heresy in the church. Jude urgently says:
Jude 3,4 It was needful for me to write unto you, and exhort you that you should earnestly contend for the faith which was once delivered unto the saints. For there are certain men crept in unawares, who were before of old ordained to this condemnation, ungodly men, turning the grace of our God into lasciviousness, and denying the only Lord God, and our Lord Jesus Christ.

And all of this was not surprising insight to the apostles, because, Jesus, himself, had forewarned of the falling away.
*Matthew 24:5,10-12 For many shall come in my name, saying, I am Christ; and shall **deceive** many...And then shall many be offended, and shall betray one another, and shall hate one another. And many false prophets shall rise, and shall deceive many. And because iniquity shall abound, the love of many shall wax cold.*

Matthew 24:24,25 For there shall arise false Christs, and false prophets, and shall show great signs and wonders; insomuch that, if it were possible, they shall deceive the very elect. Behold, I have told you before.

The Lord was telling them that apostasy would be a testing for the saints.
Mark 13:21-26 And then if any man shall say to you, "Lo, here is Christ;" or, "Lo, he is there;" believe him not: For false Christs and false prophets shall rise, and shall show signs and wonders, to seduce, if it were possible, even the elect. But take heed: behold, I have foretold you all things. But in those days, after that tribulation, the <u>sun</u> shall be darkened, and the <u>moon</u> shall not give her light, and <u>the stars of heaven</u> shall fall, and the powers that are in heaven shall be shaken. And then shall they see the Son of man coming in the clouds with great power and glory.

Herein, the Lord was predicting just how bad the apostasy would be. The "sun" and the "moon" are the *New* and the *Old Testaments*, the understanding of which would "fall" (decline) and descend into darkness. The "stars of heaven" are the ministers of the church, who would lose understanding of the *scriptures* and fall also into false teaching and immorality. The church world, "heaven," Jesus foretells, will be shaken, and congregations will split. Paul gave a final exhortation:

> *Hebrews 12:25-29 See that you refuse not Him that speaks. For if they (Israel) escaped not who refused him (Moses) that spoke on earth, much more shall not we escape, if we turn away from Him that speaks from heaven (Jesus): Whose voice then shook the earth (at Mt. Sinai): but now He has promised, saying, "Yet once more I **shake** not the earth only, but also heaven." And this word, "Yet once more," signifies the removing of those things that are shaken, as of things that are made, that those things which cannot be shaken may remain. Wherefore, we, receiving a kingdom which cannot be moved, let us have grace, whereby we may serve God acceptably with reverence and godly fear. For our God is a consuming fire.*

The children of Israel were the first to experience the shaking of God. When God promised:

> *Haggai 2:6,7 For thus says the Lord of hosts; "Yet once, it is a little while, and I will **shake** the heavens, and the earth, and the sea, and the dry land; And I will shake all nations, and The Desire Of All Nations shall come: and I will fill this house with glory," says the Lord of hosts.*

This is the passage referred to in *Hebrews* above, to "shake" Israel; God also promised to "shake the heavens," which is the religious world. What cannot be shaken is what will be left, those whom God can use in His eternal kingdom. Jesus is "The Desire-Of-All-Gentiles," (*Hebrew, khem-dat' kawl ha-goy'-im*) and after everything is shaken, then shall he return in glory.

A Brief History of the Synagogue

It was in 722 BC that the northern kingdom of Israel was conquered by Assyria. This was more than a shaking; it was devastation. Samaria was destroyed, and the people of the ten tribes were removed from their country and transported far away to Assyria and resettled. The people of the southern kingdom of Judah attempted to stay in contact with their captive kinsmen, but in little time, they completely lost communication and connection with them. They were thereafter referred to as The Lost Tribes of Israel. Either they had migrated further or had totally amalgamated with the surrounding populations. Whatever, their identity has been totally obscured to this day. Only lately have there been purported discoveries of these peoples.

It was for their waywardness that God destroyed the Kingdom of Israel, so debauched had they become with pagan deities and heathen ways. To have permitted them to stay in their land a moment longer would have led to the corruption of Judah and imperiled the God-plan of bringing forth the Messiah, the Christ, from the Israelite nation. So, it was the direct intervention of the Almighty that led to the utter erasing of a nation.

Perhaps the expulsion had not occurred soon enough, for the poison had already infected Judah, Benjamin, and the Levites. So far into corruption they had also progressed with absolute disregard for morals and adherence to the *Law of God*, that it became necessary that they also be shaken to the very core of their national identity.

A new power arose in the place of Assyria, the Babylonians, who in short order conquered the known world, scattering their vanquished foes hither and yon. The Hittites and the Persians were defeated. Ultimately, King Nebu-khadnezzar marched upon little Judah. In the bloody end, Jerusalem was burned, and the nation removed to Babylon. It was here that the expression "Jew," from the word "Judah," was first used.

The Jews had been so confident that they were God's people; they had felt they were invincible. They were stunned by their captivity. They were devastated.

Psalm 137:1-4 By the rivers of Babylon, there we sat down, yea, we wept, when we remembered Zion. We hung our harps upon the willows in the midst thereof. For there, they that carried us away captive required of us a song; and they that wasted us required of us mirth, saying, "Sing us one of the songs of Zion." How shall we sing the Lord's song in a strange land?

I hope you can sense the *pathos* of this passage. Among the leaders of the Jews there was this haunting worry that the fate that had befallen the northern tribes would shortly befall them. What could be done to keep the people from forgetting their heritage and melting in with this brutish horde? What's more, how would the eternal plan of God Almighty to bring forth a messiah from these people be affected? The Psalmist lamented:

Psalm 137:5-8 If I forget you, O Jerusalem, let my right hand forget her cunning. If I do not remember you, let my tongue cleave to the roof of my mouth; if I prefer not Jerusalem above my chief joy. Remember, O Lord, the children of Edom in the day of Jerusalem; who said, "Rase it, rase it, even to the foundation thereof." O daughter of Babylon, who is to be destroyed; happy shall he be, that rewards you as you have served (treated) us.

It was in the year 586 BC that the elders of the Jews met in the town of Tel Aviv, a community located on the Khebar Canal which connected the Tigris and Euphrates Rivers in what would today be southern Iraq.

What could be done to maintain the national identity of the Jewish people in the midst of gentiles? How could the integrity of Judah be kept? The plan that came forth was the construction of "synagogues." Ultimately three architectural styles were adopted, the most common being a rectangular shape. Rows of benches (pews) were placed facing in the direction toward Jerusalem. At the Jerusalem end of the room, called the sanctuary, was a raised platform, called the "*bema*." Chairs for the officials of the congregation were placed on the *bema*. Certain chairs became placed in such arrangement for the president of the congregation and other notables, that these chairs became known as "chief seats." At the rear of the platform was a chest called, the ark, wherein were the congregation's copies of the Torah law and the Prophetic scrolls. There was a baptistery, the *mik'-vah*, for new converts and for purification, especially for the women after child-birth and monthly. There was a lectern, the *lu-ach*, also called the *pulpitum* in *Latin*.

The architecture is so similar to that of a Christian church building that often in history one building has served alternately as a church and then a synagogue or visa versa. In my own state of Kentucky this has been the case. In 1903 the Brith Sholom congregation outgrew its synagogue on First Street in Louisville and moved into a building that had been the College Street Presbyterian Church. Similarly did the United Hebrew Congregation in Newport, and Beth Hamedrash in Louisville, and Temple Adath Israel in Lexington. Lexington's Ohavay Zion Synagogue moved into what had been a Presbyterian church. In 1917 Louisville's Agudath Achim moved into what was formerly St. John's Episcopal.

In no case did a Jewish congregation remove a stained glass window. Nor have Christian churches much altered Hebraic motifs when they have moved into former synagogues. Louisville's Adath Israel on Third Street is now the Greater Bethel Apostolic Pentecostal Church [Photo, page 36]. The Ten Commandments still appear in both English and Hebrew on the front wall of the sanctuary. The verses "Hear O Israel, the Lord our God, the Lord is One" in English and "The Lord is God" in *Hebrew* still appear in gold lettering over the ark where Torah scrolls once sat.

The Ashland, Kentucky, Agudath Achim Temple is now a church. The niche where was once the ark now contains a depiction of Jesus. Calvary Pentecostal Cathedral in Louisville, once Keneseth Israel, has two suspended doves in the ark with the inscription "Jesus is Here."

At Louisville's Unity Temple, once congregation Adath Jeshurun, the dome still displays a giant Star of David. (This information has been taken from Lee Shai Weissbach's excellent book, <u>The Synagogues of Kentucky</u>.) One might suspect that Christian church buildings actually have their origin in the synagogue architecture.

Now, in the time of the Babylonian captivity, not only did the synagogue come into being, but a new class of people called "Rabbis." It became their function to sermonize on the day's scriptural reading. Many rabbis became very adept at "stringing pearls," putting one scripture passage with another and another to make a point. Jews today still thrill at a minister who does this so masterfully. You have probably heard Christian preachers do this, too. It was perhaps fortunate for the religion that grew out of the synagogue, called "*Judaism*," that this institution came into existence when it did, because, within one generation of their Babylonian captivity, the people adopted the *Aramaic* language and forgot *Hebrew*. *Aramaic* had been the language of Damascus. When the Syrians were brought into captivity, the Empire took up their *Aramaic* tongue and ceased to speak *Khaldee*. *Aramaic* became the language of Babylon, and then that of the Jews.

The Rabbis began to study and to make comment and explanation upon the Torah law, eventually compiling the most-noted analyses into a written volume called the *Talmud*. Eventually, they claimed the origin of these writings, this "Oral Law," had been God, Himself, spoken directly to Moses at the time He gave Moses the "written" Law. The two bodies of law, they alleged, went hand-in-hand. For instance, the Torah says:

Exodus 20:8 Remember the sabbath day, to keep it holy.

The *Talmud* gives thirty eight laws regarding sabbath-keeping.

So now, the Jews could not understand their own *holy scriptures*. The International Standard Bible Encyclopaedia tells us that a new official came into being in the synagogue, called a *me-thur'-ga-man*, whose duty was to interpret into "*Aramaic* the passages of the *Law* and the Prophets which were read in *Hebrew*." Notice, it did not say "translate," but, "interpret." The rabbis regarded the *Hebrew scriptures* too holy to "translate" into another language. The *methurgamans* could only give the "sense" of what the *Bible* meant, which was called "*tar'-gum-ming*." Eventually this prohibition was waived, and the *scriptures* were finally written in *Aramaic* and entitled, *The Targum* in about 200 AD.

The *Aramaic* and *Hebrew* languages sprang from the same source and were similar in somewhat the same way that *Dutch* and *German* are alike. However, just as no one from Holland understands German, neither did the Jews understand the old *Hebrew*. Although they referred to their new language as "*Hebrew*," they were actually speaking in *Aramaic*. The holiest music of Jewish liturgy was written, not in *Hebrew*, but in *Aramaic* in 1492 in Portugal during the Catholic Inquisition era. It is today sung in every synagogue in the world, in *Aramaic*, on the Eve of *Yom Kip-pur'*, the Day of Atonement. As a matter of fact, no other song is regarded by the Jews in the same category of sacredness as *Kol Ni'-dre*, "All The Vows." It is a song of repentance for the breaking of one's word, not only to God, but to other men. This is a time of deep inner-reflection and tears.

Is it not interesting that *Hebrew* was a dead language from 500 BC until 1948, when the new state of Israel adopted it as its national language? No other extinct language has ever revived twenty five centuries after its demise! (Please see our article: The Languages of the Jews.)

The *Talmud* claims that God spoke this to Moses, which was passed down, mouth-to-ear, over the centuries till written down in the *Talmud*. The *Talmud* implies the existence of the synagogue in the time of Jacob:
> *Genesis 25:27 ...Esau was a cunning hunter, a man of the field; and Jacob was a plain man, **dwelling in tents**.*

By giving such ancient origin to the Oral Law and to the Synagogue, the rabbis hoped to add credence to their own creativity. *Judaism* is based on the Oral Law of rabbinic traditions, rather than the *Bible*. Judaism is based on the rabbi's Oral Law, rather than the *Bible*!

As we said above, the Jews referred to their new language as "*Hebrew*," although it was actually *Aramaic*. For example:
> *John 5:2 Now there is at Jerusalem by the sheep market a pool, which is called in the* Hebrew *tongue Bethesda, having five porches.*

John clearly said it was "*Hebrew*." However, in Strong's Concordance, it states:
> NT:964 Bethesda; of *Aramaic* origin; house of kindness; a pool in Jerusalem.

The expression "the *Hebrew* tongue," is used nine other times in the *New Testament* (*Luke* 23:28; *John* 19:13,17,20; *Acts* 21:40; 22:2; 26:14; *Revelation* 9:11; 16:16), but, in every case, the word or sentence is actually *Aramaic*!

When Jesus was dying on the cross he quoted *Psalm* 22:1 in *Aramaic*, not *Hebrew*.

Had he spoken in *Hebrew*, no one would have understood him.

> (*Psalm* 22:1 in *Hebrew*: *Eli, Eli, law-maw zab'-taw-ney.*)

> *Mark 15:34 And at the ninth hour Jesus cried with a loud voice, saying, "Eloi, Eloi, lama sabachthani?" which is, being interpreted, "My God, my God, why have You forsaken me?"*

(One might question why it is slightly different in
> *Matthew 27:46:* Eli, Eli, lama sabachthani? Instead of "Eloi, Eloi...")

The reason for this difference is that Mark was from Judea and spoke in the Judean accent (dialect) of *Aramaic*, whereas Matthew was a Galilean, who's accent was like Peter's (as you may recall when he denied Christ three times before the cock crowed):
> *Mark 14:70 Surely you are one of them: for you are a Galilean, and **your speech** agrees thereto.*

Peter spoke the Galilean dialect of *Aramaic*. (Isn't language an amazing thing? When God confounded the tongues, He really did a good job!)

Now, the Babylonian captivity lasted seventy years till that empire was conquered by the Persians and Medes. The Jews were permitted to return to their Promised Land. And so, some did. But, actually, only a remnant returned, about ten percent. The rest had discovered prosperous lives in the *Di-as'-po-ra*, the "Lands of Dispersion." No longer were they a pastoral people. Now, they were merchants and artisans, traits learned in Babylonia, which are still with the Jews world-wide to this day.

Those who did return brought with them some new things: 1) the *Aramaic* language; 2) *Judaism*; 3) rabbis; 4) a belief in one God; and 5) the synagogue. All over Judea and Galilee there were synagogues built. Even, the half-breed Samaritans built synagogues. There were the new Temple and also new synagogues. To illustrate: there were thirteen synagogues in Tiberias, Galilee, not a big city. Jerusalem had four hundred eighty. As the Jews continued to spread out over the known world, they took the synagogue-concept with them.

In about 330 BC another momentous change took place, the downfall of Persia and the rise of the new, Greek empire of Alexander the Great. The avowed purpose of Alexander's conquests was to spread *Hellenism*, the Greek culture, around the world. *Hellenism* is about as opposite to Hebrew culture as anything could be, yet some of the Jews took to it like no other people in the world. All through Judea, Galilee, Perea, and the Decopolis the new, Greek culture was exalted. The entire Jewish population spoke the *Greek* language now, as well as *Aramaic*. They were bi-lingual.

Before his death, Alexander had laid out the plans for a new city at the mouth of the Nile River in Egypt, Alexandria, which was quickly to become the greatest city of the ancient world. Even years later at the height of the Roman Empire, Alexandria was one-and-one-half times larger than Rome. Broad boulevards ran through the city down to the harbors. People of all nations resided there. It soon became a haven for the Jews, as well. The largest synagogue was located there. It was so vast that the people in the rear could not hear nor see what was going on in the services. An ingenious system of flag signals was invented. About half way back at the sides of the pews were flag wavers who gave signals informing the congregants just where they were in the service.

There were many other synagogues in Alexandria. There was a synagogue for those families who were tanners. There was one for those who were blacksmiths. There was one for those with a Syrian background. There was one for Jews from Spain and others for Jews of a myriad of national origins, backgrounds, and occupations. And all these Jews, and those in Babylon, and those scattered everywhere else were quite faithful to make at least one pilgrimage a year to worship the Lord at the Temple in Jerusalem.

When Jesus came on the scene, it was his practice to go to the Temple in Jerusalem, which was also the custom of his family.
> *Luke 2:41 Now his parents went to Jerusalem every year at the feast of the Passover.*

And Jesus also frequented the synagogue:
> *Luke 4:16 And (Jesus) came to Nazareth, where he had been brought up: and, <u>as his custom</u> was, he went into the synagogue on the sabbath day, and stood up for to read.*

It had become the custom that the entire *Law* was read completely through in the course of a one-year cycle of abbath services. On the day after the Feast of Tabernacles the year's cycle ended with the reading of the end of *Deuteronomy* and beginning again with *Genesis* 1:1. This day is called *Sim-chat' Torah*, that is, "the Joy of the Law."
> *Acts 15:21 For Moses of old time has in every city them that preach him, being read in the synagogues every abbath day.*

It also became established that following each week's reading of the *Law of Moses* that a portion of the *Prophets* was also read.
> *Acts 13:13-15 Paul and his company...came to Antioch in Pisidia, and went into the synagogue on the sabbath day, and sat down. And after the reading of the **Law and the Prophets**...*

It was not just any portion from the prophets, but a particular prophetic portion became attached to each week's Torah portion, and this did not vary from year to year, but was always the same. It became tradition.

Seven readers were called to the *bema*, one priest, one Levite, and five other men, each reading in *Hebrew* at least three verses. It became customary in mock-humility for a reader to decline until being begged twice more to come forth to the platform.

The Torah portion that day (in Nazareth) (*Luke* 4:16) would have been from *Numbers*. The prophetic reading was from *Isaiah* 61. Jesus did not choose his passage to read; it had long ago been established by tradition, and it was read in every synagogue in the world that day. Think of it. He was to read a passage that spoke of himself, and it was the Providence of God that had set that particular scripture for that particular day. Everyone thought it was just tradition, but it was the Almighty God who had moved behind the scene.
> *Luke 4:17-20 And there was delivered unto him the book of the prophet* Esaias (Isaiah). *And when he had opened the book, he found the place where it was written, "The spirit of the Lord is upon me, because He has anointed me to preach the gospel to the poor; He has sent me to heal the brokenhearted, to preach*

deliverance to the captives, and recovering of sight to the blind, to set at liberty them that are bruised, to preach the acceptable year of the Lord. And he closed the book, and he gave it again to the minister, and sat down. And the eyes of all them that were in the synagogue were fastened on him.

The drama of this situation was intense. Jesus had upset the money-changers in the Temple; then, he had performed a miracle at a wedding in Cana that had everybody buzzing. He had healed a lame man in Capernaum. And now he had returned to his home town on the sabbath. Their eyes were fixed on him.

After reading the scripture in *Isaiah*, he closed the book. This was not a book like you would see today, but was a scroll attached to two wooden rollers. "Closing the book" meant that he rolled up the scroll, placed upon it the cloth cover, which had two holes in the top for the rollers, hung upon the rollers a chain to which was attached a silver pointer, all done very ceremoniously. Then he handed the scroll to the rabbi or congregation president. And then he exclaimed:
Luke 4:21,22 "This day is this scripture fulfilled in your ears." And all bare him witness, and wondered at the gracious words which proceeded out of his mouth. And they said, "Is not this Joseph's son?"

The people were very familiar with this passage. They well-knew that it was speaking of the coming-messiah. They clearly understood that Jesus was claiming to be him, the Christ, the very fulfillment of the prophecy. You can imagine the stir that went through the sanctuary.

Yet, that was not the only strange thing that had occurred. Jesus had read but one-and-one-half verses before closing the book. They knew he had not completed his assigned portion. He had stopped before he read
Isaiah 61:2 and the day of vengeance of our God...

Although Jesus did not complete that verse, the knowledgeable congregation finished the passage in their minds. Here Jesus had employed a technique employed in the Academy: one actually was speaking of the passage which he did NOT read. When he then said, "This day this scripture is fulfilled in your ears," they new Jesus was claiming divinity. "Kill him!"

Not only did Jesus preach to crowds of people out in the open, by the Lake, or in the desert, but the synagogue was also his venue.
Matthew 9:35 And Jesus went about all the cities and villages, teaching in their synagogues, and preaching the gospel of the kingdom, and healing every sickness and every disease among the people.

However, when the Assembly of Jesus was inaugurated on the Day of Pentecost in about the year 30 AD, there was a different kind of protocol. The worship of the *New Testament* did not fit the old synagogue. The new Christians met any place they could, in homes, in the courtyard of the Temple, itself, on the streets, in amphitheaters. There is not one instance in *scripture* where a church met in a synagogue. Never did an early Christian congregation meet in a synagogue!

When the apostle Paul began his ministry it seems that he always went to the Jewish synagogue first thing. Although Paul was

the apostle to the gentiles, he gave first consideration to the Jews.
> *Romans 2:10 But glory, honor, and peace, to every man that works good, to the Jew first, and also to the Gentile.*

Paul began this custom shortly after his conversion in Damascus.
> *Acts 9:20 And straightway he preached Christ in the <u>synagogues</u>, that he is the Son of God.*

It seems Paul always began his ministry in any city in the synagogue. Please see a complete list of scripture-references (Chapter 2).

Paul went first to the synagogues, but he brought his converts out of them. The synagogue buildings were not conducive to spirit-filled worship. They did not lend themselves well to intimate Christian devotion and adoration and fellowship. It would be impossible to fit a "holy-ghost" meeting into the canned services in the synagogue repeating the same rituals and traditions week after week. Can you imagine trying to squeeze into a synagogue service speaking in tongues, interpretations, prophecies, discerning of spirits, words of knowledge, healings, and vociferous, energetic, enthusiastic worship? The churches were alive, on fire, vigorous. Programmed, synagogue "services" were just dead.

We have much evidence that the earliest meetings of the church were often held in homes.

It was in the upper room of a home in Troas where "the disciples came together to break bread, Paul preached...until midnight." A young man named Eutychus fell asleep and was killed falling from the third loft, but Paul raised him up alive (*Acts 20:7-12*).

I think the pattern for church gatherings was set in the very beginning days of the church.
> *Acts 2:46 And they, continuing daily with one accord in the temple, and breaking bread **from house to house**, did eat their meat with gladness and singleness of heart...*

> *Acts 5:42 And daily in the temple, and in **every house**, they ceased not to teach and preach Jesus Christ.*

How different was the fellowship of the assembly compared to the "services" of the synagogue! Certainly, meetings in homes and meetings in larger gatherings of "the whole church" (*1 Corinthians* 14:23) were led by the holy spirit. Paul mentions churches in the homes of different saints in his letters.

Toward the end of Paul's ministry on his way to Jerusalem for the last time, he stopped in Miletus and sent for the elders of the church in Ephesus to meet with him, to whom he gave exhortation and warning, to which we earlier referred (page 2):
> *Acts 20:20 ...I kept back nothing that was profitable unto you, but have showed you, and have taught you publicly, and **from house to house**...*

Of all the problems which the apostle Paul faced in his years of serving the Lord, the most persistent was that of the Judaizers. Were they his "thorn-in-the-flesh?" These people were Christians who sincerely felt that many of the things of the *Law of Moses* were not only meaningful for the church, but that their observances were incumbent for Christians.

Paul taught that the rituals and ceremonies of the *Law* were to be regarded as teachers and pictures of things pertaining to Christ, who had fulfilled the *Law* by his death at Calvary. It was the heartfelt opinion of the synagogue party that Paul, himself, had **fallen away** from the faith.

For example, the question of circumcision had been dealt with in a conference in Jerusalem in about 52 AD in which an official letter was sent to the congregation in Antioch stating:

> *Acts 15:24 Forasmuch as we have heard, that certain which went out from us have troubled you with words, subverting your souls, saying, "You must be circumcised, and keep the Law:" to whom we gave no such commandment...*

But, in no way did this fix the problem, but it only increased. Even some of the leaders of the Jerusalem assembly were not sound in their doctrine or behavior, most notably James, Jesus' brother, and Peter, who was adversely influenced by James. This was more than enough opposition to Paul's teaching to eventually subvert the truth.

When Paul finally reached Jerusalem the last time, he gave a grand report of his monumental work among the gentiles, which evoked glorious praise from James and the elders, who then said to Paul, in almost the same breath:

> *Acts 21:20,21 And when they heard it, they glorified the Lord, and said unto (Paul), "You see, brother, how many thousands of Jews there are which believe;* and they are all zealous of the* Law*: And they are informed of you, that you teach all the Jews which are among the Gentiles to forsake Moses, saying that they ought not to circumcise their children, neither to walk after the customs..."*

(* *James* 2:2 may indicate that some of the churches in Jerusalem met in synagogues.)

The Falling Away

Incidentally, the word "forsake," *Acts* 21:21 is the *Greek* word *apostasia*. These Judaizers felt that Paul had "fallen away" and forsaken Moses. A great deal of the blame for the Judaization of the Church must be laid upon the leadership of the mother church in Jerusalem for having not clearly taught the fulfillment and conclusion of the legal rituals of the *Law of Moses*.

Paul was shortly thereafter removed to Rome where he ministered some brief time before his death. And now, there was little to hold back the influence of the synagogue party. It was not long until "church worship followed the synagogue pattern with Scripture-reading, prayer, and a sermon" (Nelson's Illustrated Bible Dictionary, 1986, Thomas Nelson Publishers).

"Going-to-church" is an expression originated in the synagogue. (Jews commonly refer to going to synagogue by the term "going to *shool*," which is so similar the English word "school," as to leave no doubt to its meaning. Indeed, the synagogue was, in many aspects, a school.)

Soon synagogue-type buildings were used for church gatherings. "The oldest Christian meetings and meeting-places were modeled on the pattern of the synagogues." "Having-services" is a synagogue term. (International Standard Bible Encyclopedia, 1996)

Soon, also, the system of administration of the church was altered, no longer led by ordained elders, but by preachers in the rabbinic mold. "The government of the church evidently came from the synagogue, not from the Aaronic priesthood. So also did the worship; with the addition of the new doctrines, the gifts of the spirit, and the supper of the Lord." Actually "services" was a terminology borrowed from the original Temple "service." (Fausset's Bible Dictionary, 1998)

The Epistle of Ignatius to the Magnesians (about 100 AD) refers to Sunday as "the Lord's day, the queen and prince of all days." Chrysostom said, "It was called the Lord's day because the Lord rose from the dead on that day." Justin Martyr wrote, "On Sunday we hold our joint meeting." So, it would seem conclusive that by the second century that the church met on Sundays, and this done partly in contrast to the Jewish seventh-day observance. It also seems that Sunday was referred to as "the Lord's day." Almost all biblical commentators concur.

"Elder-shepherd/pastors" were integral parts of the early church and were very early in Israelite history, but not part of the synagogue. Then the apostatizing church, emulating the synagogue, practically did away with a multiple elder-pastors, as well as all the other offices of the ministry. Two thousand years later the offices of apostle, prophet, teacher, and evangelist are still not employed according the new-testament pattern. Repeat: Two thousand years later the offices of apostle, prophet, teacher, and evangelist are still not employed in the Church.

The evolution from "elders" to one prominent, rabbi-style, head-preacher was the origin of bishops, who claimed authority over assemblies in a particular region. The local churches had completely lost their autonomy to the bishops. Dominant bishops prevailed over larger geographical areas and became known as "arch-bishops." In the ultimate "falling-away," the Bishop of Rome achieved preeminence over all the ecclesiastical hierarchy becoming Pope.

After the reign of Emperor Constantine, *Roman Catholicism* became the state-religion of the Roman Empire. Wherever the dominion expanded it encountered peoples with strange pagan religions and deities. Rather than expunge these false gods and doctrines, the church graciously accommodated them into the Christian faith, until a pantheon of divine saints and their statues were worshipped and adored by Christians.

Later Popes claimed to be Vicars of Christ, i.e. vice-Christs. They asserted that they were Christ on earth. The church continued its falling away for over a thousand years until the Protestant Reformation began a reversal of the apostasy.

When John Calvin visited Rome, he was given a tour of the grand palaces and church edifices there. His guide proudly proclaimed, "So, you see, we can no longer say, 'Silver and gold have we none' (*Acts* 3:6)." To which Calvin replied, "And, neither can we say, 'Such as we have, we give unto thee'."

The Result and God's Solution

The worst cause and effect of the fall of the church was paganization, the introduction into the Christian faith of Babylonian ideas, and also, anti-Semitism which was the despicable invention within the Christian Church. But, the preceding evil was the subversion of the authority of the local church elders to one principal "rabbi"-preacher, the loss of autonomy of the local church, and the establishment of a hierarchy of international church officials.

And, it was the Judaization of the church that opened the door for the falling-away. The mimicry of synagogue ritual and Jewish custom by and in the early church translated into practices with a Christianized flavor. And these became embellished with pomp and grandeur. This was an incredible Babylonious departure from the simple faith that Christ had espoused.
> *2 Corinthians 1:12,13 For our boasting is this: the testimony of our conscience (is) that we conducted ourselves in the world in <u>simplicity</u> and <u>godly sincerity</u>, not with fleshly wisdom but by the <u>grace</u> of God, and more abundantly toward you.*

Oh, what a radical deviation the church made from the lofty ideals of the apostle: simplicity, godly sincerity, and grace. But, Paul was not ignorant of what lay ahead, nor was he slack in forewarning.
> *2 Corinthians 11:2,3 For I am jealous over you with godly jealousy: for I have espoused you to one husband, that I may present you as a chaste virgin to Christ. But I fear, lest by any means, as the serpent beguiled Eve through his subtlety, so your minds should be corrupted from the **simplicity** that is in Christ.*

Could the saints be polluted from the simplicity of the *Gospel*? Paul could already see this tendency in the people.
> *2 Corinthians 11:4 ...If (one) comes (and) preaches another Jesus, whom we have not preached, or if you receive another spirit, which you have not received, or another gospel, which you have not accepted, you might well bear with him.*

These were saints who came into Christ through Paul, people well-grounded in the truth, yet they were subject to hearing something different and accepting it. Listen to this verse in *The Living Bible*:
> *You seem so gullible: you believe whatever anyone tells you even if he is preaching about another Jesus than the one we preach, or a different spirit than the holy spirit you received, or shows you a different way to be saved. You swallow it all.*

Indeed. The church swallowed it all. Down it went. Ultimately, God made a reverse move, the Reformation. God has not been in a hurry since the 1500's, and, at this writing. We're still unlike the early church.

The noted twentieth century Pentecostal theologian William Sowders was one who saw the reformation as a continual process toward the restoration of the original glory and power of that church. He felt that the Restoration would have to pass through all the stages of the falling-away, but in <u>reverse order</u>.

It is, therefore, with this idea in mind that I wanted to lay out the serious depravity of "the synagogue movement" in the early church and the spiritless evil of the Judaizers. (Making such comments, perhaps, one of Jewish background, as myself, would less-likely be charged with anti-Semitism than anyone else.)

If Sowders were correct, that the phases of the falling-away would be revisited and corrected in reverse order, then we need to note those errors closely and clearly, so that we will know just what yet needs to be eradicated or amended. (See *Joel* 1:4;2:25)

I believe that the early church and the ultimate restored church were and will be vastly different than the organism we call "the church" today.

Will we be bold enough to come out of the comfortable, warm, dark cocoon of yesterday's Tradition? Will we be able to break the shackles of the habits and fashions and customs and observances in which we have grown up and with which we are so familiar? Will we dare to change the cherished, but flawed, tainted, and imperfect things that have been handed down to us by our honored predecessors?

In fact, there <u>will be</u> those who will be so brave. And brave they will have to be, for theirs will not be a welcome task. They will surely suffer in the worst ways as the foregone martyrs of Jesus have.

But, before the second coming, they will present the world one brief glimpse of the glorious Body of Christ and one momentary, unadulterated, opportunity to
> *Hebrews 6:5 taste the good Word of God, and the Powers* (ministers) *of the world to come.*

Once upon a time there was a woman; she was the Congregation of God.
> *Rev 12:6,14 Then the woman fled into the **wilderness**, where she has a place prepared by God, that they should feed her there one thousand two hundred and sixty days…where she is nourished.*

All those years (of days) the woman was in this "wilderness" condition. Then, God began to make a move and reverse her flight. Here is what Solomon saw.
> *Song of Solomon 8:5 Who is this coming up from the wilderness leaning upon her Beloved?*

Since the time of the Protestant Reformation, the woman, the church of God, has been coming out of the wilderness. Restoration has been God's objective. She shall be magnificent when you see her again.

All the glory that she had in early Jerusalem she shall have again. Once she witnessed to the Jewish nation, who in rejecting her testimony brought upon Israel the judgment of God. Thus, shall it be at the end of the day, a restored church, having come all the out of Babylon. She shall present her testimony to the *goyim*, the gentiles. Then the righteous God shall bring His Judgment upon those who reject her, too.

The Jews had become very comfortable with their traditions and modes of worship: the Temple, the synagogue, Judaism. But, Jesus was bringing them something new, something for another world. He declared:
> *Mark 2:22 No one puts new wine into old wineskins; or else the new wine bursts the wineskins, the wine is spilled, and the wineskins are ruined. But new wine must be put into new wineskins."*

No, the new-covenant order could not function in the confines of Judaism. Yet, over the centuries, Judaistic traditions, Constantinian paganizations, Lutheran appendages and customs have Babylonianized the faith once again, rendering it incapable of receiving heavenly changes. It is "new wine from Pentecost" that is needed, not that it is <u>brand</u> new; it was new from the upper room, and it must be renewed today to receive heaven's work of restoration. We must get out the new wine skins. Our synagogic, Lutheran model WILL NOT WORK.

As I said earlier that I have been asked where I got this notion meet in homes. I know Who gave it to me. My question to you is: Where did you get the notion to build and to meet in synagogues?

Chapter 6. The Fate and The Destiny of Churches

Wherever the Church of Jesus Christ goes, the seed of God's Word is spread plentifully. Jesus is the sower, and he is never stingy. Neither is he picky upon what kind of ground the seed is sown.

> *Mark 4:3-8 There went out a sower to sow. And it came to pass, as he sowed, some fell by the way side, and the fowls of the air came and devoured it up. And some fell on stony ground, where it had not much earth; and immediately it sprang up, because it had no depth of earth. But when the sun was up, it was scorched; and because it had no root, it withered away.*
>
> *And some fell among thorns, and the thorns grew up, and choked it, and it yielded no fruit. And other fell on good ground, and did yield fruit that sprang up and increased.*
>
> *Some fell by the wayside, some on stony ground, some among thorns, and a fourth on good ground. This would seem not to be a good return on the investment, but such is the way of the Kingdom of God.*

Jesus gives us another parable.

> *Matthew 13:24-27 The kingdom of heaven is likened unto a man which sowed good seed in his field. But while men slept, his enemy came and sowed tares among the wheat, and went his way. But when the blade was sprung up, and brought forth fruit, then appeared the tares also. So the servants of the householder came and said unto him, "Sir, did you not sow good seed in your field? From whence then has it tares?"*

The Kingdom of Heaven is the Church. Notice in the above passage that all the seed that was sown was "good seed." But, we see that everyone in the church is not "wheat;" some are "tares," that is, weeds. Everyone in the Church is either one or the other, wheat or weeds. I am either a wheat or a tare; you are either a wheat or a tare.

It is very tempting to look around and start pointing fingers and judging: "There's no way that busy-body is going to make heaven her home!" But, wait! The Lord cautions us against that impulsive idea. We might be the very one that would say:

> *Matthew 13:28-30 "Shall we go and gather them up?" But he said, "No, lest while you gather up the tares, you root up also the wheat with them. Let both grow together until the harvest. And in the time of harvest I will say to the reapers, "Gather together first the tares, and bind them in bundles to burn them; but gather the wheat into my barn."*

He is saying that there will come a time of Judgment, and at that time the decisions will be made on which are which. You might think that it isn't very tidy for the church garden to be growing weeds among the good crop. But, there are several reasons why this is, not only permitted, but is normal for the Church.

One reason for the tares is to test, approve, sanction, and ratify those who are wheat. It is necessary for there to be Bad so that the Good will shine out. Paul was not surprised to hear that there were bad things happening in the Corinthian church.

1 Corinthians 11:18,19 I hear that there are divisions among you; and I partly believe it. For there must be also heresies among you, that they which are approved may be made manifest among you.

Not only were there divisions, but he anticipated false teaching would be given, as well. It was a key in differentiating the wheat from the tares.

The apostle John had a strong word for these folks: anti-christs.

1 John 2:19 They went out from us, but they were not of us; for if they had been of us, they would no doubt have continued with us: but they went out, that they might be made manifest that they were not all of us.

While the ministry today is to judge "matters" within the church (*1 Corinthians 6:2,4*), John is saying that the tares eventually prove what they are. In the Judgment there will not be any "close decisions," no "five to four decisions." It will be "manifest." It will be clear. But, YOU be very careful not to judge who is which. Why? You're not The Judge; Jesus is. You do not know which is which; it has not been revealed to you. He knows; and, guess what? He's not telling now.

But, here is what he IS telling:

John 13:34 A new commandment I give unto you: That you love one another; as I have loved you, that you also love one another.

1 Peter 1:22 Since you have purified your souls in obeying the truth through the spirit in sincere love of the brethren, love one another fervently with a pure heart.

You don't know who is wheat and who are tares. Some tough old miser may end up with a wonderful, generous heart, who leads many to Christ. Some popular pillar of the church may end up being a betrayer. You don't know. All kinds of folks in the church are giving you many opportunities to love.

1 Thessalonians 3:12 The Lord make you to increase and abound in love one toward another.

We are given many occasions to express Christ's love, and the wheat and the tares have many situations to manifest whom they really are.

Another reason for not uprooting the tares in the church, but waiting till God is ready for the Judgment, is that in exposing the tares and rebuking them or dis-fellowshipping them, you may damage one of their close friends or relatives or spouse. God has plenty of time. Unless there is serious corruption, the ministry knows that some things are best left alone. The Judge will take care of them in His time.

We had earlier indicated that Jesus is rather indiscriminate and sweeping in the sowing of his seed. Please consider this parable:

Matthew 22:2,3 The kingdom of heaven is like unto a certain king, which made a marriage for his son and sent forth his servants to call them that were bidden to the wedding: and they would not come.

The "kingdom of heaven" is the church; the "king" is God, and "his son" is Jesus. The "servants" are the ministers of the earliest days of the church. The invited guests were the Jews, who would not come. They rejected the Good News of Jesus Christ.

Therefore, God cast off the Jewish nation, destroyed their country, and scattered the Jews around the world.

Matthew 22:7 But when the king heard thereof, he was wroth: and he sent forth his armies, and destroyed those murderers, and burned up their city.

This opened the way for the gentiles to be invited to enter into the church.

Matthew 22:8-10 Then (the king) said to his servants, "The wedding is ready, but they which were bidden were not worthy. Go therefore into the highways, and as many as you shall find, bid to the marriage." So those servants went out into the highways, and gathered together all as many as they found, both bad and good: and the wedding was furnished with guests.

We are to see here how broad is the invitation, how generous, how encompassing is the opportunity to find Christ. Everybody gets invited: "both bad and good." You mean "bad" people get into the church? Yes. Look at Jude's lament for what these "bad" Christians did:

Jude 4,8,12,13 For certain men have crept in unnoticed, who long ago were marked out for this condemnation, ungodly men, who turn the grace of our God into lewdness and deny the only Lord God and our Lord Jesus Christ...(They) defile the flesh, reject authority, and speak evil of dignitaries...These are spots in your feasts of charity, when they feast with you, feeding themselves without fear: clouds they are without water, carried about of winds; trees whose fruit withers, without fruit, twice dead, plucked up by the roots, raging waves of the sea, foaming out their own shame; wandering stars, to whom is reserved the blackness of darkness forever.

Certain people in the church are determined to cause trouble. Yes, they're in the church; their entry went unnoticed. They're right in there with everybody else. They cause problems. They promote false teaching. They undermine the ministry. They are also destined for "condemnation" in the Day of Judgment.

Say! Do you know which ones they are in your church? No. You don't know which ones they are. So, you most looooooooove everybody!

Today we are nearing the end of an age. It is reported that there are now two billion Christians in the world, all this from a single lone Jesus. As the world's population is increasing by leaps and bounds, it must be noted that over half the people who have ever lived in the history of the world are living today. As the community of the world is multiplying, the same is true of the church, which is increasing in numbers at an astonishing rate.

Most of these new Christians are in "Third World" countries, Africans, Latinos, and Asiatics. Missionaries are fanning out across the globe. Bennie Hin had one service in India in 2005 with two million Christian worshippers, it is said.

Some skeptics charge: "As long as you're offering them food, clothing, and medicine you'll draw a crowd; there are always those seeking after the loaves and fishes."

But, this is a dangerously smug and erroneous view. The natural benefits that are dispensed to these new converts are very minimal. The poverty and diseases in these countries are so enormous that the great charity being directed to them is like a drop in the ocean. If you go to these places, you will find throngs of Christians, still economically depressed. There simply isn't enough wealth and generosity to make that much of difference.

Haiti is an example: huge evangelistic efforts have been going on there for decades. Haiti was the poorest country in the world then, and it still is today. But, there are hundreds of thousands of fervent, new, poor Christians; they've not come for the hand-outs, after all.

What is happening is merely a fulfillment of God's Word to "compel them to come in."
> *Luke 14:23 And the lord said unto the servant, "Go out into the highways and hedges, and compel them to come in, that My House may be filled."*

"My house" is the church. The enormity of the size of the church was even forecast way back in the *Law of Moses*.

You are aware that in the Jewish Feast of Passover that the bread that is eaten is made without leaven. Paul wrote about leaven, calling it "malice and wickedness." He referred to the people of the church as a loaf of leavened bread.
> *1 Corinthians 5:6-8; 10:17 Don't you know that a little leaven leavens the whole lump? Purge out therefore the old leaven, that you may be a new lump, as you are unleavened. For even Christ our Passover is sacrificed for us. Therefore let us keep the feast, not with old leaven, neither with the leaven of malice and wickedness; but with the unleavened bread of sincerity and truth...For we being many are one bread, and one body: for we are all partakers of that one bread (that is, we have all eaten of Jesus).*

By Jesus' suffering and self-sacrifice, and his death on the cross at Calvary, he fulfilled the type of the Passover lamb. He was sacrificed for our sins, our wickedness, our spitefulness. Having become believers in Christ, these old evils have been purged from our lives. We're being made unleavened. Paul urged the church to walk in sincerity and truth, without leaven in our lives.

While Passover foreshadowed the salvation that would come to those who believed in Jesus' death, burial, and resurrection, the following Jewish feast, Pentecost, commemorated the giving of the *Law*, and looked forward to the inauguration of Church of Christ. Bread was also a significant part of the ritual of this festival. But, there was something quite different, it was made WITH leaven.
> *Leviticus 23:17 You shall bring from your dwellings two...loaves of two-tenths of an ephah. They shall be of fine flour; they shall be baked WITH leaven.*

The offering of "two" loaves at Pentecost was quite significant. One loaf represented the Church of Moses; the other represented the Church of Jesus, which includes the gentiles.

But, note that they were baked "with leaven," so that they would rise. The great increase in the size of the leavened loaf predicted the great size of the church. It also foreshadowed something very negative: the church was to be leavened; it was to have within it malice and wickedness and hypocrisy.

The "leavened bread" of Pentecost envisioned a huge church, one with wickedness in it. Certainly, it's not difficult in reading the annals of church history to discover the horrendous, vile acts perpetrated by and in the church. There have been many who have crept in unawares who have propagated murder, looting, and pillaging on a monstrous scale. The deaths and robberies executed by Christians have been incalculable. The church has had no shortage of wickedness and malice. It has surely been baked with leaven.

In like manner Jesus thus described his church:
*Luke 13:20,21 Whereunto shall I liken the kingdom of God? It is like leaven, which a woman took and hid in three measures of meal, till the whole was **leavened**.*

This is a dire prediction for the church: not only was it to tremendously increase in size, but there was to be a time when the entire church was given to leaven, to malice and wickedness. The church surely fell into this state during the Dark Ages. There was little visible holiness and righteousness.

Now, let us pursue some more parables about church-growth; here is another one where Jesus foretells the future enormity of the church:
Luke 13:18,19 Unto what is the kingdom of God like? And whereunto shall I resemble it? It is like a grain of mustard seed, which a man took, and cast into his garden; and it grew, and waxed a great tree; and the fowls of the air lodged in the branches of it.

Some have fabricated stories of having seen such great trees of the mustard family. However, the members of this genus of flowering plants grow to a height of six inches to a couple of feet. The seeds of the black mustard plant are ground into a powder and prepared as a paste for a pungent seasoning for foods. Some other plants of this group are cabbage, turnip, broccoli, radish, celery, and horseradish.

It would certainly be an oddity for a vegetable to grow into "a great tree," wouldn't it? In fact, this parable illustrates an absolutely abnormal growth. Surely, the church is a fulfillment of this parable. Having begun with a tiny seed, that is, Jesus, it now is burgeoning with two billion adherents.

Let us call our attention to the passage: "and the fowls of the air lodged in its branches." This same expression was used in a parable by Ezekiel referring to the pagan Assyrian Empire which disseminated false religion all over the world:
Ezekiel 31:6 All the fowls of heaven made their nests in his boughs.

And in another place, the Babylonian King Nebuchadnezzar had a dream about an enormous tree, which Daniel said represented the King and his kingdom:
*Daniel 4:20-22 The tree that you saw, which grew, and was strong, whose height reached unto the heaven, and the sight thereof to all the earth, whose leaves were fair, and the fruit thereof much, and in it was meat for all; under which the beasts of the field dwelt, and upon whose branches the **fowls of the heaven** had their habitation: It is you, O king, that are grown and become strong: for your greatness is grown, and reaches unto heaven, and your dominion to the end of the earth.*

We know that the pagan Babylonian Empire, the place of the origin of false religion, encompassed the known world. It was like a tree that grew unto the heaven, picturing the exalted place the King and Empire came to believe they were: divine!

Ancient Babylon is a picture of the eventual magnificent power of corrupt religion. The apostle John had a vision of this mystery Babylon, false religion around the world, much of which claims to be Christian. Pay particular attention to the "birds" mentioned here:
> *Revelation 18:1-3 And after these things I saw another angel come down from heaven, having great power; and the earth was lightened with his glory. And he cried mightily with a strong voice, saying, "Babylon the great is fallen, is fallen, and is become the habitation of devils, and the hold of every foul spirit, and a cage of every* **unclean and hateful bird***. For all nations have drunk of the wine of the wrath of her fornication, and the kings of the earth have committed fornication with her, and the merchants of the earth are waxed rich through the abundance of her delicacies."*

What are these fowls of heaven? Are they pheasants? Are they geese or ducks? What are these unclean and hateful birds? They are vultures. They are ravens. They are buzzards. They are scavengers, unclean fowls of the air. They were represented in the dream of pagan Babylon. They are in the vision of Mystery Babylon, the Great, at the end of the age. They are a picture of corruption, of unruly, unrestrained disorder and obscene debauchery.

Mystery Babylon has had her reign of power and horror for thousands of years. Her counterfeit influence has coiled its way throughout human history. God intends to destroy Her in the end.

I would like you to imagine for a moment the apostle John near the end of his life, living on the Isle of Patmos. In his vision he sees the Great Whore of false religion:
> *Revelation 17:6 And I saw the woman drunken with the blood of the saints, and with the blood of the martyrs of Jesus: and when I saw her, I wondered with* **great admiration** *(KJV).*

One might be surprised that a great apostle could come to admire false religion personified in his vision as the Whore. John did not admire her as you may think. Here only is John's wonder called forth: not the beast of civil power become corrupt, but the woman sunken into the harlot, the Church of Jesus Christ become a world-loving apostate, move his astonishment at so awful a change. That the world should be beastly is natural; but that the Church should become the whore is monstrous, and arouses his amazement. John is absolutely astonished that the Church he, himself, saw come purely out of the upper room and be witness to marvelous signs and wonders become what he sees in his vision. He did not admire, as the *KJV* renders, but was amazed, horrified, astonished.

The early church of Jesus Christ had a glorious, but brief season, before she began to leaven and apostatize and fall away. She gave way to false doctrine and opened herself up to paganization. She merged with Babylon. May we repeat a previous scripture?
> *Luke 13:20,21 Whereunto shall I liken the kingdom of God? It is like leaven, which a woman took and hid*

*in three measures of meal, till the **whole** was leavened.*

Virtually unseen on the pages of history is a thin thread of righteous Christians. Her saints are unknown. She existed, mostly recognized only by her founder, Jesus Christ. She has been hidden for lo these many years.
Revelation 12: 6 Then the woman (the church) fled into the wilderness, where she has a place prepared by God.

All these centuries she was hidden, hidden, as it were, in seclusion on the back side of the desert. But, with the Protestant Reformation in the sixteenth century, she began her trek out of the wilderness with her beloved Jesus. God has been making a move of restoration for five hundred years. Then comes the inspired question:
Song of Solomon 8:5 Who is this coming up from the wilderness, leaning upon her Beloved?

THIS woman is the true Church of Christ leaning on her beloved Jesus. In these last years, as we have said, there has been an explosion in the numbers of people who have become converted to Christ around the globe. There have been many moves of God as He progresses to the conclusion of the age. Even in those movements that have been corrupted or tainted by false doctrine and Babylonious teaching, God has been moving. In the midst of the corrupt woman of Babylon, even there, God has been nurturing a multitude of people ignorant of His next action. They are oblivious to the fact that they are even dwelling in Babylon; they don't realize it, yet. But, very soon the Almighty shall issue forth His Call:
Revelation 18:4,5 And I heard another voice from heaven saying, "Come out of her, My people, lest you be partakers of her sins, and lest you receive of her plagues. For her sins have reached to heaven, and God has remembered her iniquities."

Come out of false, Babylonian religion, MY PEOPLE!

As you can see, there are two different symbolic woman mentioned in the *Bible*, one is the true, holy church of God, the other being false religion. We have seen the fate of the Babylonian woman. But, what of the holy church? God has been preparing within her womb a very special group. These are they who have overcome all that is evil and all that is impure in their individual lives. Many have been martyred for their faith and their testimonies. These overcomers have a unique and distinguished role to play in the future history of the world.
Revelation 12:2,4 And she being with child cried, travailing in birth, and pained to be delivered... And she brought forth a man child, who was to rule all nations with a rod of iron: and her child was caught up unto God, and to his throne.

You will note that the woman's child "was to rule." This indicates the purpose this child (i.e., these overcomers) is destined to have.

In the womb of the church, God is producing a select group of saints, who are to "rule all nations with a rod of iron." This "rod of iron" is far stronger than just any metal; it is *The Word of God*; that is the "rod of iron." They are to reign over the earth with Jesus for one thousand years.
Revelation 5:9,10 They sang a new song, saying: "You are worthy to take the Book, and to open its seals; For You were slain, and have

redeemed us to God by Your blood out of every kindred and tongue and people and nation, And have made us kings and priests to our God. And <u>we shall reign on the earth</u>."

Many scriptures in the *Bible* detail the ultimate fate of false religion, but the following vision of John is about as descriptive of her horrible end as there is:

Revelation 18:7-10 In the measure that she glorified herself and lived luxuriously, in the same measure give her torment and sorrow; for she says in her heart, "I sit as queen, and am no widow, and will not see sorrow." Therefore her plagues will come in one day – death and mourning and famine. And she will be utterly burned with fire, for strong is the Lord God who judges her. The kings of the earth who committed fornication and lived luxuriously with her will weep and lament for her, when they see the smoke of her burning, standing at a distance for fear of her torment, saying, "Alas, alas, that great city Babylon, that mighty city! For in one hour your judgment has come."

"The kings of the earth" represent all the nations that have been complicit with her and her deception. That list includes all of the nations on the planet. False religion has plagued the world for millennia. The vision shows that it shall come to total and tragic demise. This is the fate of Babylonian religion: Destruction. Judgment. Smoke.

If that be the fate of the false woman, what then is the destiny of the other true and righteous woman, whose heart is inclined toward God?

Daniel 7:27 And the kingdom and dominion, and the greatness of the kingdom under the whole heaven, shall be given to the people of the saints of the Most High, Whose Kingdom is an everlasting kingdom, and all dominions shall serve and obey Him.

Revelation 20:6 They shall be priests of God and of Christ, and shall reign with him a thousand years.

"Fate" and "destiny" are two similar words. They both refer to an inevitable course of events determined beyond human control. "Fate" usually implies a negative end: death, destruction, and doom, which is to be the conclusion of everything ungodly. "Destiny" is a necessary succession of events and usually implies a favorable outcome.

For the past two thousand years Jesus has been sanctifying and cleansing a people by washing them with His Word. He has been getting all the "leaven" out of their lives. Their destiny is eternal life with Jesus.

Ephesians 5:26,27 That He might sanctify and cleanse (her) with the washing of water by the Word, that He might present (her) to Himself a glorious church, not having spot, or wrinkle, or any such thing; but that (she) should be holy and without blemish.

1 Thessalonians 4:16,17 For the Lord himself shall descend from heaven with a shout, with the voice of the archangel, and with the trump of God: and the dead in Christ shall rise first. Then we which are alive and remain shall be caught up together with them in the clouds, to meet the Lord in the air: and so shall we ever be with the Lord.

We are nearing the conclusion of all things. Are you making yourself ready? Is your heart inclined toward God?

***

I have often heard it said by those who desire to see the "restoration of the church" mention that it should be after the pattern of the assembly in Jerusalem. After I realized that the Jerusalem assembly was "zealous of the *Law*," I disagreed with that goal. What was the zeal of those believers? They were still going to their synagogues; they were still going to the Temple; they were still practicing animal sacrifices; they were still tithing to the Temple. It bothered me that James was supporting such adherence to the "old" faith. Then, I realized that there was no way to get those Jews to change their patterns ingrained over the centuries. They would have never been a part of Christ if they had to abandon their old institutions. I see that there was never any attempt made by the leaders in Jerusalem to do otherwise. These believers were regarded as another Jewish sect of the day, the Nazarenes, and that they remained.

When these believers tried to foist the old system on the gentile believers, however, there was trouble. The gentiles were not going to practice those rituals which Paul had clearly taught were to be understood spiritually and symbolically. They also received a more complete understanding from Paul regarding "grace," which the Jerusalem congregation had not.

Therefore, I think Jerusalem is not the typical pattern to be copied. Since, this is still the "gentile times," I think the pattern that Paul laid out should be pre-eminent.

Saint Peter's, Rome, Italy

Chapter 7. The Sanhedrin

There are those who trace the origin of the Sanhedrin to Moses:

*Numbers 11:16,17 So the Lord said to Moses: "Gather to Me **seventy men** of the elders of Israel, whom you know to be the elders of the people and officers over them; bring them to the tabernacle of meeting, that they may stand there with you. Then I will come down and talk with you there. I will take of the spirit that is upon you and will put the same upon them; and they shall bear the burden of the people with you, that you may not bear it yourself alone*

This was approximately 1500 BC. But, a more appropriate founding date would be 191 BC. The word "Sanhedrin" comes from the Greek word *sun-he-dri-on*. This word is used twenty three times in the *New Testament* and is rendered in English versions as "the council."

The Sanhedrin was often the occasion of bitter debate between adherents of the Sadducee and Pharisee sects. In the early years the Sadducees, the aristocratic priestly element, were dominant, but later the Torah-scholars, the Pharisees got the upper hand. In the last days of the Temple, under the rule of Rome, the Sadducees re-gained the majority.

The official name for this organization was: "The Great Sanhedrin which sits in the hall of hewn stone." Its building straddled the north wall of the courtyard of the Temple in Jerusalem, half of it protruding into the courtyard and half of it outside the Temple complex. The stones of its construction had been cut or hewn with iron instruments in contrast to the unhewn stones of the Temple. The seating arrangement of the Sanhedrin was in rows in the shape of a crescent moon.

The great Sanhedrin was composed of seventy-one priests and sages. The president of the group was called the "nasi," or prince. There was a vice-president of the council, as well, who was called the *Av Bet Din*, the Father of the House of Judgment. When the Sanhedrin sat as a criminal court, it was he who presided.

Usually, a Lesser Sanhedrin of twenty three members convened. In general, the full panel of seventy one judges only met when the twenty-three-member panel could not reach a conclusive verdict or in matters of national significance.

The Maccabees, the Hasmoneans

In 166 BC, the Greco-Syrians over-ran Judea. King Antiochus Epiphanes outlawed sabbath-worship, the rite of circumcision, and the Temple service. A priest named Matathias raised up a rebellion which was captained by his five sons. Judah, known as the Maccabee, was the leader. The sect of the Pharisees supported the Maccabees at first. However, Judah signed a treaty with Rome, which was roundly opposed by the religious party who believed that the people of God ought not be aligned with heathens.

Simon was the only one of the five brothers who survived this successful, twenty-years guerilla warfare, perhaps the first war in world history waged for religious freedom. Simon did something that antagonized the Pharisees again; he made himself both king and also high priest. The Pharisees believed that only the coming-messiah could bear both titles.

Simon's son, King John Hyrcanus, succeeded him to the throne <u>and</u> to the high-priesthood. He angered the Pharisees yet again. He forcibly converted the Edomites to Judaism. The Pharisees were very evangelistic, but forced-conversion was abominable to them. Incidentally, this conversion to Judaism of the descendants of Esau came back to haunt Israel, for in the next century an Edomite, Herod, became King of the Jews.

The Hasmonean kings presided over the Sanhedrin until 75 BC when King Alexander Jannaeus was succeeded by his wife, Queen Salome Alexandra, a Pharisee.

Authority of the Council

At various times, the Sanhedrin had more or less authority. It had the authority to rule on religious laws, rituals, and scriptural controversies. It ruled on civil cases and even in capital cases such as murder. In Jesus' day the Romans took away the council's authority to execute criminals, which certainly affected the outcome in Jesus of Nazareth's case. Please note what authority the Sanhedrin gave to Saul of Tarsus:
Acts 8:3 As for Saul, he made havoc of the church, entering every house, and dragging off men and women, committing them to prison.

Acts 9:1,2 Then Saul, still breathing threats and murder against the disciples of the Lord, went to the high priest and asked letters from him to the synagogues of Damascus, so that if he found any who were of the Way, whether men or women, he might bring them bound to Jerusalem.

Every city in Palestine had a Sanhedrin of twenty three members; small villages had councils of only three. Appeals were all referred to the court in Jerusalem. (There may have been two Sanhedrins at the Temple, one for religious matters and one for secular concerns.)

Members of the Sanhedrin were said to possess "*sh'mi-hah*," authority. When a member died, hands were laid upon a new man to bring him in as a replacement. It should be noted that the Pharisee contingent of members was composed of scribes and rabbis.

In many instances the "Council" violated their own rules and regulations. They were a "kangaroo court." They were not authorized to meet on holy days; to meet at night; or to meet without a quorum. The leadership of the Sanhedrin had become corrupt and self-serving. The Greek word *Sunhedrion* is rendered in the following verses as "council."
*John 11:47 Then the chief priests and the Pharisees gathered a **council** and said, "What shall we do? For this Man works many signs.*

Here is an example of how corrupt leaders can take over a Council and include only their cronies. You will notice that Joseph of Arimathea was not present. Nicodemus had not been invited. *King James* added "the elders," but that was not in the original text.
*Matthew 26:59 Now the chief priests, ~~the elders~~, and the **council** all sought false testimony against Jesus to put Him to death.*

Caiaphas, the high priest, was the head of a *cabal*, a secret group within the organization, which conspired to convict Jesus by corrupt means. Jesus was arrested

at night <u>and</u> on the sabbath of Unleavened Bread.
> *John 18:3 So Judas came to the grove, guiding a detachment of soldiers and some officials from the chief priests and Pharisees.*
>
> *Mark 15:1 Immediately, at daybreak, the chief held a consultation with the elders and scribes and the whole **council**; and they bound Jesus, led Him away, and delivered Him to Pilate.*
>
> *Luke 22:66,67 And as soon as it was day, the elders of the people and the chief priests and the scribes came together, and led him into their **council**, saying, "Are you the Christ? Tell us.*

Since proclaiming oneself messiah was not forbidden by the *scriptures* (there were many springing up in those days), but, since it was illegal under Roman law to challenge imperial authority, the Sanhedrin confronted Pilate with that strategy:
> *John 19:12 From then on Pilate sought to release Jesus, but the Jews cried out, saying, "If you let this Man go, you are not Caesar's friend. Whoever makes himself a king speaks against Caesar."*

Detractors of the authenticity of the *Bible* argue that since it was forbidden for the Council to meet at night or on a holy day, the *Gospels* could not be accurate, and that this could not have happened to Jesus. But, this was certainly not the only time the Sanhedrin bent its rules: the Council, later on, also arrested the disciples at night.
> *Acts 4:2-3 Being greatly disturbed that (Peter and John) taught the people and preached in Jesus the resurrection from the dead. And they laid hands on them, and put them in custody until the next day, for it was <u>already evening</u>.*
>
> *Acts 5:27,28 And when they had brought the apostles, they set them before the **council**. And the high priest asked them, saying, "Did we not strictly command you not to teach in this name?*
>
> *Acts 6:12 And they stirred up the people, the elders, and the scribes; and they came upon him, seized him, and brought him to the **council**.*
>
> *Acts 23:14,15 We have bound ourselves under a great oath that we will eat nothing until we have killed Paul. Now you, therefore, together with the **council**, suggest to the commander that he be brought down to you tomorrow, as though you were going to make further inquiries concerning him; but we are ready to kill him before he comes near.*

With malice the Sanhedrin convicted Jesus of blasphemy and delivered him to the Romans. Alas! Their troubles were multiplied when the disciples increased greatly in numbers until they filled the city with the messiah's teaching. The Council was an ever-present threat to Jesus and to the Church, as much as the menace of the Romans.

When Jerusalem was destroyed by the Romans in 70 AD, the Temple and the ministering priesthood ended, but, Rabbi Yochanon ben Zacchai had struck a deal with the Roman General Titus to permit the Sanhedrin to move to Yavneh (Jamnia) in Galilee. The Sadducees and all the other Jewish sects ceased at that time, that is, all except the Pharisees from whom modern-day Judaism stems. Ultimately the Council ended up in Tiberius, on the Sea of Galilee. It continued to hold religious authority in Jewish life, to some degree or another into the fifth century AD. Almost all the nasis for the last three hundred years were descendants of Hillel and Gamaliel.

The last known official act of the Sanhedrin was in 358 AD when Hillel II proposed that hence-forth, the Jewish calendar be mathematically-based, which scheme is used to this day.

The last nasi was Gamaliel VI who was executed by Emperor Theodosius II in 425 for illegally erecting new synagogues. The Sanhedrin was then outlawed.

There were occasional attempts to revive the Sanhedrin through the ages. It was briefly accomplished by Emperor Napoleon Bonaparte, who reconstituted *Le Grand Sanhedrin* in Paris in 1806. The French Assembly of Notables issued a proclamation to all the Jewish communities of Europe, inviting them to send delegates to Paris two weeks hence on October 20. The proclamation was written in *Hebrew, French, German*, and *Italian*. The action of Napoleon aroused fervor in the Jews that rights of citizenship which had been achieved by other groups might also become a reality for them.

Napoleon presented the first twelve questions for the new Sanhedrin. The questions presented were:

1. Is it lawful for Jews to have more than one wife?
2. Is divorce allowed by the Jewish religion? Is divorce valid, although pronounced not by courts of justice but by virtue of laws in contradiction to the French code?
3. May a Jewess marry a Christian, or [May] a Jew [marry] a Christian woman? or does Jewish law order that the Jews should only intermarry among themselves?
4. In the eyes of Jews, are Frenchmen not of the Jewish religion considered as brethren or as strangers?
5. What conduct does Jewish law prescribe toward Frenchmen not of the Jewish religion?
6. Do the Jews born in France, and treated by the law as French citizens, acknowledge France as their country? Are they bound to defend it? Are they bound to obey the laws and follow the directions of the civil code?
7. Who elects the rabbis?
8. What kind of police jurisdiction do the rabbis exercise over the Jews? What judicial power do they exercise over them?
9. Are the police jurisdictions of the rabbis and the forms of their election regulated by Jewish law, or are they only sanctioned by custom?
10. Are there professions from which the Jews are excluded by their law?
11. Does Jewish law forbid the Jews to take usury from their brethren?
12. Does it forbid, or does it allow, usury in dealings with strangers?

The decisions of the Grand Sanhedrin, formulated in nine articles and drawn up in *French* and *Hebrew*, were as follows: "polygamy had been authorized but…should cease to be… in the West; that Jews, under *Moses' Law*, considered that only Jews were their brothers… The Sanhedrin decided that all men are brothers, irrespective of their religion, as long as they were not idolatrous, and if Israelites, living among them, enjoyed the same rights which they themselves enjoyed;

having established the fraternity between all men, Israelites had the obligation to defend the land in which they lived (even if the *Law* had only mentioned the duty to defend the Temple of Jerusalem); marriages between Jews and Christians are not *anathema* but represent a necessity to be encouraged...; it is a duty to hold property, etc.; and that *Judaism* does not forbid any kind of handicraft or occupation;..."

The next year Bonaparte invaded Poland against Prussia, and the Jews rendered great services to his army, to which the emperor remarked laughing, "The Sanhedrin is at least useful to me."

In October 2004, a group of rabbis representing various communities in Israel undertook a ceremony in Tiberias, where the old Sanhedrin had once been located. How this new body will fit into the Israeli political scheme of things is a subject of intense debate in Israel these days, since it already has a civil court system and also religious organizations such as the one which sanctions and regulates kosher food.

There are at this time perhaps fifty thousand Christian (messianic) Jews living in Israel. They are among the most avid supporters of the new Sanhedrin. Their reasoning is that it was the Sanhedrin which had originally condemned Jesus, and that it is the only authority having the power to reverse the judgment made two thousand years ago. They believe the Sanhedrin's exoneration of Jesus must and will precede the re-fulfillment of the following prophecy:
> *Zechariah 12:10 And I will pour on the house of David and on the inhabitants of Jerusalem the spirit of grace and supplication; then they will look on Me whom they pierced.*

The Council of Jerusalem

In the books of *Acts* and Paul's epistles, the church elder governed each of the local assemblies. It has been reckoned by some that the meeting mentioned in the fifteenth chapter of *Acts* gives sanction for trans-local authority for global groups of leading ministers. However, close consideration of this passage reveals that "judaizers" from the Jerusalem assembly had gone to Antioch declaring that one had to become a Jew to be a Christian and must observe sabbath and circumcision. This created such havoc in the Antioch assembly that the problem ultimately was confronted in a meeting in Jerusalem, the place of the problem's source. This, however, ought not be construed as license for decision-making by regional, national, or international ecclesiastical courts. The *Scriptures* reveal no higher authority than the elders of each local assembly.

Which of the two assemblies do you think benefitted from the meeting in Jerusalem? Of course Antioch profited in that they now had plenty of ammunition to ward off the judaizers. You can be sure that Paul referred to this conclusion in his instructions in all the churches.

But, the Jerusalem assembly was also the beneficiary in that it learned about the spirit of grace they were to have toward gentile believers. This became the staunch position of Jerusalem regarding gentile believers. They would never again countenance their members to go to Paul's works or to undermine his doctrine (although such did eventually happen). They were taught that Paul's teaching was correct, and that it was in no way inferior to the beliefs in Israel.

We might note that the word "council" is NOT used in *Acts* 15.

Acts 15:6 Now the apostles and elders <u>came together</u> to consider this matter.

They considered this matter and made an equitable decision. They "came together." <u>There were not representatives from **any** other assemblies</u>, only the two. Furthermore, please note that through the years and with all the serious situations that occurred in the Jerusalem assembly and also in Paul's works which are recorded in the *Bible*, we have no record they were ever dealt with in a meeting such as this one which had been in Jerusalem.

General church fellowship meetings around the world, as well as, ministers' meetings have always been of enormous value in digging out old truths, giving guidance and direction for the day, and very importantly, holding the "fellowship" together (not altogether well) for decades.

Historically, at different times, world-wide Body-of-Christ-wide rules have been laid down by a group of ministers. This is nothing more than a usurpation of the rule of the local church elders.

Can a nation-wide or world-wide meeting of ministers and churches discipline an erring minister or saint? Can this meeting determine rules or to shun or to dis-fellowship someone?

The "general body" cannot discipline an erring minister or saint, but only the local elders. It seems that Paul rebuked the entire local Corinthian church for not dealing with certain matters. His words resulted in a tremendous change in that assembly. His words have become to be regarded as "scriptures," even. But, that was Paul; he was the founding apostle; he **did** have authority.

Another question one might ask is how can one reconcile that Peter, for example, was an apostle and also an elder? Was he a local minister or was he a traveling minister? It may be that apostles, prophets, evangelists, and teachers, when they were functioning in their local assemblies, were regarded as "elders. However, in that elders govern the local church, these men did not carry that kind of authority when they were "on the road." Thus, the authority that Peter had when he was away from Jerusalem, was <u>not</u> the authority by virtue of his eldership, but of his apostleship. Peter was not an apostle to Jerusalem; Jesus was. But, the twelve were <u>sent</u> into all the world.

The word *apostolos* means "one who is sent." This word is used in the church entirely differently from an "ambassador" in the world. For example, Saul of Tarsus was an emissary (*sha-li-akh*) of the Sanhedrin. Just as Saul was beholden to the Sanhedrin which sent him out, similarly Paul and Barnabas were "sent out" from Antioch. In both examples, they were responsible to the bodies that were commending them. However, their purposes were entirely different. Saul was sent with authority to pass on regulations and legislations, to arrest, and to punish; Paul and Barnabas were <u>sent forth</u> by the holy ghost (*Acts* 13:4) to spread the *Good News* and to establish new works. They were both "sent," but oh! How differently!

Ministers from a local church may minister elsewhere, but they have no jurisdiction in another assembly.

Sanhedrin in the Christian Church

This limitation of authority, which we have just discussed, has not been adhered to by the *Roman Catholic Church*, which met in Nicea, [present-day Turkey] in 325 AD to discuss and rule upon the supposed heretic words being propagated by Arius. History records that the "leadership" of the Council had already determined the guilt and the death penalty.

Certainly, Jesus had taught that the *Word of God* would often be the means by which the Church would be judged and divided:
> *Matthew 10:34 Do not think that I came to bring peace on earth. I did not come to bring peace but a sword* [the Bible].

The Lord did not advocate weeding out false teaching. Heretics and unrighteous people in the church are not to be rooted out. They are even necessary.
> *Matthew 13:28-30 Do you want us then to go and gather them up? But (Jesus) said, "No, lest while you gather up the tares you also uproot the wheat with them."*

> *Luke 9:49,50 Now John answered and said, "Master, we saw someone casting out demons in Your name, and we forbade him because he does not follow with us." But Jesus said to him, "Do not forbid him, for he who is not against us is on our side."*

Neither "expel" did the apostle Paul, who wrote:
> *1 Corinthians 11:19 For there must also be heresies among you, that those who are approved may be recognized among you.*

Thus, one of the means of establishing truth is allowing false doctrine to remain, considering that
> *Psalm 33:11 the counsel of the Lord stands forever.*

Ultimately, when left to the good pleasure of God, the truth will prevail.
> *Matthew 15:13 Every plant which My heavenly Father has not planted will be uprooted.*

Please consider how Jesus treated the disciples' complaint about the man who was casting out evil spirits in Jesus' name, but was not a member of their fellowship. Jesus declared:
> *Luke 9:50 "Forbid him not,*

but rather encourage him, for he is carrying on the same design that you are, though, for reasons best known to himself, he does not follow with you; but, he will meet you in the same end, though he does not accompany you now in the same way. You do well to do as you do, but it does not therefore follow that he does ill to do as he does, nor that you do well to put him under an injunction or a court order, for he that is not against us is for us, and therefore ought to be countenanced by us."

We need not lose any of our friends, while we have so few, and we have so many enemies. Those may be found faithful followers of Christ, and, as such, may be accepted of him, though they do not follow like us. O what a great deal of harm to the church, even from those that boast of relation to Christ, and pretend to envy for his sake, would be prevented, if this passage of story were not duly considered!
> *Mark 9:40,41 For he that is not against us is on our part. For whosoever shall give you a cup of water to drink in my name, because you belong to Christ, verily I say to you, he shall not lose his reward.*

Now, returning to the Catholic Church Councils: In 381, the Council of

Constantinople authenticated the divinity of the holy ghost. In all, the *Roman Church* has had twenty-one such councils in its long history. We must concede, however, that often their decrees were wrong and not led by the spirit.

The Councils of the *Church* have proven to be just as ornery and vile as their Jewish predecessors. They have reared up military campaigns which have run amok over Europe and the Middle East. They authorized the burning of opponents at the stake. They have engaged in genocide. They have initiated drives to raise vast fortunes for Church coffers.

The *New Testament* does not recognize such meetings or such deliberative bodies. But, it does teach us some important things about the elders of the local church:

> *1 Thessalonians 5:12,13 And we urge you, brethren, to recognize those who **labor** among you, and are over you in the Lord and admonish you, and to esteem them very highly in love for their work's sake.*
>
> *Hebrews 13:7,17 Remember those who **rule** over you, who have spoken the Word of God to you, whose faith follow...Obey those who **rule** over you, and be submissive, for they watch out for your souls, as those who must give account.*
>
> *1 Timothy 5:17 Let the **elders** who **rule** well be counted worthy of double honor.*

The elder/shepherds of the church are strictly local ministers. Their prime function as shepherd/pastors is to council and to teach the saints in their charge. Their other role as "elders" is magisterial and organizational in the local assembly. They do not function beyond their city's borders. Other Bible-names for shepherds are overseers and bishops. These titles are often incorrectly used to describe a minister who has authority over multiple churches or ministers in other cities. The *Bible* does not recognize "arch-bishops" or "popes." Regarding the church, let us be very clear: only founding apostles have trans-local authority.

However, in these day of restoration, ministers have come to realize the great necessity of "being under authority," and they have accordingly placed themselves "under" someone in another locale. No fault could be found with that. This must be an individual thing and not under the auspices or umbrella of a governmental council.

To reiterate: shepherd/pastors are local ministers. Prophets, teachers, and evangelists, on the other hand, may function trans-locally. But, their authority does not extend into the realm of church business in another city.

Apostles, who are sent out from a local church to found new works, do have authority over the assemblies they found, and their authority may be delegated, as Paul did to Titus.

> *Titus 1:5 For this reason I left you in Crete, that you should set in order the things that are lacking, and appoint elders in every city as I commanded you.*

After the passing of the founding apostle, other ministers may visit and support and serve a local church, but the ruling authority thereafter always remains in the hands of the local elders. Any new disciples must be contributed to the local work. There may not be a separate new work in one locality.

There cannot be an outside "Sanhedrin" to deal with the misconduct of a local minister. Ministerial misconduct is only safe-quarded against by the presence of a multiplicity of local elders, which is often not present in most modern assemblies. Where there is only one shepherd/pastor/minister in a local church, there will be great opportunity for unbridled wrongdoing.

The temptation to have an authoritative body within a church organization has not escaped the Protestant Churches, either. They have relished synods, conferences, convocations, symposiums, seminars, congresses, denominations, and federations. They have developed regulatory organizations. The spirit of sanhedrin reeks in their caucuses and deliberations. The presence of the holy spirit in their debates is non-existent. They not only sit in condemnation upon those whom are in error or whom are their political foes, but they completely disregard the spirit which Christ presented and which he requires in all those who will rule and reign with Him.
> *Matthew 5:44,45 But I say to you, "Love your enemies, bless them that curse you, do good to them that hate you, and pray for those who despitefully use you, and persecute you that you may be the children of your Father Who is in heaven.*

> *Galatians 6:1-3 Brethren, if a man is overtaken in any trespass, you who are spiritual restore such a one in a spirit of gentleness, considering yourself lest you also be tempted. Bear one another's burdens, and so fulfill the law of Christ. For if anyone thinks himself to be something, when he is nothing, he deceives himself.*

Had the *Roman Catholic Church* and all her off-shoots observed the biblical parameters mentioned above, much havoc would have been avoided, and their development into the Beast of *Revelation* would have been circumvented; but then, this was/is not the Plan of God. As a result, *Rome* and her daughters have acted and will continue to perform in a similar manner as the Sanhedrin, which persecuted the early Church and opposed Jesus. This must also be *Rome's* destiny: to persecute true believers and to oppose Jesus.

We had earlier introduced the word *ca-bal'*, a small number of people together in some close design, usually to promote their self-righteous views and interests in a church, state, or other community, often by intrigue. *Cabals* are sometimes secret societies composed of a few designing persons. The term can also be used to refer to the designs of such persons or to the practical consequences of their evolving behavior, and also holds a general meaning of intrigue and conspiracy. Its usage carries strong connotations of shadowy corners, back rooms and insidious influence. As the end of the age nears, you will see them manifest and carry the day as they promote their narrow self-interests. *Cabals* are the destructive products of sanhedrins.

Chapter 8. The Restoration of the Church

"Restoring" implies a need to be fixed or mended. One might have thought that the glorious church that came out of the "upper room" on the Day of Pentecost would have remained glorious, I mean, with such auspicious beginnings!!!

> *Acts 2:40-43 And with many other words did Peter testify and exhort, saying, "Save yourselves from this untoward generation." Then they that gladly received his word were baptized: and the same day there were added unto them about three thousand souls. And they continued steadfastly in the apostles' doctrine and fellowship, and in breaking of bread, and in prayers. And fear came upon every soul: and many wonders and signs were done by the apostles...And they, continuing daily with one accord in the Temple, and breaking bread from house to house, did eat their meat with gladness and singleness of heart, praising God, and having favor with all the people. And the Lord added to the church daily such as should be saved.*

> *Acts 4:32,33 The multitude of them that believed were of one heart and of one soul: neither said any of them that ought of the things which he possessed was his own; but they had all things common. And with great power gave the apostles witness of the resurrection of the Lord Jesus: and great grace was upon them all.*

> *Acts 5:14,16 And believers were the more added to the Lord, multitudes both of men and women...There came also a multitude out of the cities round about unto Jerusalem, bringing sick folks, and them which were vexed with unclean spirits: and they were healed every one.*

> *Acts 5:42 Daily in the temple, and in every house, they ceased not to teach and preach Jesus Christ.*

> *Acts 8:5-8 Philip went down to the city of Samaria, and preached Christ unto them. And the people with one accord gave heed unto those things which Philip spoke, hearing and seeing the miracles which he did. For unclean spirits, crying with loud voice, came out of many that were possessed with them: and many taken with palsies, and that were lame, were healed. And there was great joy in that city.*

This is a taste of the purity and power of the Church of Jesus Christ in its earliest beginning.

It was not long, however, before it was discovered that all the members of the Church were not going to behave properly.

> *Acts 5:1,2 But a certain man named Ananias, with Sapphira his wife, sold a possession, and kept back part of the price, his wife also being privy to it, and brought a certain part, and laid it at the apostles' feet.*

For their deception they were both struck dead. But, this only served to enhance the reputation of the Church.

> *Acts 5:11 And great fear came upon all the church, and upon as many as heard these things.*

In due season, the Church finally began to spread out around the world. Most of the saints in the mother church in Jerusalem had been of the ultra-religious Pharisee persuasion, and many of them had not been convinced that it was not "Jewishness" and "Temple rituals" by which salvation rested. With all the fervor that they possessed they went out to all the new assemblies in other countries insisting that Sabbath-keeping, circumcision, and other Jewish customs be observed by gentile believers.

From Antioch, Syria, Paul and Barnabas brought this controversy back to its source, the Jerusalem assembly. The contention was abated only for a short time, and then it blew up with greater ardor all over the Mediterranean world in all the Churches of Christ. After Paul's departure it seems that the Judaizing party carried the day. Their influence after 65 AD led to the church to take on the form of the Jewish synagogues in their services and in their government. Some assert that these similarities existed from the beginning.

Predictions of Apostasy

Even before that, there crept in teaching in the churches that the Day of Christ's return was near. The apostle Paul corrected their mistaken notion:
2 Thessalonians 2:2,3 Be not soon shaken in mind, or be troubled, neither by spirit, nor by word, nor by letter as from us, as that the day of Christ is at hand. Let no man deceive you by any means: for that day shall not come, except there come a falling away first...

Others began to teach that the resurrection had already occurred:

2 Timothy 2:17,18 Hymenaeus and Philetus...have strayed concerning the truth, saying that the resurrection is already past; and they overthrow the faith of some.

Yet others
1 Corinthians 15:12 say...that there is no resurrection of the dead.

Paul gave warning that
1 Timothy 4:1 in the latter times some shall depart from the faith, giving heed to seducing spirits, and doctrines of devils.

Acts 20:29,30 For I know this, that after my departing shall grievous wolves enter in among you, not sparing the flock. Also of your own selves shall men arise, speaking perverse things, to draw away disciples after themselves.

The apostles Peter and John also alerted the believers:
2 Peter 2:1 There will be false teachers among you, who will secretly bring in destructive heresies.

1 John 2:18,19 Even now are there many antichrists; whereby we know that it is the last time. They went out from us, but they were not of us; for if they had been of us, they would no doubt have continued with us: but they went out, that they might be made manifest that they were not all of us.

The Lord Jesus Himself, while He was still here on earth, had already forecast these problems for His Church:
Matthew 24:5,10-12,24 Many shall come in My Name, saying that I am Christ; and shall deceive...Many shall be offended, and shall betray one

another, and shall hate one another. And many false prophets shall rise, and shall deceive many. And because iniquity shall abound, the love of many shall wax cold...There shall arise false Christs, and false prophets, and shall show great signs and wonders; insomuch that, if it were possible, they shall deceive the very elect.

We have earlier said that it was surprising that Jesus could not keep His Church straight. But, if we had paid more attention to these scriptures, we would have <u>expected</u> it instead. Besides, these deviations served a purpose:
*1 Corinthians 11:18,19 When you come together in the church, I hear that there are divisions among you...There **must** be also heresies among you, that those who are approved may be made manifest among you.*

It was absolutely necessary that errors occur in the Church; in this way, those who remained faithful to the truth and did not deviate became obvious and noticed and marked by the Lord.

Other Events in the Falling Away

As the government of the Church began to change, the offices of the ministry of apostles, prophets, evangelists, and teachers disappeared. The multiplicity of elders became a thing of the past. Pastoral counseling vanished. In the place of counseling, the pastors began to emulate the preaching of the rabbis. In due season, there was but one preacher per church, and he not a shepherd in the original sense.

In time, some preachers rose to prominence and took upon themselves the title of "bishop." Then, some bishops acquired much influence over large areas and were recognized as "arch-bishops." Ultimately the Bishop of Rome took for himself the title of "pope."

Gone now was the autonomy of the local Churches of Christ; now, authority was vested in Rome.

By decree of Emperor Constantine the entire empire became Christian. As it expanded, the Church began to adapt many pagan teachings into its doctrine. The more Rome swelled, the more false teaching entered in. The Church began to canonize saints and to venerate them, especially Mary.

Legal corruption and immorality became commonplace in all levels of the *Catholic Church*. Deals were struck with civil governments in country after country until there was no line of demarcation between church and state; they became one.

The Church then began to raise military forces. Between 1095-1295 there were seven Christian Crusades coming out of Western Europe into the Holy Land. As these forces made their ways they marauded and pillaged the Jewish communities along the way. Anti-Semitism became part of the church. This was a major, Babylonious deviation from original truth.

Pope Urban II was responsible for assisting Emperor Alexus I of Constantinople in launching the first crusade. He made one of the most influential speeches in the Middle Ages at the Council of Clermont, calling on Christian princes in Europe to go to rescue the Holy Land from the Turks.

Raymond of Aguiliers described the capture of Jerusalem by the Crusaders:

> Some of our men cut off the heads of their enemies; others shot them with arrows, so that they fell from the towers; others tortured them longer by casting them into the flames. Piles of heads, hands and feet were to be seen in the streets of the city. It was necessary to pick one's way over the bodies of men and horses. But these were small matters compared to what happened at the temple of Solomon, a place where religious services were once chanted. What happened there? If I tell the truth, it will exceed your powers of belief. So let it suffice to say this much at least, that in the temple and portico of Solomon, men rode in blood up to their knees and bridle reins.

Alfonso Borgia became Pope Callistus III in 1455. His nephew, Rodrigo, became Pope Alexander VI in 1492. It was he who divided the New World between Spain and Portugal by "papal bull." Lucrecia Borgia brought great opulence to the Vatican palaces along with the lowest degree of sexual depravity. Lewd behavior in the palace was the rule. And, bishoprics were sold at great prices of bribery.

A new deviation entered during the Middle Ages; it became Catholic doctrine that sinners must not only repent of sins that they've committed, they must also confess these sins and pay some sort of retribution. This eventually led to the selling of "Indulgences."

The Church had taught that punishment for sin would be either temporal, that is while the sinner was still living, or in the burning of hell. The Council of Trent, 1545, taught that every sin must be purified either here on earth, or after death in the state called "Purgatory." It evolved that a monetary payment of penalty could be made, which, supposedly, absolved one of past sins and/or released one from purgatory after death. Eventually, one could purchase Indulgences for departed relatives.

Martin Luther

On a trip to Rome in 1511, Priest Martin Luther was horrified by the wealth and luxury of the Roman Catholic Church, compared to the poverty of the people in Germany. Further, his study of the *Bible*, particularly the books of the *Psalms*, *Romans*, *Galatians*, and *Hebrews*, convinced him that good works and confession could not earn salvation, but that justification was by faith alone, and was the gift of God. He came to believe that the Church's teaching – that pilgrimages, relics, and penances could earn salvation – was wrong. When the Dominican friar Johann Tetzel was sent around Germany in 1516 selling Indulgences (payments to secure remissions of punishment for sin) to raise funds for the work on St. Peter's Basilica in Rome, Luther was disgusted that the Church seemed to be trying to sell salvation to raise money for Herself.

It is told that on October 31, 1517 Luther nailed on the church door in Wittenberg a statement of 'Ninety-five Theses' attacking these practices and suggesting that religion was an inward relationship with God, and the following year he was summoned to Rome to defend his action. His reply was to attack the papal system even more strongly, and in 1520 he published his three greatest works. In the first he attacked the authority of the pope and called on Germans to unite against papal exploitation and to reform the church. In the second, On Christian

Liberty, he expounded the nature of Christian faith and argued that 'the soul...is justified by faith alone, and not by any works' – the doctrine that became the founding principle of Reformation theology. In the third, On the Babylonish Captivity of the Church, he rejected five of the seven contemporary sacraments and the doctrine of transubstantiation (the transformation of bread and wine into the body and blood of Jesus during the Eucharist). When a papal bull (edict) was published against him, he publicly burned it.

At the Diet of Worms in 1521 the Holy Roman Emperor Charles V demanded that he retract his objections – Luther's reply: "Here I stand", marked the start of the Reformation. Originally intending reform, his protest led to a split in the church, the Augsburg Confession (1530), leading to the foundation of a new Protestant Church.

Restoration Continues

Prior to Luther, John Huss (1373-1415) of Bohemia (Czeckoslavakia), had promoted right-living over sacraments. He opposed veneration of images.

Ulrich Zwingli (1484-1531) of Switzerland, said that the *Bible* should be the only authority for beliefs and practices.

John Calvin (1509-1564), Geneva, Switzerland, developed the doctrine of the sovereignty of God. His work led to establishing the Presbyterian Church.

Menno Simons (1496-1561) taught believer's baptism and non-resistance. He urged the Eucharist was only symbolic. The Mennonites and Amish came from him.

John Knox (1514-1572) led Scottish reformation.

George Fox (1624-1691) England, founded the Quaker movement. He emphasized the Inner Light of Christ.

John Wesley (1703-1791), England, emphasized living a sanctified life for Christ. His work led to the Methodist Church.

In 1801 Barton Stone minister of Cane Ridge Church near Paris, Kentucky traveled to Logan County to witness the spiritual happenings in the churches there. He was so impressed he organized a camp meeting at Cane Ridge the next August. There began the Great Revival. The ungodly frontier atmosphere of the area was changed by the work of the holy spirit. By 1802 all the brothels and saloons in Lexington had gone out of business. One person from Frankfort, Kentucky wrote: "It is a very comfortable thing to be in a country where religion has obtained the pre-eminent influence."

For the next hundred years most of the ministers in the Midwest and South were the result of this Revival.

After the Civil War a full-fledged Holiness revival broke out within the ranks of Methodism, and in 1867 the National Camp Meeting Association for the Promotion of Holiness was formed.

At a Bible school in Topeka, Kansas, founded by a Holiness evangelist, the "gift of the spirit" came to a student in 1901, and the practice of *glossolalia* (speaking in tongues) quickly spread. The Pentecostal revival made its greatest inroads in areas where Holiness movements were already prospering, and it attracted far more non-

Methodists than had the earlier forms of perfectionism. Besides the emphasis on the baptism of the holy spirit, Pentecostalism recognized divine healing and demanded highly puritanical standards of personal conduct. It spread throughout the world.

The modern day "Tongues Movement" began in the 1970's and is spreading throughout Christendom with amazing speed. It created more excitement than any other religious movement did in the twentieth century. Thousands of people in almost every denomination say they have spoken in "tongues."

The tongues movement, also known as the "charismatic renewal," because of the emphasis on the restoration of spiritual gifts (*1 Corinthians* 12:1-11) in the Church, has come into the main line denominations: Episcopalians, Methodists, Baptists and Roman Catholics are speaking in tongues. These tongues groups are now staying in these denominations and through classes, prayer groups, and home-studies, they are making converts. Theodore Epp observed: "Major doctrinal differences are often overlooked by those in the movement as long as a person has seemingly experienced the gift of the spirit and speaking in tongues."

The explosion of the charismatic movement is world-wide. On January 5, 2005 in Los, Nigeria, five Muslim men, crippled or blind, received miraculous healings at a meeting of the German evangelist Bernhard Bonnke. In the course of these meetings, more than four-and-a-half million attended, so it is said.

It is now almost six hundred years since the beginnings of the Reformation in Europe. As we are nearing the end of the Gentile Age and the coming of the Judgment Day, where is all this heading? What is God doing?

A Restored Church

As the Pentecostal Revival was gaining adherents in the United States and other countries, the First World War began. However, this did not stop the move of God. In particular were the revelations of understanding given during those years and following to William Sowders. In camp meetings at Elco, Illinois and later at Shephardsville, Kentucky and in his church in Louisville between 1927 and 1952, Sowders introduced many of his divinely revealed teachings, including those regarding the restoration of Jesus' Church to the glory it had held in Jerusalem two thousand years ago.

Without mentioning his name any further, what follows are some of the insights he has passed on.

As the age draws to a conclusion, it seems to many that what Epps observed, the blurring of doctrinal and other differences between denominations, is a good thing. At the very center of it all is the Pope of the *Roman Catholic Church*. I believe it is he to whom Paul refers:

> *2 Thessalonians 2:2-12 Be not soon shaken in mind or troubled, either by spirit or by word or by letter, as if from us, as though the day of Christ had come. Let no one deceive you by any means; for that Day (of the second coming of Jesus) will not come until the falling away comes first (the apostasy of the church), and **the man of sin** (the Roman Pontiff) is revealed, the son of perdition, who opposes and exalts himself above all that is called God or that is worshipped, so that he*

sits as God in the temple of God, showing himself that he is God.

Do you not remember that when I was still with you I told you these things?

*And now you know what is restraining (that is, the holy spirit of God), that he (the man of sin) may be revealed in his own time. For the mystery of lawlessness is already at work; only he who now restrains (the holy spirit) will do so until he is taken out of the way. And then **the lawless one** will be revealed, whom the Lord will consume with the breath of His Mouth and destroy with the brightness of His coming. The coming of the lawless one is according to the working of satan, with all power, signs, and lying wonders, and with all unrighteous deception among those who perish, because they did not receive the love of the truth, that they might be saved. And for this reason God will send them strong delusion, that they should believe the lie, that they all may be condemned who did not believe the truth but had pleasure in unrighteousness.*

Paul had taught this in the churches and was now reminding them. The Pope and his office did not exist until the third century, but he is referenced throughout the *Bible*. For example:

Isaiah 4:1 And in that day seven women shall take hold of one man, saying, "We will eat our own bread, and wear our own apparel: only let us be called by Thy Name, to take away our reproach."

The "one man" will be the Pope. "Seven" is the perfect or full number. The "women" are religious orders and churches. "Seven women" means "all religions." We are seeing today in the early part of the twenty-first century, all these women coming together in an ecumenical movement. The prophecy says they will take hold of the one man, that is, the Pope. The different churches will continue to "eat" their "own bread," that is, they will continue to teach their own special doctrines; they will continue to "wear" their "own apparel," that is, they will keep their own church organizations. But they will want to join with this man so their individual groups would not be left out.

But yet, there will be those who will not compromise their doctrinal beliefs, but will continue to strive to comprehend all the teachings of the *Word of God*.

Isaiah 52:7,8 How beautiful upon the mountains are the feet of him who brings good tidings, who publishes peace; who brings good tidings of good, who publishes salvation; who says to Zion, "Thy God reigns!"

Your watchmen shall lift up the voice; with the voice together shall they sing: for they shall see eye to eye, when the Lord shall <u>bring again Zion</u>.

The beautiful feet are those of Jesus. The mountains are churches. The "watchmen" are Jesus' ministers. Today they do not see eye-to-eye. As a matter of fact, there are probably not any of those seeking to know God's Word perfectly, who agree on every doctrine. The prophecy foresees a day when they all will see eye-to-eye. That day will be "when the Lord shall bring again Zion." Notice the "when" and the "again."

What is Zion? It is not referring to that mountain in the land of Israel. Zion is an Old Testament symbol for the Church of Jesus Christ. Paul taught this:

*Hebrews 12:22,23 But you have come to **Mount Zion** and to the city of the living God, the heavenly Jerusalem, to an innumerable company of angels, to the general assembly and Church of the firstborn.*

Mount Zion is a symbolic name for the Church. The expression "bring again Zion" (*Isaiah* 52:8) implies that Zion has been here and has left its place and will be brought back again. This shows us that Jesus' Church, which has fallen, gone into apostasy, will be brought back, that is, restored.

At that time the watchmen will see eye-to-eye:
Isaiah 30:26 in the day that the Lord binds up the breach of His people, and heals the stroke of their wound.

Zephaniah 3:9 For then will I turn to the people a pure language, that they may all call upon the Name of the Lord, to serve Him <u>with one consent</u>.

This kind of unity and "pure language" was present in the early Church:
*Acts 2:1 When the day of Pentecost was fully come, they were all with **one accord** in one place.*

*Acts 4:32 The multitude of them that believed were of **one heart and of one soul**.*

The apostle Paul urged this kind of unity to the church in Corinth:
*1 Corinthians 1:10 Now I beseech you, brethren, by the Name of our Lord Jesus Christ, that you all **speak the same thing**, and that there be no divisions among you; but that you be perfectly joined together **in the same mind** and in the same judgment.*

He alerted the church in Rome:
Romans 16:17 Mark them which cause divisions and offenses contrary to the doctrine which you have learned; and avoid them.

The unity of the Church is critical, not only for the power of the Church, but for its witness. Jesus prayed to His Father for this kind of unity:
*John 17:22,23 And the glory which You gave Me I have given them, that they may **be one** just as We are one: I in them, and You in Me; that they may be made perfect in one, and that the world may know that You have sent Me, and have loved them as You have loved Me.*

With the Church being in unity, it would be a witness of two things:
1) that God had indeed sent His Son to the world; and
2) that God loves the Church as much as He loves His Son.

We know what the world thinks of the Church today with all its thousands of denominations and sects: they laugh. They ask: "Is your Jesus divided?"

Paul saw how crucial unity was. He exhorted the brethren:
*Ephesians 4:3 Endeavoring to keep the **unity of the spirit** in the bond of peace.*

The more passionate men are about the Truth of God's *Word*, the more difficult it is for them to maintain unity. In the zealous quest for truth, men are apt to become divided from one another. This has happened countless times, because men have strayed from the pathway of charity, that precious bond of peace, that perfect

bond. Paul knew that the only way for the Church to hold together, or for that matter, come BACK together, was to manifest the love of God
> *Ephesians 4:13 TILL we all come in the unity of the faith.*

That great, ecumenical, world system that is also coming together at the end of this age is willing to sacrifice their beliefs merely for the sake of unity, peace, and safety. Jesus is not asking His Church to sacrifice principles for unity, but He wants Charity to be above all.
> *Ephesians 4:3,13 Endeavoring to keep the unity of the spirit in the bond of peace...till we all come in the unity of the faith.*

To have acquired all doctrinal truth with the absence of charity would negate all the truth. But, it is not even possible without charity. God will not bring back the captivity of Zion without the love of the brethren. The bond of charity is a prerequisite for restoration:
> *Ephesians 4:3,13 Endeavoring to keep the unity of the spirit in the (love) bond of peace...TILL we all come in the unity of the faith.*

It was perhaps three decades after the inauguration of the Church that Jude, the brother of James (as well as of the Lord Jesus), became very concerned about the serious conditions of apostasy that were worming their ways into the Church.
> *Jude 3 I found it necessary to write to you exhorting you to earnestly contend for the faith which was once delivered to the saints.*

Jude was urging the Church to recover what It was losing. He did not imply that would come easily. He said "earnestly contend." Here are some synonyms for "contend:"

debate	struggle
combat	strive
clash	grapple
wrangle	dispute
argue	

We understand that the day is coming when men of God will again see eye-to-eye. Are we to suppose that the ones who will arrive at that unity will be those who are passively sitting by and waiting? Will God just suddenly shower His Favor upon them, and all of the sudden they will all have perfect understanding of the Bible? Or will the Almighty be please with those who studying and seeking and grappling and caring and contending?

This is a warfare in which we find ourselves; ambivalence will not get the done; equivocating is done by deceitful me. Here is Paul's position:
> *Philippians 1:27 Stand fast in one spirit, with one mind striving together for the faith of the Gospel.*

Paul saw that salvation was to be striven for, not something that one passively sat around and awaited. I said that this is a warfare. Paul wrote:
> *1 Thessalonians 2:2 We were bold in our God to speak unto you the Gospel of God with much contention.*

Seeking God and being faithful in the face of flak is serious business. Encountering clamorous criticism is not for the weak-hearted. But, the reward for earnestly contending for the faith is enormous. The King says:
> *Revelation 2:10 " Be faithful unto death, and I will give you a crown of life."*

A crown of life!!! It's worth the contending in love, is it not?

The Woman in the Wilderness

There is a woman mentioned in the *Bible* who is the Church.
> *Revelation 12:1 There appeared a great wonder in heaven; a **woman** clothed with the sun, and the moon under her feet, and upon her head a crown of twelve stars.*

The woman represents the people of God. Another place they are referenced is:
> *Revelation 19:1 I heard a great voice of <u>much people in heaven</u>, saying, "Alleluia; Salvation, and glory, and honor, and power, unto the Lord our God."*

The location of "much people" in "heaven" does not put them in "third heaven," the habitation of God,
> *Isaiah 57:15 the high and lofty One who inhabits eternity, whose Name is Holy.*

Nor is it
> *1 Kings 8:27 the heaven and heaven of heavens.*

But, it is the "church heaven," the place where spiritual and religious things occur among men and women, both divinely inspired and also demonically inspired. The woman appeared in heaven clothed with the "sun," the *New Testament* of God's *Word*. She is standing upon the "moon," the foundation of the *Old Testament*. The light of the Old Covenant moon is a reflection of the New Covenant sun. The *Law* was a shadow of *Grace*. The twelve apostles are the woman's starry crown.

The purpose of the Church is to bring forth and nurture children. And that is just what she has been doing for two thousand years.
> *Revelation 12:2 And she, being with child cried, travailing in birth, and pained to be delivered.*

Paul, as a minister of the Church, was part of the travailing in birth:
> *Galatians 4:19 My little children, of whom I **travail** in birth again until Christ be formed in you.*

> *1 Thessalonians 2:7 I was gentle among you, even as a nurse cherishes her children.*

One might be taken aback that a man would speak in such a feminine way about himself, but this is the symbolic language in which the *Bible* is cloaked.
> *Revelation 12:3,4 And another sign appeared in heaven: behold, a great, fiery red dragon having seven heads and ten horns, and seven crowns on his heads. His tail drew a third of the stars of heaven and threw them to the earth. And the dragon stood before the woman who was ready to give birth, to devour her Child as soon as it was born.*

Alas, the Church Woman is <u>not</u> the only one in heaven! The *Scriptures* had earlier identified another <u>woman</u> in heaven. This woman is "false religion." And yes, she's in the religious heavens, too. She's been there since the Tower of Babel, dispensing her counterfeit religion. The prophets of Israel all declared God's hatred of her:
> *Nahum 3:4,5 Because of the multitude of the whoredoms of the well-favored harlot, the mistress of witchcrafts, who sells nations through her whoredoms, and families through*

her witchcrafts. "Behold, I am against you," says the Lord of hosts.

What may seem surprising at first is that the great dragon is in heaven, too! The dragon represents the great conglomeration of national governments in one huge civil power. But, how did this world administration get into heaven? It was the whore of false religion uniting with this world government that has brought civil power into heaven. This is not the first time in world history that this has happened.

You may recall in our earlier discussion of the "falling away" of the Church in the Middle Ages, that there was a union of church and state that happened back there. The two were so blended together as to be inseparable. The symbolic language of the *Bible* refers to this kind of union as "a dragon" or "a beast." All the world powers throughout history who combined church and state in one entity have been called "beasts." The ancient government of Egypt was a "beast." The Pharaoh was not only the head of the government, but also of the religion. The Assyrian, Babylonian, Persian, Greek, and Roman Empires, each in succession, were likewise "beasts." In the Middle Ages the Holy Roman Empire employed the union of church and state. Its emperors went to Rome to be crowned in the Vatican. But, such a system has not existed on the earth for hundreds of years. But, a new beast is now reviving and coming into existence.

God has permitted all these beasts to form throughout human history. He is not surprised by it all. For one thing, He has used them to concentrate all the wicked into one nice little package. He has also used the fiery trials the beasts have breathed out upon the Church over the ages as a means of purifying the saints.

Likewise has God used the whore through the ages as a place of amalgamation of those who were enemies of God. Her judgment is soon approaching:

Revelation 17:1,2 Come, I will show you the judgment of the great harlot who sits on many waters, with whom the kings of the earth (that is, "the nations") committed fornication, and the inhabitants of the earth were made drunk with the wine of her fornication.

The "many waters" upon which the whore sits refers to the "sea of humanity." Almost the whole human race has she corrupted. The whore sits on the sea of humanity.

When John had the vision of the woman in heaven and the dragon there, he actually saw the dragon throwing the stars out of the sky to the ground:

Revelation 12:4 the third part of the stars of heaven, and did cast them to the earth.

You will recall that the church woman had a crown of twelve stars. The stars represented church leaders, and perhaps a century later one third of the church's leadership were seen to have become corrupt. The dragon gathered them up and tossed them out of heaven and to the earth.

In the mean time back in heaven, the woman was ready to give birth. And the dragon was waiting for the delivery so he might gobble up the child. But, the woman delivered and

Revelation 12:5 brought forth a man child, who was to rule all nations with a rod of iron.

Millions and millions of people through the centuries have been part of the church

woman. But, not all of them will have eternal life. Many in the church have been unworthy. As Jesus said:
Matthew 22:14 Many are called, but few are chosen.

The woman in heaven represents the "many." But, from the womb of this Church there are developed those that God calls "overcomers;" they are the product, the offspring of the church; they are the "few" who are "chosen" for eternal life. This is the "man child," who was to rule the nations. (Yet another name for the "man child" is the "Bride.") [Some see the "woman" to be "Israel."]

The prophet Daniel saw the same group of overcomers:
Daniel 7:27 The kingdom and dominion, and the greatness of the kingdom under the whole heaven, shall be given to the people of the saints of the most High, whose kingdom is an everlasting kingdom, and all dominions shall serve and obey Him (that is, King Jesus, the most High).

So, we see that man child, the overcomers of the church, shall have dominion, that is, they shall rule.

And, they shall rule with a rod of iron. The man child is to rule the nations with this rod. The rod of iron is the *Word of God*; It cannot be broken. But, the rod of iron breaks everything it hits.
Psalm 2:9 You shall break them with a rod of iron; You shall dash them in pieces like a potter's vessel.

This seems awfully rough, but that's exactly what we need; we need to be broken by God's *Word*, and to be dashed into pieces. We're no good to God, if we're left whole.

Matthew 21:44 Whoever falls on this Stone will be broken.

Now, returning to John's apocalypse:
Revelation 12:5 She (the Church) brought forth a man child (the overcomers), who was to rule all nations with a rod of iron: and her child was caught up unto God, and to his throne.

We are not to misunderstand that the man child literally went to God's throne in third heaven, but that the man child was preserved by the protective power of the Almighty, understanding that
Romans 13:1 there is no power but of God.

When the beast of the Holy Roman Empire, the great red dragon, threatened the man child, the child was caught up to God's throne, that is into God's safe-keeping. The man child is the product or off-spring of the Church. The man child represents the overcomers, and that number has not been completely made up; there are still more to come forth before the end of the age. Thus, it is God's design to secure the man child till the coming of the Lord.

Not only is the man child being preserved, but the church woman has also been protected from the beast:
Revelation 12:6,14 And the woman fled into the wilderness, where she has a place prepared of God, that they should feed her there a thousand two hundred and threescore days...To the woman were given two wings of a great eagle, that she might fly into the wilderness, into her place, where she is nourished for a time, and times, and half a time, from the face of the serpent.

When the church woman went into the wilderness, nothing more was seen of her for twelve hundred sixty years, that is, until the Protestant Reformation began. But, God has had a place for the true woman; He did not permit her to be exterminated. The pages of history record little of her. We are not to suppose that she was non-existent; we are not to suppose, 'though her numbers were few, that she did not continue to have some truly righteous men and women. There is but a thin thread of these virtuous and devout Christians during this wilderness period.

Since the early day of the Church, there has been a battle going on in the Church, in "the heavenly places;" it has been a warfare between those who were attempting to walk in charity and those who were greedy, between those who were contending for the *Word* that was once delivered to the saints and those who wanted to compromise with the dragon and the whore.
> *Revelation 12:7 There was war in heaven: Michael and his angels fought against the dragon; and the dragon fought and his angels.*

We are not to imagine a war going on the third heaven with God and Jesus being spectators of the combat; we are to see the conflict in first heaven, that is, the church heaven, a clash between the righteous and the unrighteous, between the wheat and the tares. The "wheat" are Michael's angels (messengers). "Michael" in *Hebrew* means: the One Who is like God.

God did not stop the warfare; He did not block out heresies; He did not prevent the saints from being persecuted. But, He was the continual preserver of His saints. But, the accusers and adversaries and all those who were carnal-minded were thrown out of heaven. They still thought they were in control; not only were they deceived, but they have been deceived and have been deceiving since the Tower of Babel. John saw their over-throw:
> *Revelation 12:9,10 The great dragon was cast out, that old serpent, called the devil (accuser), and satan (adversary), which deceive the whole world was cast out into the earth, and his angels were cast out with him. And I heard a loud voice saying in heaven, "Now is come salvation, and strength, and the kingdom of our God, and the power of his Christ: for the accuser of our brethren is cast down, which accused them before our God day and night."*

Here is the secret of how the saints overcame the dragon, the devil, and the satan:
> *Revelation 12:11 They overcame him by*
> *1) the blood of the Lamb, and*
> *2) by the word of their testimony; and*
> *3) they loved not their lives unto the death.*

To the end, the dragon has not given up, but has continued to try to corrupt and to persecute. The rest of the man child shall also be persecuted.
> *Revelation 12:17 The dragon was wroth with the woman, and went to make war with the remnant of her seed, who*
> *1) keep the Commandments of God, and*
> *2) have the Testimony of Jesus Christ.*

Lo, these last two thousand years the Church of Jesus Christ has existed, almost always under pressure from an enemy, the imposition of false teaching and conflict, battles within, attacks from without. But, God has had a place prepared for her in the wilderness, in the desert, on the back-side.

For nearly six hundred years the woman has been recovering; she has been making her way back from the wilderness. King Solomon had a vision of this woman:

> *Song of Solomon 3:6; 8:4,5 Who is this coming out of the **wilderness** like pillars of smoke, perfumed with myrrh and frankincense, with all the merchant's fragrant powders?...I charge you, O daughters of Jerusalem, that you stir not up, nor awake my love, until He please. Who is this coming up from the **wilderness**, leaning upon her Beloved?*

Perhaps, never have there been written such words of passion and romance. Who is this? Just who is this woman? It is the Church. After all the years in the wilderness she is seen emerging. She is leaning upon her beloved Jesus. She has the fragrance upon her of her prayers, of her sufferings, and of the holy spirit.

She is the Church of Jesus; she's still producing the rest of her man child. She's getting rid of her Babylonish and Judaistic garments. She's coming out of her captivities. Her captivity is being restored to the glorious liberty of the children of God.

> *Psalm 126 When the Lord brought back the captive ones of Zion, we were like those who dream. Then our mouth was filled with laughter and our tongue with joyful shouting. Then they said among the nations, "The Lord has done great things for them."*
>
> *The Lord has done great things for us; we are glad.*
>
> *Restore our captivity, O Lord, as the streams in the South. Those who sow in tears shall reap with joyful shouting. He who goes to and fro weeping, carrying his bag of seed, shall doubtless come again with rejoicing, bringing his sheaves with him.*

It was the Dark Ages in Europe. Magnificent cathedrals were being built in every nation. Many arch-bishops were becoming wealthy. If we might repeat: John Calvin was being toured around Rome by a Vatican official, who stopped and proudly proclaimed: "So you see, we can no longer say, 'Silver and gold have we none'!!"

Calvin responded: "Neither can we say, 'Such as I have I give to you. In the name of Jesus Christ of Nazareth rise up and walk'."

It is the fondest hope and expectation of the "restoration movement" that the glory of the earliest days of the Church will be manifested just before Jesus' return. It was the Jewish nation who witnessed the power of God manifested by the disciples of Christ. The Jews had no excuse; God favored them with the evidence documenting the authenticity of the words of Jesus' followers. Israel saw. Most of Israel rejected. Because of that, the Jewish nation has been cast

> *Matthew 13:50 into the furnace of fire: there shall be wailing and gnashing of teeth.*

Before the flood, God gave witness to the world. Before the exodus God gave witness to the truth and power of His Word. Before the destruction of the northern kingdom of Israel, God sent many, many prophets performing signs and wonders. Before Nebuchadnezzar destroyed Jerusalem and its Temple, He gave abundant witness. Before the Kingdom of Babylon was overthrown, God showed them the handwriting on the wall.

Likewise, in the last days before Armageddon, God will have a people, a kingdom of priests and a holy nation full of the truth, full of charity, and full of power. The gentile nations will not be able to say: "We were uninformed."

John Huss and Zwingli began to speak in about the year 1400. The woman began coming out of the wilderness. Martin Luther spoke, and she stepped up her stride. When Calvin showed the sovereignty of God in the sixteenth century, the woman kept coming. When Anabaptists like Menno Simons said that baptism was only for believers...When John Knox said the Catholic Mass was idolatry in 1550 and compared it the sin of Nadab and Abihu, who offered strange fire (*Leviticus* 10:1-3)...When George Fox in the 1600's spoke of the Inner Light, the woman continued making her way out of the wilderness. In the eighteenth century John Wesley preached "holiness or hell," and that woman advanced. At the beginning of the nineteenth century there was the Great Revival at Cane Ridge. She kept coming. In the twentieth century the woman moved forward by the restoration to the church of the baptism of the holy ghost. Later the charismatic gifts began to be emphasized. People in all Christian denominations and sects became spirit-filled, and the woman came near the edge of the wilderness. God has His people sown all over the place.

> *Joel 2:1 Blow the trumpet in Zion, and sound an alarm in My holy mountain: let all the inhabitants of the land tremble: for the day of the Lord comes, for it is nigh at hand.*

> *Revelation 18:4-8 And I heard another voice from heaven saying, "Come out of her, My people, lest you share in her sins, and lest you receive of her plagues. For her sins have reached to heaven, and God has remembered her iniquities.*

> *Render to her just as she rendered to you, and repay her double according to her works; in the cup which she has mixed, mix double for her. In the measure that she glorified herself and lived luxuriously, in the same measure give her torment and sorrow; for she says in her heart, "I sit as queen, and am no widow, and will not see sorrow."*

> *Therefore her plagues will come in one day -- death and mourning and famine. And she will be utterly burned with fire, for strong is the Lord God who judges her.*

Many of God's people are now in false religion. "Come out of her," cries the Church. "Blow the trumpet in Zion." Charity now prevails. The men of God will, at last, be permitted to perfectly understand God's Holy *Word*. What is more, they shall preach in one accord. As the apostle Paul has exhorted:

> *Philippians 2:2 Be like-minded, having the same love, being of one accord, of one mind.*

There will actually be that witness again, as the Jews had seen two thousand years ago. Signs and wonders will be manifested. This time they will witness to the gentile nations of the glory of serving the true and living God. The prophecy of Isaiah will have its greatest and ultimate fulfillment:

> *Isaiah 60:2,3 The Lord shall arise upon you, and His glory shall be seen*

upon you. And the Gentiles shall come to your light, and kings to the brightness of your rising.

Then the world shall be fairly judged by Jesus Christ, of whom God has testified Himself by raising Him from the dead.
Acts 17:31 God has appointed a day on which He will judge the world in righteousness by the Man whom He has ordained. He has given assurance of this to all by raising Him from the dead.

The Almighty, in all His fairness would not be just in judging the world without first having raised up a true witness. He did this for the Jewish nation, who glimpsed a glorious church. He is about to do this to the world. None will be with excuse; they shall see the true witness, Jesus' Church restored. Because there is a restored church, judgment can then come.
Psalm 9:8 God shall judge the world in righteousness, He shall minister judgment to the people in uprightness.

Everything that is opposed to Jesus will come to a terrible end. He will sit, abiding enthroned forever, and that as Judge: He has prepared His throne for the purpose of judgment. This same God, who has just given proof that He lives and reigns eternally, will judge the nations still more comprehensively, strictly, and impartially. The gentiles shall have their fair opportunity to view a glorious church.

Those ministers who had pegged themselves to be the powers of heaven shall come crashing down to earth like falling stars. Of this Jesus foretold:
Matthew 24:29,30 The stars shall fall from heaven, and the powers of the [religious] heavens shall be shaken. And then shall appear the sign of the Son of man in heaven: and then shall all the tribes of the earth mourn, and they shall see the Son of man coming in the clouds of heaven with power and great glory.

Paul has said that they will have witnessed
Hebrews 6:5 the powers of the world-to-come.

Who are these "clouds of heaven?" And, who are these "powers of the world-to-come?" They are that very "man child" whom God has been preparing all along. The restored church has within it "the powers of the world-to-come." God said that He will "bring again Zion."
Isaiah 52:8 Your watchmen shall lift up the voice; with the voice together shall they sing: for they shall see eye-to-eye, when the Lord shall bring again Zion.

The earnest expectation of all creation awaits their ultimate manifestation. We shall conclude
with the vision Daniel had of the end.
Daniel 7:13,14,18 I saw in the night visions, and, behold, one like the Son of man came with the clouds of heaven, and came to the Ancient of Days, and they brought him near before Him. And there was given Him dominion, and glory, and a kingdom, that all people, nations, and languages, should serve Him. His dominion is an everlasting dominion, which shall not pass away, and His kingdom that which shall not be destroyed...The saints of the Most High shall take the kingdom, and possess the kingdom forever, even forever and ever.

Chapter 9. Establishing a Local Church Again
A Pattern for Restoration

There are many, many churches of the Body of Christ today with mere handfuls of people, mostly elderly and not a great deal of God's spirit. Is it just the age in which we presently live? Is there something that is hindering the blessing of God? Is there something that can help these anemic situations? Why are they floundering?

In many cases the founder of a local assembly was not "sent out" to do a work; he merely started out on his own. That means he had no one, no church to whom he was responsible, no one to whom he had to report.

Secondly, he founded a church like an apostle would have, but then he did something different than an apostle. Instead of founding a local work and moving on to another city, continuing to function in the apostolic office, he settled down in that city, and there remained. He lived off the work he had established. Some might use the expression: "He feathered his nest."

But, a true apostle never settles down for long. The spirit of God compels him to get up and move on to another place and build another church. He has left behind in every place an established ministry to continue the care of the assembly. The life of an apostle is not easy; he's always on the move; comfort is not his goal.

We find in many cities, the founder of the work ultimately passed away, not having ordained elders/pastors/shepherds to carry on the work. It had been as if the life-blood of Heaven to that work all had to pass through him to the people. Now, he's gone, and the people are left starving and fatherless.

So, a pastor from a nearby city comes to oversee the work. He, himself, may settle down and live off the work the rest of his life, a work which he had no share in originating. Seldom do these situations flourish; they usually fritter away.

What to do! Is it possible to get these assemblies back in order? Is it likely that they can return to vibrant health? What to do!

Some may suggest these churches are not in "apostolic order." We are all accustomed to using the expression "apostolic order," and we suppose our own church has it, or we, at least, think that such a thing actually exists.

However, when one considers the New-Testament accounts of local churches, he notices great variations in their organization and order. But, with all the great diversity of models, little of which I am aware in this "latter day" comes close to Biblical examples. Think about it: can you locate a twenty-first-century congregation anywhere in the world that is similar to a first-century church? And the funniest thing: everybody wants to keep on doing the same thing tomorrow that they are doing today and did yesterday. Why? I think it's because we haven't got the foggiest idea of how to get out of our rut!

Surely, anyone who is interested in an "end-time restored church" would want to employ the *Bible* as a guide-line. I assure you, the solutions to these puzzles most likely lie hidden within the pages of the *Bible* (plus a heavy dose of the holy spirit's anointing). Let's get back to the *Bible*. Let's just get back to the basics. However, even this is difficult to do, since the early churches sprang up in so many diverse ways. Which early-day congregation would you like to emulate?

When the church in Jerusalem was conceived on the Day of Pentecost it began in the power of the holy spirit. Peter explained to three thousand people about the death and resurrection of Jesus and the outpouring of the holy spirit:

Acts 2:23,24 This Man (Jesus) was handed over to you by the determinate counsel and foreknowledge of God; and you, with the help of wicked men, put him to death by nailing him to the cross. But God raised him from the dead...

v36 God has made this Jesus, whom you crucified, both Lord and Christ.

v18 I will pour out My spirit in those days...

They inquired:
Acts 2:37 What shall we do?

Peter responded:
Acts 2:38 Repent, and be baptized every one of you in the name of Jesus Christ for the remission of sins, and you shall receive the gift of the holy ghost.

Paul explained that the baptism of the holy ghost is one's entrance into the Church, which Paul called the Body of Christ:
1 Corinthians 12:13 For by one spirit are we all baptized into one Body.

When Paul says, "one Body," he means that there is only one church for Jewish and gentile believers. It is not race, but by the spirit that one gains membership into the church.

We should note that the initial outpouring of the spirit occurred on the Jewish holiday of Pentecost, and that a large part of those three thousand people had made a journey to Jerusalem from many distant parts of the world. And, it would be safe to speculate that most of them did not remain in Jerusalem, but afterward returned to their homes and families. Undoubtedly neither did they remain silent about their experience.

Oh, the infinite wisdom of God! To have the inauguration of Jesus' Church to be on the holy day of Pentecost, when there would be thousands of visitors present from around the world! This thing was NOT done in secret.

The *Bible* makes absolutely no mention of this, but, if those three-thousand did not remain silent, it is certain that there sprang up from these original believers groups of disciples of Christ all over the world. These holy pilgrims were like so many torches, lit by the fire of the spirit, spreading everywhere the holy blaze by which they themselves had been ignited.

How they were organized we do not know. We can say for sure, that since the apostles never left Jerusalem for three-and-one-half years, these scattered groups of followers of Jesus may not have had organizational input from the apostles unless they might have made later pilgrimages there to inquire of the apostles about "order." But, what kind of order did they have? We don't know.

For that matter, what kind of organization did the Jerusalem church have?

Firstly, God, Himself, sent His son Jesus from heaven to earth.
1 John 4:9 God sent his only begotten Son into the world.

The word "sent" is translated from the Greek word *a-pos-tel'-lo*, from which we derive the word "apostle." Jesus was God's apostle to the earth.
Hebrews 3:1,2 Consider the Apostle and High Priest of our profession, Christ Jesus, Who was faithful to Him that appointed Him.

Jesus was the faithful apostle <u>appointed</u> by God particularly <u>to the church in Jerusalem</u>; Jesus labored for three-and-one-half years, and then he sent back the holy spirit by which He begat that church. Jesus, Himself, dug that work out.

During His ministry Jesus ordained twelve more apostles.
Luke 9:2 He sent them to preach the kingdom of God, and to heal the sick.

Mark 6:7 He gave them power over unclean spirits.

Matthew 10:6 Go rather to the lost sheep of the house of Israel.

Mark 3:14 He ordained twelve, that they might be with Him and that He might send (a-pos-tel'-lo) *them out to preach...*

The word "preach" is from the *Greek* word *ke-ru'-so*, which means "to proclaim" or "to publish." "Preaching" does not necessarily mean speaking out loud; declaring the *Good News* may be made, for example, by the life a Believer lives, without a specific word being spoken.

Jesus commissioned them:

Mark 16:15 Go into all the world and preach the gospel to every creature.

Matthew 28:19,20 Go therefore and make disciples of all the nations, baptizing them in the name of the Father and of the Son and of the holy spirit, teaching them to observe all things that I have commanded you.

It was their commission to "go" and "preach," to "teach," to "make disciples." They were SENT (*a-pos-tel'-lo*). However, at first, they did NOT go into all the world, but, they remained in Jerusalem.
*Acts 6:7 And the word of God increased; and the number of the disciples multiplied **in Jerusalem** grew.*

Ultimately there arose an oppression of the church.
Acts 8:1 At that time there was a great persecution against the church which was at Jerusalem; and they were all scattered abroad throughout the regions of Judea and Samaria, except the apostles.

Some suppose that the scattering of the saints was in fear, and that it was only the apostles who stood their ground. However, this persecution had been foretold by the Lord, Who gave specific instructions that the members of the church were to remove to another city and to continue the Work. He said:
Matthew 10:22,23 You will be hated by all for My Name's sake. But he who endures to the end will be saved. <u>When they persecute you in this city</u> (Jerusalem), <u>flee to another</u>.

The word "flee" could also be rendered: to shun, to vanish away, to escape. Their actions were not cowardice, but rather obedience to the Lord's directions.

> *When they persecute you in this city, get yourselves to another city!*

The following proves that the saints did not flee "this city" in fear:

> *Acts 8:4 Therefore those who were scattered went everywhere **preaching** the Word.*

When the persecution arose in Jerusalem, they were not scared to death; they left there "preaching the Word!!!" What may have seemed like a victory for the enemies of Christ

> *Philippians 1:12 actually turned out for the furtherance of the Gospel.*

The Church began spreading, just as Jesus had planned. He had said:

> *Acts 1:8 You shall receive power when the holy spirit has come upon you; and you shall be witnesses to Me in Jerusalem, and in all Judea and Samaria, and to the end of the earth.*

So, not out of fright, but in obedience, they moved on. Down to Samaria went Philip.

> *Acts 8:5,6 Then Philip went down to the city of Samaria, and preached Christ to them. And the people with one accord gave heed to those things which Philip spoke, hearing and seeing the miracles which he did.*

Please consider how extraordinary this was. Philip, a Jew, would have never gone into Samaria; Jews did NOT go there. But wait! Jesus had done so, [the woman at the well (John 4:4)], and He ordained that the Church do this, too:

> *in Jerusalem, in Judea, in **Samaria**, and to the end of the earth.*

So, Philip went, and, no doubt, at the behest of the holy spirit.

> *Acts 8:14-17 Now when the apostles which were at Jerusalem heard that Samaria had received the Word of God, they sent unto them Peter and John...Who, when they were come down, prayed for them...Then they laid their hands on them, and they received the holy ghost.*

The scattering of the Church was even much broader than that.

> *Acts 11:19-22 Now they which were scattered abroad upon the persecution that arose about Stephen traveled as far as Phenice, and Cyprus, and Antioch, preaching the Word to none but to the Jews only. And some of them were men of Cyprus and Cyrene, which, when they were come to Antioch, spoke to the Grecians (Hellenized Jews), preaching the Lord Jesus. And the Hand of the Lord was with them: and a great number believed, and turned to the Lord. Then tidings of these things came unto the ears of the church which was in Jerusalem: and they sent forth Barnabas, that he should <u>go as far as</u> Antioch.*

In spite of the persecution, the Church in Jerusalem had continued to grow. They then sent Barnabas, a prophet, to Antioch. He was authorized to "go as far as Antioch."

Before leaving Jerusalem, let us continue to consider our question: What kind of order did the church there have? The greatest distinguishing factor was the affect of the infusion of God's spirit in the lives of the saints.

> *Acts 4:31 They were all filled with the holy ghost, and they spoke the Word of God with boldness.*

They were ALL filled with the holy ghost. If there is one thing that a restored church will have is that the members will be full of the spirit. Paul was able to say:
> *Romans 15:19 Through mighty signs and wonders, by the power of the spirit of God.*

Should we today expect to see an abundance of signs and wonders when the church is NOT in order? when the member's lives are NOT in order? Why no! These manifestations are God's Witness of His approval. If we are not in order, why would the Almighty signal His approval?

When it says "they spoke the *Word of God* with boldness," it does not mean in a Sunday church meeting; it means that they spoke everywhere; they ALL spoke everywhere, all the time, about their Jesus. Not only were they powerful, but they humbly trusted in God. You will see this happen again as present-day assemblies are brought back to God's order.

Here is something else peculiar about that early Jerusalem assembly:
> *Acts 4:32 No one claimed that any of his possessions was his own, but they shared everything they had.*

That was powerful! Remember now, we're talking about church order. What did they do? They avowed that their possessions were really God's. And, they all acknowledged the apostles' authority. They brought money and
> *Acts 4:37 laid it at the apostles' feet.*

Despite persecution, the Jerusalem assembly continued to flourish. Many years later, possibly twenty five years later, James and the elders of the church declared to the apostle Paul:

> *Acts 21:20 You see, brother, how many thousands of Jews believe.*

A better rendering would have been "tens of thousands."

This was not a little anemic church; it was alive; it was vigorous. (Remember, we're talking about copying an early-day assembly in the latter day.)

Of the government of the local church we have scant information. We know that at the very beginning they met in homes AND out in the open in the porches of the Temple.
> *Acts 2:42,46 They continued steadfastly in the apostles' doctrine and fellowship, and in breaking of bread, and in prayers.*

> *Acts 2:46 They, continuing daily with one accord **in the temple**, and breaking bread from house to house.*

> *Acts 5:42 Daily **in the temple**, and **in every house**, they ceased not to teach and preach Jesus Christ.*

We may ascertain somewhat from this:
1) They separated their lives from the world, and lived in a holy Christian fellowship, strengthening and building up each other in their most holy faith.

2) They frequently ate together and met together at their respective lodgings.

3) They yielded themselves readily to the instructions of the apostles.

4) They had a great deal of mutual conversation with each other; they were much together.

5) If the "breaking of bread" refers to more than eating their meals together, they did not think fit to "take communion" in the environs of the Temple. If "breaking of bread" means eating meals together, they did not do it at the Temple, either.

6) They gave generously to one another, but were under no obligation nor command to do this (*Acts* 5:4).

7) The apostles left all to follow Christ, and gave themselves wholly to the *Word* and prayer.

8) We may speculate and wonder if they ever did meet together in one large congregation.

> *Acts 4:31,33 When they had prayed, the place was shaken where they were assembled together; and they were all filled with the holy ghost, and they spoke the* Word *of God with boldness...With great power the apostles gave witness of the* **resurrection** *of the Lord Jesus.*

1) The resurrection of the Lord Jesus was the main point to be established. Do you think churches in the latter day will have a different message? We hear little preaching these days about Jesus' resurrection. Neither do we witness the "power" that attended their teaching. No doubt there was much to say about the resurrection and about resurrection life in Christ. And the Almighty was pleased to manifest His approval with power. So,

2) Striking miracles were performed giving proof of the resurrection and confirming the doctrine.

Some folks say that it is not yet time for the manifestation of this power; it will happen in God's Time. That is absolutely correct. But, were the Body of Christ, or even a local assembly, right now today in such a condition, I cannot see why there would not be a demonstration of power in their presence. Right now today!

So, don't make the excuse that the power and witness of God is not available today. Don't say that it is not possible for the people of God to be over-comers today. Don't put off the prospect for another generation. God is the same today as He was and will be. We can be equipped as well today as any day. If you want to preach a powerful message, preach that!

Deacons

Just as in the rest of Jewish society, the church was composed of Hellenized Jewish believers (Grecians) and traditional Jewish believers (Hebrews). It was specifically to these Hebrew believers that Paul wrote an epistle. He, himself, was one of them (*Philippians* 3:5). It was one of his credentials.

> *Acts 6:1 And in those days, when the number of the disciples was multiplied, there arose a murmuring of the Grecians against the Hebrews, because their widows were neglected in the daily ministration.*

In its benevolence the church had grace to serve the widows, but the Grecian widows were being over-looked. Necessity being the mother of invention, it was quickly determined to do something that had never been done before: to ordain seven deacons.

> *Acts 6:6,7 When they had prayed, they laid their hands on them. And* <u>the</u> Word *of God* <u>increased</u>; *and the number of the disciples multiplied in Jerusalem greatly; and a great*

company of the priests were obedient to the faith.

Do you think perhaps in the latter day, the spirit may lead to do something that had never been done before? How much of what we do now needs to be discarded while striving to remain true to the Bible's model? Well, here was something new. The ordination of deacons was employed later in all the Churches of Christ (*1 Timothy* 3:8, *Philippians* 1:1) with prayer and the laying on of hands. Though all the members were to be "servants" according to Christ's example, special deacons (servants) were ordained to carry out the churches' non-spiritual and administrative functions.

We could make a long dissertation on serving, service, ministering, ministry, administering, and administrating, but suffice it to say that ALL the saints "serve," and, furthermore, certain members are pointed out for specific functions in the church. Some have duties that are on-going; some have a function that is specific and temporary, perhaps even for one-time only. These deacons, whether long-term or short-term, were publicly acknowledged in the inauguration of their work by prayer and the laying-on-of-hands.

Acts 6:6 When they had prayed, they laid their hands on them.

We're speaking of "order" here. In no other place does it mention that hands were laid upon deacons, but it would seem from this initial ordination ceremony it is likely that this practice was employed everywhere in the Body of Christ. Some deacons may later go on to be ordained to a ministerial "office."

It would seem that "deacons" should be common-place in the church. *Di-a-ko-ne'-o*, a verb (serve, minister, administer) is found thirty seven times in *scripture*. Do you think that *di-a'-ko-nos*, a noun, used thirty times in the *New Testament* (servant, minister, deacon), should be in the latter-day church? I believe the non-deployment of deacons to be one of the greatest short-comings of the modern Church of Christ. Repeat: the non-employment of deacons is a great short-coming of today's Church.

Acts 6:2,4 It is not reasonable that we should leave the Word of God, *and serve tables...But we will give ourselves continually to prayer, and to the ministry of the Word.*

We often find pastors these days doing all sorts of busy things, tending to the upkeep of the church property, dealing with church finances, etc, instead of studying the *Bible* and counseling the members of the church with the *Word*. They are often so occupied with "things," they have little time for their primary function in the church. Let the deacons do their work! Where are the deacons?

Antioch

It happened that the Grecians in Antioch, the Hellenized Jews, were the first to receive Christ in that city.

*Acts 11:21 And the hand of the Lord was with them: and **a great number** believed, and turned to the Lord.*

This assembly was NOT started by an apostle; it began from the scattering of believers from the mother church in Jerusalem and now had "a great number."

Acts 11:22-26 Then tidings of these things came unto the ears of the church which was in Jerusalem: and they sent forth Barnabas, that he should go as far as Antioch. Who, when he came, and had seen the grace of God, was glad, and exhorted them all, that with purpose of heart they would cleave unto the Lord. For he was a good man, and full of the holy ghost and of faith: and much people was added unto the Lord. Then Barnabas went to Tarsus, to find Saul. When he had found him, he brought him unto Antioch. And it came to pass, that a whole year they assembled themselves with the church, and taught much people. And the disciples were called Christians first in Antioch.

When Jerusalem heard that a church had begun in Antioch they ordained one of their members named Barnabas to go there. He was thrilled to see what the Lord was accomplishing. As a prophet he admonished the people to fix their love upon Jesus. His ministry was powerful, and his faith was so great. Many additional people came to Jesus as a result, yet Barnabas knew the church was lacking teaching. Off he went to Asia Minor and brought Saul back with him. Together they worked with the church for a year, explaining the "types" and "shadows" of the *Law* and the messages of the Prophets and how to live a holy life in this present world.

At this time church prophets began to circulate foretelling the coming of a terrible famine that was soon to come upon the world.
Acts 11:27,28 In these days came prophets (plural) from Jerusalem to Antioch. And there stood up one of them named Agabus, and signified by the spirit that there should be great dearth (famine) throughout all the world: which (actually) came to pass in the days of Claudius Caesar.

The *Bible* tells us that this prophecy came to pass just as it was spoken. The significant thing was the famine would be the worst in Palestine. The prophets were not just warning of the famine, however, but had another purpose: to stir up a heart of charity in the saints so they would have compassion and benevolence for the church in Jerusalem.

The Office of the Prophet

We learn something about the ministry from that incident: that prophets in the Early Church were mobile; they did not always stay in their local assemblies, but they moved about as directed by the spirit. (Please see Chapter 18.)

Some years later there arose a problem in Antioch: certain members of the Jerusalem assembly were going to Antioch teaching them they must necessarily obey the Jewish *Law* in order to be a Christian. In particular, they taught that circumcision was required.

The elders in Antioch pondered what to do about this false-teaching. Since its origin had been in Jerusalem, they had no choice but file a complaint there, not because the global church leadership was there. After much controversy, Jerusalem agreed, and they wrote a letter of apology to Antioch and with instructions and explanations that these teachings had not been the true faith of Jesus Christ.

To add weight and stress to this letter, <u>two prophets</u> from Jerusalem, Judas and Silas, were authorized to go to Antioch.
Acts 15:30-35 They came to Antioch; and when they had gathered the multitude together, they delivered the letter. When they had read it, they rejoiced over its encouragement.

*Now Judas and Silas, themselves **being prophets** also, exhorted and strengthened the brethren with many words. And after they had stayed there for a time, they were sent back with greetings from the brethren to the apostles.*

However, it seemed good to Silas to remain there. Paul and Barnabas also remained in Antioch, teaching and preaching the *Word of the Lord*, with many others also.

Again, we see the mobility of the office of a prophet. We have record of this relationship between two assemblies of the Church of Christ, Jerusalem and Antioch, and the infusion into their activities of four prophets, Barnabas, Agabus, Silas, and Judas. We also know that there were other prophets in the Early Church, for Paul spoke of them in Corinth.

*1 Corinthians 14:29-32 Let two or three **prophets** speak, and let the others judge. But if anything is revealed to another who sits by, let the first keep silent. For you can all prophesy one by one, that all may learn and all may be encouraged. And the spirits of the **prophets** are subject to the **prophets**.*

Without any comments on this passage, we merely want to point out that the prophets were not only moving about from city to city, but they were vitally important in the functions and meetings of their local assemblies, too.

At the time of this writing, prophets have not functioned in Jesus' Church for about two thousand years. I personally believe that this office of the ministry, since it did not exist in the synagogue, was excised from the church as it underwent judaization and apostasy. But, if the office of prophet had been so vital in Jerusalem, Antioch, and Corinth, do you think it will be essential, important, and necessary in the Latter-day Church? For that matter, the functioning of all five offices of the ministry will be found in a restored church.

We enthusiastically look forward to the interposition and recovery of the prophets into the life of the church again. We could not even guess what profound affects they will have upon the Church and the world in the end time.

The Office of the Evangelist

We had earlier (Page 80) mentioned Philip going to Samaria with the *Word*. Philip was an evangelist:

Acts 21:8 Philip the evangelist...

There is very little mention of this office in the *Bible*, so we have much to learn about its role and function. We do know that miracles were performed by Philip that confirmed to the crowd that what he was preaching was ordained from Heaven.

*Acts 8:6,12 Hearing and seeing the **miracles** which he did...they believed... Philip preaching the things concerning the Kingdom of God, and in the Name of Jesus Christ, they were baptized, both men and women.*

Many ministers in the nineteenth, twentieth, and twenty-first centuries have dubbed themselves as "evangelists." Some even do or did perform miracles. We do not know what miracles Philip actually did, but we are suggesting that we have yet to see in our day a real, full-blown evangelist. We appreciate everything any Christian does to advance the cause of Christ in the earth today. We do not intend to demean any of their labors. But, as someone said, "If they're not quacking, they're not ducks!"

After these events in Samaria
> *Acts 8:26* ***the angel of the Lord*** *spoke to Philip, saying, "Arise and go toward the south along the road which goes down from Jerusalem to Gaza."*

So, "the angel of the Lord" intervened with this evangelist. [Ought we to expect angelic visitations to twenty-first century evangelists?] Philip came upon a chariot driven by an Ethiopian eunuch, who was returning home from Jerusalem. And then, the spirit spoke:
> *Acts 8:29* ***The spirit said*** *to Philip, "Go near and overtake this chariot."*

This is not suggesting that Philip was a super athlete, but we can see that the spirit of God helped him super-naturally. These kinds of things must likely happen with evangelists! They will also be very sensitive to "the still-small-voice" of the spirit.

The eunuch was reading *Isaiah*, and Philip was adept in the *scriptures*, and explained that the man had been reading a prophecy about Jesus Christ. The Ethiopian was just as persuaded as the people of Samaria had been. He wanted to be baptized:
> *Acts 8:38-40 Both Philip and the eunuch went down into the water, and he baptized him. Now when they came up out of the water, the spirit of the Lord caught Philip away, so that the eunuch saw him no more; and he went on his way rejoicing.*

Suddenly, the spirit of God removed Philip from that location, and he was found at Azotus. And passing through, he preached in all the cities till he came to Caesarea.

Again, the super-natural accompanied the evangelist: Azotus was fifty miles away. Did Philip arrive there in an instant? And then, he kept on preaching.

Many people call themselves "preachers," but, we must conclude that they are the prophets and the evangelists who are the ministers who do the preaching. Repeat: prophets and evangelists preach. We would not want to exclude anyone who wants to say they are a preacher, although the *scriptures* refer to no one with such a title. But, the *Bible* clearly tells us that the prophets and the evangelists do preach.

The work of Philip was accompanied with miracles and super-natural signs. As we are looking forward to the manifestation of the latter-day prophets and teachers, we are just as anticipatory of the latter day evangelists.

The Office of the Elder

We have previously noted Agabus' prophecy of a coming famine and the offering made by the church in Antioch to be sent to Jerusalem. This charity was of such momentous import that Barnabas and Saul themselves were given the duty of transporting this generosity.
> *Acts 11:30 They did, and sent it to the elders* (pres-boo'-ter-os) *by the hands of Barnabas and Saul.*

Some say the "presbytery" in the Jerusalem church were the "aged men." Some say they were "the seventy" which Jesus had sent out. Others say this referred to the "hundred and twenty." Still others opine that it refers to the "seven deacons." The following is from the *Wycliffe Bible Commentary:*

Here is the first mention in *Acts* of these Christian officials. Luke gives no hint as to how the office of elder came into existence or by what means elders were chosen. A group of elders ruled over each Jewish synagogue, and it is probable that the Christian church adopted the Jewish pattern. Probably the believers constituted a number of house congregations in several homes, and the elders may have been the leaders of these several congregations.

Later on Barnabas and Saul went again to Jerusalem regarding the controversy of the teaching of the Judaizers of the requirement of circumcision.
*Acts 15:4 When they were come to Jerusalem, they were received by the church, and by the apostles AND **elders**.*

(We had previously noted that THE apostle of the Jerusalem church was Jesus Christ, Who was sent from heaven by God, the Father. Although the apostles mentioned in this passage are the twelve, whom had been with the Lord, they actually served the local Jerusalem assembly as <u>elders</u>, that is, as pastors, like all the rest of the local elders. Peter even commented:
1 Peter 5:1 The elders which are among you I exhort, who am also an elder...

Not until the twelve left Jerusalem did they function as apostles, fulfilling their charge to "Go!")

We agree that the elders were likely the leaders of their respective "house congregations" in Jerusalem. This same pattern was employed by Barnabas and Saul on their missionary journeys:
*Acts 14:23 They had ordained **elders** in every church.*

On Paul's last trek to Jerusalem
*Acts 21:18 Paul went in with us unto James; and all the **elders** were present.*

On this last journey Paul had earlier stopped in Miletus and sent a message to the elders in Ephesus to meet with him:
*Acts 20:17 From Miletus he sent to Ephesus, and called the **elders** of the church.*

Knowing he would not see them again, he had some parting instructions:
Acts 20:28-29 Keep watch over yourselves and all the flock of which the holy spirit has made you overseers (ep-is'-ko-pos). *Be shepherds* (poi-main') *of the church of God, which He* (Jesus) *bought with his own blood.*

The elders are also referred to by Paul as "overseers" and "shepherds." *Ep-is'-ko-pos* is also rendered in the *KJV* several times by the word "bishop" (*1 Timothy* 3:1,2; *Titus* 1:7; *1 Peter* 2:25; *Acts* 1:20). *Poi-main'* is always (sixteen times) given as "shepherd," except in *Ephesians* 4:11, where it is rendered "pastor." Another word for "shepherds" is "feeders." We are demonstrating that these words are all referring to essentially the same office of the ministry.

pres-boo'-ter-os   elders, presbytery
ep-is'-ko-pos   overseers, bishops
poi-main'   shepherds, pastors, feeders

This office is ALWAYS in the plural in every city. *Scripture* never mentions "one pastor" in a church, "one bishop," one "overseer," one "elder." They are always plural. For example, Paul instructed Titus:
*Titus 1:5 For this reason I left you in Crete, that you should set in order the things that are lacking, and appoint **elderS** in every city.*

I have been asked, "When did the church change from multiple shepherds in the church to having only one?" After considerable study, it is my conclusion that after the passing of Paul, the Judaizers brought the influence of the synagogue to bear in all the churches around the world, including a singular rabbi-like preacher-pastor and the ultimate elimination of all the other offices of the ministry. However, as long as some of the original apostles were still on the scene, the original order and pattern for the New-Testament church was holding. Note that James also referred to "elders" in the plural:

*James 5:14,15 Is anyone among you sick? Let him call for the **elderS** of the church, and let them pray over him, anointing him with oil in the Name of the Lord. And the prayer of faith will save the sick, and the Lord will raise him up. And if he has committed sins, he will be forgiven.*

This passage demonstrates the great power resident in the shepherds of the church, not only in the early days, but in this latter day. See how they prayed for the sick together, but each one, as a shepherd, each one worked among his own respective flock; they also prayed together at times for an ill member of the congregation. Their lives were examples for all to emulate. They were (and are) to teach (*1 Timothy* 3:2), not just the *scriptures*, but teach about living life in the church, in their families, and amongst the world.

Shepherds are to be held responsible to God for how they care for their flocks. They are to be led by the spirit in their counseling; they will be super-naturally supported by the gift of the word of knowledge and the gift of the world of wisdom. They will be super-naturally supported by the charismatic gifts of words of knowledge and wisdom.

1 Thessalonians 5:12-15 We beseech you, brethren (of the church), to know them which labor among you, and are over you in the Lord, and admonish you...Esteem them very highly in love for their work's sake. And be at peace among yourselves. Now we exhort you, brethren, warn them that are unruly, comfort the feebleminded, support the weak, be patient toward all men. See that none render evil for evil unto any man.

1 Peter 5:2,3 Shepherd the flock of God which is among you, serving as overseers, not by compulsion but willingly, not for dishonest gain but eagerly; nor as being lords over those entrusted to you, but being examples to the flock.

If ever it were true that "preaching" be done by example more than by words uttered, it would apply to the shepherds. In establishing a local church again, it is paramount that pastors plural be trained and raised up in the assembly, have oversight for a limited number of saints (I will say up to thirty, including but a handful of adult males [Jesus, himself, discipled twelve men]). One of their objectives will be the raising up of more ministers.

<u>There is not one *scripture* where pastors preach</u>. Nor is there one mention where pastors even <u>spoke</u> in a church meeting. Not that they were forbidden to speak, but that was not their purpose. Then what? They were/are to admonish their flocks. They are to warn. They are to comfort. They are to be patient. They are to be living, breathing examples of Jesus Christ. It is in this way that a church will grow, increase, multiply. The burden of the office

of shepherd is enormous. The final salvation of each individual pastor will be judged in large part by how he, himself, dealt with every saint in his oversight. I think the failure of doing those things was the reason that William Sowders asserted that few pastors would be saved.

Just as parents will be judged on the upbringing of their children, so will pastors on how they handle their sheep.
Ephesians 6:4 Fathers, provoke not your children to wrath: but bring them up in the nurture and admonition of the Lord.

As I indicated earlier, if you hanker to preach, perhaps you are not a pastor, but a prophet or an evangelist. Preaching pastors came into the apostatizing church by Jewish influence copying the rabbis in the synagogue. It is my conclusion that in a re-established New-Testament assembly, the shepherds will basically not preach; they will counsel.

In another chapter (*The Ministry of Melchizedek Today*) it is clearly demonstrated that the elders are to be supported by the saints. The ministers will not become wealthy, but they will be as well-off as those in their oversight.

The Office of the Teacher

Here the weakness of this chapter is exposed. The only information on which we have to go is that found in the *Bible*. There is even less about the "teacher" than the others. While there are specific teachers in the church, the necessity for ALL ministers to do some teaching is required.
1 Timothy 3:2 A bishop then must be blameless, the husband of one wife, vigilant, sober, of good behavior, given to hospitality, apt to teach.

2 Timothy 2:24,25 And the servant of the Lord must not strive; but be gentle unto all men, apt to teach, patient, in meekness instructing those that oppose themselves.

All Christian ministers teach, but the ordained teacher is a special minister of the Lord; he is anointed in his teaching in such a way that the most-simple mind may clearly understand the *Word*. Teachers are clearly a distinct and separate office of the church.
*Acts 13:1 There were in the church that was at Antioch certain prophets **and teachers**; as Barnabas, and Simeon that was called Niger, and Lucius of Cyrene, and Manaen, which had been brought up with Herod the tetrarch, and Saul.*

These five ministers were either prophets or teachers, two of one and three of the other. Barnabas likely was one of the prophets and Saul one of the teachers. This was before these two men were ordained as apostles and sent out from Antioch. Paul said he was a minister to the gentiles,
*2 Timothy 1:11 to which I was appointed a preacher, an apostle, and a **teacher** of the gentiles.*

Though we have little information, we know that teachers were extremely important men in the assembly:
*1 Corinthians 12:28 And God has set some in the church, first apostles, secondarily prophets, **thirdly teachers**, after that miracles, then gifts of healings, helps, governments, diversities of tongues.*

We would suggest that this verse is speaking of the general Body of Christ more than a particular local assembly. Whereas the shepherds were and are committed to the local church, we have seen that the apostles, prophets, and evangelists would also be itinerant. We would suggest that teachers are to be travelers, also. Whether their ministry is accompanied by signs and wonders as are the others, we cannot say.

It may be worthy of remark that the churches in early New England had, at the first, a class of people who were called "teachers." One was appointed to this office in every church, distinct from the pastor, whose proper business it was to instruct the congregation in the doctrines of religion. It was an office of great importance to the church; and the exhortation given to the apostle may be applied to teachers: that they should be devoted, careful, constant, and diligent in their teaching; that they should confine themselves to their appropriate place; and should feel that their office is of great importance in the church of God; and remember that this is the Almighty's arrangement, designed to promote the edification of his people.

The Office of the Apostle

We have written more extensively on "apostles" in other chapters than we shall here. Apostles are "sent ones." The *Latin* word *mitto*, meaning "to send" is applied to them by our modern word, "missionary." Yet, little of the way of present-day missionaries is scripturally based.

Apostles are the first rank of Jesus' Church. Some of the talent of all the other offices is present in them. They are sent out from a local church for the purpose of establishing Christian works where none exist. They also have the function of "confirming" the saints in existing works.[*1]

While the prophets and teachers in Antioch were worshipping and fasting the holy spirit spoke to them:
Acts 13:2-4 "Set apart for me Barnabas and Saul for the work to which I have called them." So after they had fasted and prayed, they placed their hands on them and sent them off. The two of them, sent on their way by the holy spirit, went down to Seleucia.

Apostles must be ever-guided by the holy spirit. They must be so sensitive to hearing "the still small voice" of God, that they will be able to change their direction, even not doing the very thing on which their heart was set;
*Acts 16:6,7 Now when they had gone through Phrygia and the region of Galatia, they were **forbidden by the holy spirit** to preach the* Word *in Asia. After they had come to Mysia, they tried to go into Bithynia, but the spirit **did not permit** them.*

Paul and Barnabas and all the other apostles established many works around the world. We see that they resided in different cities for a season until the spirit bade them move on. It is the on-going labor of the apostle to keep planting. We have mentioned earlier that most ministers go to a certain city, start a work and remain there. Their work ceases to match their calling. It should be that as they were/are teaching the new Christians about Jesus, they have their eyes on those whom the Lord was raising up for the ministry. Once this objective had been met the spirit sent them to the next city.

[*1] Please see Chapter 9, "Confirming the Saints."

Acts 14:23 When they had ordained elders in every church...

As an example, the work in Crete had not been completed. Paul sent Titus there to finish the job.
Titus 1:5 I left you in Crete, that you should set in order the things that are lacking, and ordain elders in every city as I commanded you.

The saints are also known as disciples, that is, learners. Jesus established the pattern for discipleship:
Mark 3:14 He ordained twelve, that they should be with him, and that he might send them forth to preach.

Jesus chose twelve that they should be with him constantly, to be witnesses of his doctrine, his manner of life, and his patience, that they might fully know it, and be able to give an account of it; and especially that they might attest the truth of his miracles; they must have been with him to receive instructions from him, that they might be qualified to give instructions to others.

The same means of discipling Paul did as well:
2 Timothy 2:2,3 The things that you have heard from me among many witnesses, commit these to faithful men who will be able to teach others also.

By this means is the *Gospel* spread, not by the preaching to the multitudes, but by the pains-taking process of <u>discipleship</u>. The elders who were ordained by Paul and Barnabas taught likewise their own disciples.

Some suppose that the church can come under the discipleship of Jesus Christ by ministering from the pulpit. This was/is not Jesus' way; he taught them by personal example. The thing that is most accomplished by sitting in a pew is endurance. But not discipleship!

It is no telling what wonders might have come about had some of the great preachers of the twentieth century not settled down, but kept planting!

***

We have our ways of doing things in the church; we learned them from our predecessors; the church has operated this way for centuries; the ways have been handed down from generation to generation. But, so many things do not match the Biblical pattern.

Should we suppose that we will replicate the early church's ministry and results by NOT conforming to their pattern? It seems sheer idiocy to keep doing things that we know are not scriptural and expecting different results. Shall we be content with mediocrity?

Re-ordering a Local Church

One time there was a church whose founder and pastor died. He had not ordained any elders over the years; he was the IT of the church. He had asked a trusted minister friend from another city to take over his work when he died. But, the other minister already had his own church.

For a while this man tried to travel back and forth preaching from both pulpits alternately. This trekking back and forth began to wear on him and was not producing positive results. Here are some things that were not according to *Bible* standards:

1. He was trying to be the pastor of two congregations;
2. He had <u>not</u> been raised up in the second church, thus lacking intimacy;
3. He became a <u>custodian</u> of the second church, just trying to keep it alive.

Following were the suggestions made to rectify the situation. I will use the fictitious names of Bro. Blue and the church in Centerville.

Now that the church in Centerville is pastor-less, what must be done to make the situation right? (Many churches are in similar circumstance.)

1. There can be no apostle to "start" the work there, since it has already been established, and the Founder is deceased. It is possible, however, for apostolic work to yet be done there. We see in *scripture* that apostles went to cities in which churches had already been established. Paul went to Rome. Peter and Apollos were in Corinth; Timothy went to Cyprus, John to Ephesus. Nothing is wrong with apostles coming to the city of another man's work. However, everything they do/did there contributed to the original work. A new and separate work in a city is not recognized in *scripture*.

2. But, to get this Centerville church back on track, perhaps some artificial means must be undertaken, something that might not be exactly scriptural. I have prayed about this, and I think the Lord showed me that a "surrogate" or "substitute" apostle could be sent there.

3. One of his purposes would be to raise up qualified elders from amongst the brotherhood, who will henceforth lead the flock after this "surrogate" finally departs.

4. It should be publicly stated that his stay would be one or two years or so. No one should think this person will permanently reside there.

5. What kind of qualifications should he have?:

a) He does not necessarily have to have been married, but, in this circumstance, it would probably be helpful that he were or had been.

b) If he had children, it would be best that they be full-grown, so that he might devote himself principally to the ministry.

c) His wife must be in agreement with this plan.

d) It would be preferable that he be from Bro. Blue's oversight. If he were not, but "borrowed" from another work, he would have to be able to acknowledge Bro. Blue's personal, pastoral oversight for this period of time.

e) He must be a caring, disciplined, holy person.

f) As an apostle, albeit a temporary one, he must trust God for financial support. The people must be taught by Bro. Blue and others, of their responsibility to support this man. This also does not exclude possible back-up support from the outside, especially from Bro. Blue.

g) While the burden of the work is to be solely the surrogate apostle's, he is to submit to Bro. Blue. He is to keep him abreast of events, progress, and failures.

6. Hands are to be laid upon him twice.

a) first, by the brothers of his local church, who are sending him out to do a work of the ministry.

b) secondly, by Bro. Blue in the presence of the Centerville church. They are to witness the bestowing of authority upon his head. Bro. Blue is to give him full authority, directing the people to look to this man for
    1) leadership and
    2) counsel.

7. His ordained purposes are to
   a) hold the work together
   b) raise up ministers.

8. When he has accomplished his purposes he is to leave. He may return occasionally, as Paul and Barnabas did, but he will have ordained two or more elders toward whom he will have directed the hearts of the people.

This is my suggestion as a possible way to restore this congregation to New-Testament order.

Order and Authority

When new elders are raised up in the local church, they are all equal in authority. One older elder might be the pastor of the others and have spiritual over-sight for them, but, as far as governance is concerned, they are equal.

Since the elders govern the church by the holy spirit, their decisions will always be unanimous. One contrary opinion, therefore, will delay action. They must wait for unanimity. This prevents cliques from forming and taking political domination.

Many ministers have feared sharing authority with other men, dreading that the others may lure away some of the sheep or begin teaching some heresy. Be assured that these very things WILL happen. It grieved Paul when those kinds of things occurred (*Philippians* 3:2; *Galatians* 1:6; *1 Timothy* 1:20; *2 Timothy* 2:14,17; *2 Peter* 2:1,10; *Jude* 4).

Titus 1:10-11 For there are many unruly and vain talkers and deceivers, specially they of the circumcision, whose mouths must be stopped, who subvert whole houses (home churches), teaching things which they ought not, for filthy lucre's sake.

Paul recognized that these subverters were actually used by the Lord in sifting the flock.

1 Corinthians 11:19 There must also be heresies among you, that those who are approved may be recognized among you.

But, shepherds must usually deal gently with their flocks, not lording their authority. More than by words, but by example do they teach.

1 Peter 5:3 Neither as being lords over God's heritage, but being examples to the flock.

All ministers should have their own pastor/shepherd. A minister derives his authority by being under authority. When a man of God submits himself (his ministry, his life, even his family life) to another man, then erroneous things in his character and his teaching can be exposed. On the other hand, when a minister ceases to be transparent to the one man to whom he is to be accountable, then he may be deceived and walk in darkness to his detriment and to his flock, as well.

(When a minister strays into immorality, no matter how anointed is his preaching, he is disconnected from his mooring, and everything he teaches will be tainted or deceived.)

May we conclude with a word of alert. Most of us have anticipated the day when the glory of the early church in Jerusalem would be manifested in our day.
Acts 2:47   Praising God, and having favor with all the people. And the Lord added to the church daily such as should be saved.

Acts 4:21,33   All men glorified God for that which was done...With great power gave the apostles witness of the resurrection of the Lord Jesus: and great grace was upon them all.

But, the *Bible* gives ample warning that in the end of this age there will be a time of world-wide chaos, scattering, upheaval, political unrest, savage persecution, and plagues. It could be that many glorious things that will happen may never be known by the Body-of-Christ-in-General until these marvelous testimonies come forth as testimonials during the new age of Christ's reign.

That some local churches will be healed of their disorders and that the Church of Christ will be restored are assured, but perhaps not the way we may have envisioned, and not the same way in every city; there will be a variety of norms. A variety of norms? One thing will be constant: the anointing of the holy spirit will be great everywhere that good men seek God.

On the first page of this chapter I suggested that it was critical for God's people to keep digging into the *Word*. I also said that we seem to keep doing what we've always done; we're certainly grateful for what our forefathers have passed on to us. But, did they have a restored church? No. They passed on to us some practices that were not right; we just don't know which things we've been taught that were erroneous. What to do! My suggestion is that everything you know and believe--lay them on the table; pray a lot; listen for the still small voice; be prepared to change; and do not fail to love everybody unto the end of the age. Prophecy: He who thinks he's got it all figured out is due a lot of surprises.

Please consider some of my suggestions,.......and also let Him
1 Thessalonians 3:13   establish your hearts blameless in holiness before our God and Father at the coming of our Lord Jesus Christ with all His saints.

The "early" Church did not have "services" as did the Jewish synagogue, but assembled at the summons of the local elders, who were so-moved by the holy spirit. The apostatizing church developed a prescribed "liturgy," a standardized order of events observed during a religious service.

If your church's meetings follow some kind of ordered or scripted sequence of events, it is liturgical, no matter how loose it might be. But, as it was in Jerusalem, Antioch, and Ephesus, the meetings of the latter-day Church will not be standardized, ritualized, predictable, or repetitive. Every gathering of the saints will be unprecedented and extraordinary. They will be as varied as the stars of the universe, because the force that created the stars is the same force that will move upon the congregating saints.

Chapter 10. Confirming The Saints

Acts 14:22 Confirming the souls of the disciples, and exhorting them to continue in the faith, and that we must through much tribulation enter into the kingdom of God.

New church converts have to be established, strengthened, made firm, or encouraged by the presentation of truth and by the motives of the *Gospel*. In the first century they were surrounded by enemies, and exposed to temptations and to dangers; and, they had, as yet, but a slight acquaintance with the truths of the *Gospel*, and that it was therefore important that they should be further instructed in the truth, and established in the faith. This was what Paul and Barnabas in returning to their churches accomplished, as in the above verse.

Likewise, after the Council of Jerusalem a letter was sent to the church in Antioch assuring them of the decisions made there and their total acknowledgment of the brotherhood of Jewish and gentile Christians. Antioch had been shaken by the teaching that gentile believers had to keep the sabbath and the men to be circumcised. The determination declined that notion. Two prophets were commissioned to accompany Paul and Barnabas and this letter back to Antioch. By this action they were showing the great importance they had placed upon the business that had occurred. When the prophets arrived in Antioch they lent all their weight to the letter and its message:

*Acts 15:32 And Judas and Silas, being prophets also themselves, exhorted the brethren with many words, and **confirmed** them.*

The apostles and the prophets made certain that the disciples had no misunderstanding the Will of God.

The word "disciple" signifies literally, a "scholar." The church of Christ was a school, in which Christ himself was chief Master, and his apostles, subordinate teachers. All the converts were disciples or scholars, who came to this school to be instructed in the knowledge of themselves and of God: of their duty to Him, to the church, to society, and to themselves. After having been initiated in the principles of the heavenly doctrine, they needed line upon line, and precept upon precept, in order that they might be confirmed and established in the truth. Though it was a great and important thing to have their minds, their understanding, properly informed, yet, if the heart was not disciplined, information in the understanding would be of little avail; therefore they confirmed the souls of the disciples.

Acts 15:41 Paul went through Syria and Cilicia, strengthening the churches.

As there must be some particular standard of truth, to which they might continually resort, that their faith might stand in the power of God, it was necessary that they should have such a system of doctrine as they knew came from God. These doctrines were those which contained all the essential principles of Christianity, and this was called THE FAITH: and, as they must have sound principles, in order that they might have righteous practices, so it was necessary that they should continue in that faith, that it might produce that obedience, without which even faith itself, however excellent, must be useless and dead. It was and is our hearts that are in need of confirmation.

> *Isaiah 35:3,4 Strengthen the weak hands, and **make firm** (confirm) the feeble knees. Say to those who are fearful-hearted, "Be strong, do not fear! Behold, your God will come with vengeance, with the recompense of God; He will come and save you."*

For this reason the Almighty has seen fit to place His people in the Congregation of the Lord, that they might be instructed and helped.

Again, as the spirit of the world would be ever opposed to the spirit of Christ, so they must make up their minds to expect persecution and tribulation in various forms, and therefore had need of confirmed souls and strong faith, that, when trials came, they might meet them with suitable fortitude, and stand unmoved in the cloudy and dark day.

As, for example, the church in Thessalonika was undergoing opposition, Paul saw fit to send Timothy to them to confirm them. Paul wrote that he had

> *1 Thessalonians 3:2-4 sent Timothy, our brother and minister of God, and our fellow laborer in the gospel of Christ, to **establish** you and encourage you concerning your faith, that no one should be shaken by these afflictions; for you yourselves know that we are appointed to this. For, in fact, we told you before when we were with you that we would suffer tribulation, just as it happened, and you know.*

And, as the mind must faint under trouble that sees no prospect of its end, and no conviction of its use, it was necessary that they should keep in view the Kingdom of God, of which they were subjects, and to which, through their adoption into the Heavenly Family, they had a divine right. Hence, from the apostles' teaching, they not only learned that they should meet with tribulation, much tribulation, but, for their encouragement, they were also informed that these were the very means which God would use to bring them into perfection.

> *1 Thessalonians 3:13 To the end (God) may stablish your hearts unblameable in holiness before God, even our Father, at the coming of our Lord Jesus Christ with all his saints.*

If they had tribulation in the way, they had a heaven of eternal glory as the end to which they were continually to direct their views. Into these truths were the saints constantly confirmed. To have this explained to them by letter must have continually comforted the saints.

The apostle Peter also spent a great deal of his ministry, as well as his epistles for the purpose of confirming the saints.

> *1 Peter 5:10 May the God of all grace, who called us to His eternal glory by Christ Jesus, after you have suffered a while, perfect, **establish**, **strengthen**, and **settle** you.*

Not just the apostles of the church, but all of its officers are intent upon confirming the saints. Paul states that God's ministers are

> *Ephesians 4:12-16 for the perfecting of the saints for the work of ministry, for the edifying of the body of Christ, till we all come to the unity of the faith and of the knowledge of the Son of God, to a perfect man, to the measure of the stature of the fullness of Christ; that we should no longer be children, tossed to and fro and carried about with every wind of doctrine, by the trickery of men, in the cunning craftiness of deceitful plotting, but,*

speaking the truth in love, may grow up in all things into Him who is the head -- Christ -- from whom the whole body, joined and knit together by what every joint supplies, according to the effective working by which every part does its share, causes growth of the body for the edifying of itself in love.

The purposes of the ministry are to perfect, build up, and mature the members of the church. In the meantime, they are faced with trials, tests, crosses, oppositions, burdens. And for these things the saints are in need, both as a church and individually, to be confirmed.

Do not confuse the tender work of the ministry in confirming the saints with the miraculous confirmations attending the preaching of the Word.

*Mark 16:20 And they went forth, and preached everywhere, the Lord working with them, and **confirming** the Word with signs following.*

Romans 15:19 In mighty signs and wonders, by the power of the spirit of God, so that from Jerusalem and round about to Illyricum I have fully preached the Gospel of Christ.

Thus, signs and wonders are to accompany and to confirm the preached *Word*, but this is a different usage of the word "confirm" then the comfort brought by the ministry of the Church. Albeit the church will not have fulfilled its latter day mission until mighty signs and wonders attest the Truth of Jesus Christ, it is the gentle and patient work of the ministry on a day-to-day basis to confirm the saints. This church and that pastor who are not daily devoted to the ministry of confirmation are apt to miss God.

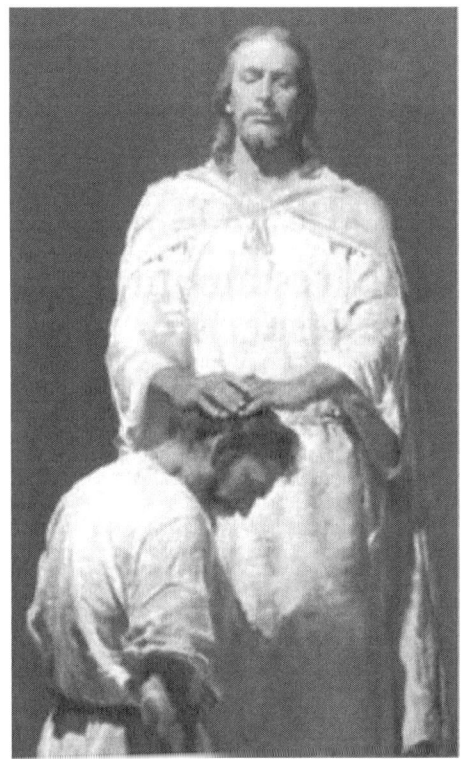

Laying on of Hands

Jesus Laying Hands on the Lame Child

Chapter 11. Making Disciples

Surely our fathers have inherited lies! Jeremiah 16:19

By all that Jesus had done--gave up His divinity, came to earth, had his life placed in the womb of an earth-woman and born of her, lived an earth-life, suffered, became perfect and obedient, was arrested, was tried and convicted, beaten, stripped, striped, crucified, bled, died, was buried, was raised from the dead, appeared to many, ascended back to the Father, and sent back the holy spirit--he had "prepared a place" and laid the foundation for the Kingdom of God. He now had all authority in heaven and on earth. And now, He was authorizing his disciples to do what he had done to them. He was commissioning them to do to others what had been wrought in them. He was sending them out to nurture others.

Mark 16:15,16 And he said to them, "Go into all the world, and preach the gospel to every creature. He that believes and is baptized shall be saved; but he that believes not shall be damned.

What was the principal intention of this commission? It was: to disciple all nations. *Math-e-teu-sa-te* is the *Greek* word meaning: "admit them as disciples." He was saying to the twelve sent ones (apostles): "Do your utmost to make the nations Christian nations." He did not say: "Go to the nations, and pronounce the judgments of God against them, as Jonah did against Nineveh, and as the other Old-Testament prophets (though they had reason enough to charge them for their wickedness), but He said: "Go, and disciple them." Christ, the Mediator, was setting up a kingdom in the world, bringing the nations into his subjection, setting up a school, bringing the nations to be His scholars, raising an army for the carrying on of the war against the powers of darkness, enlisting the nations of the earth under His Banner of love. The work which the apostles had to do was to set up the Christian religion in all places, and it was honorable work. The pagan nations had conquered the world for themselves, and made it miserable; the apostles were to conquer the nations for Christ, and made them happy.

Matthew 28:19,20 Go therefore, and teach (make disciples of matheteuo-Greek) all nations, baptizing them into (Greek: eis) the Name of the Father, and of the Son, and of the holy ghost, teaching them to observe all things whatsoever I have commanded you.

Jesus said that <u>every</u> man that is acquainted with the *Gospel* ought to carry this Truth to others. As the disciples had said that THEY had understood the truth, Jesus says that it should not be unemployed. They should bring it forth in due time, like a householder bringing out of his treasury, or place of deposit, what had been laid up there at any time, as it was needed.

Matthew 13:51,52 Jesus said to them, "Have you understood all these things?" They answered, "Yes, Lord." Then he said to them, "Therefore every scribe who is instructed <u>into</u> the kingdom of heaven is like a man who is a householder, who brings forth out of his treasure things new and old.

The new things they were to teach pertained to the grace Christ had brought to the world, the grace to overcome the world and become perfect. The old things were the rich pictures painted by Moses and the Prophets that illustrated all that Jesus had come to do in <u>discipling</u> the nations.

A disciple is a follower, an adherent, a learner, a pupil, a believer. Two examples would be:
> Matthew 27:57 ...*a rich man of Arimathaea, named Joseph, who also himself was Jesus'* **disciple**.

> Acts 14:21 *And when they had preached the gospel to that city, and had taught (***discipled***) many...*

The word "disciple" is used seventy four times in *Matthew*, twenty nine times in *Acts*. It is used altogether two hundred sixty nine times in the *New Testament*. It is a significant Christian word.

> Acts 11:26 *And the* **disciples** *were called Christians first in Antioch.*

> Acts 9:26 *And when Saul was come to Jerusalem, he tried to join himself to the* **disciples**: *but they were all afraid of him, and believed not that he was a* **disciple**.

Christian disciples learn to live their lives as Jesus did, that is, denying self. They are taught to forsake their own will in favor of the directions of the holy spirit, to live in Christ's resurrection power.
> Romans 6:4 *Therefore we are buried with him by baptism into death: that like as Christ was raised up from the dead by the glory of the Father, even so we also should walk in newness of life.*

> Colossians 2:12 *Buried with Him in baptism, in which you also were raised with Him through faith in the working of God, who raised Him from the dead.*

> Luke 14:33 *Whoever forsakes not all that he has, he cannot be my* **disciple**.

The Pattern of Teaching and Doing

Years after Luke had written his *Gospel*, he realized that he had not finished the story, rather that he had only begun it, and that, really, the story had no ending in his lifetime. But, he continued to write:
> Acts 1:1 *The former treatise have I* (Luke) *made, O Theophilus, of all that Jesus began both* **to do** *and teach...*

It was not just what Jesus had taught the twelve, but what he had **done**. When Jesus had selected them he had two purposes in mind for them, one present and one future:
> Mark 3:14 *And he ordained twelve, that (1) they should* **be with him**, *and (2) that he might* **send them** *forth to preach.*

What Jesus taught them was not just Bible lessons, but living life. They were to learn how Jesus lived, ate, walked, acted, related, and reacted. Disciples learn to become like their masters. He did not teach them for their own benefit alone, but for the salvation of the nations.
> Mark 6:7 *And he called unto him the twelve, and began to send them forth by two and two...*

> Mark 6:30 *And the apostles gathered themselves together unto Jesus, and told him all things, both what they had* **done**, *and what they had* **taught**.

Having gone out, they returned. They reported what they had "done" and had "taught." They verified to Jesus, their rabbi, their discipler, that they had done just as he would have done. They did and taught what he had done and taught, <u>because they had been with him</u>. They knew.

Acts 4:13 Now when they saw the boldness of Peter and John, and perceived that they were unlearned and ignorant men, they marveled; and they took knowledge of them, that they had been with Jesus.

This is the <u>master-plan of evangelism</u>. This is the blue print for world conquest: one-on-one teaching and relationship. Jesus spoke to the multitudes, but he invested himself in but a few. Although the church has come today to do things much differently, ought it to expect to get the same results that Jesus got? Did Jesus make disciples preaching from the synagogue pulpit to people sitting neatly in pews? Or did he diligently live and walk with his men daily demonstrating the way they were to <u>be</u>?

The first commandment given by God was: Be fruitful and multiply. This ought to have more than a natural meaning to the Church. "Be fruitful and multiply" translates in the spirit as follows: "Go, make disciples."

William Sowders saw the principle of discipleship continuing beyond the church-age on into the millennium with a Jewish-led ministry (*Zechariah 8:21-23*). Discipleship will continue.

Church Leadership

More important even than the elders of Israel were the elders of the *New Testament*, who governed the church. The elders were raised up from among their own congregations. They were servants to the members of the church, and were given honor by the members for their lowliness.

*1 Thessalonians 5:12 And we beseech you, brethren, to know them which labor **among you**, and are over you in the Lord, and admonish you*

The elders of the church were similar to shepherds who kept the flocks of sheep together and in order. The *Latin* word for "shepherd" is "pastor." They had authority to counsel and correct the church. The true Church did not have a class of Babylonious "dignitaries. In the kingdom of God, where things are just about opposite from the world, the most-lowly members were the rulers. And, they are <u>among</u> their sheep.

John 13:14,15 If I then, your Lord and Teacher, have washed your feet, you also ought to wash one another's feet. For I have given you an example, that you should do as I have done to you.

*1 Timothy 5:17 Let the **elders** that rule well be counted worthy of double honor,*

Hebrews 13:7 Remember them which have the rule over you.

v17 Obey them that have the rule over you.

Matthew 23:11 But he who is greatest among you shall be your servant.

When churches in the early days were established, the holy spirit pointed out which ones would have authority to serve the congregation.

*Acts 14:23 They ordained **elders** in every church.*

Elders were/are plural. The spirit raised up multiple shepherds in each church. This was true, not only of the churches in Europe and Asia, but in Jerusalem and Judea, as well. When the churches in Europe sent an offering to Jerusalem, it was brought by

Barnabas and Saul personally and given to the <u>elders</u> there:
> *Acts 11:29,30 Then the disciples, every man according to his ability, determined to send relief unto the brethren which dwelt in Judea, which also they did, and sent it to the **elders** by the hands of Barnabas and Saul.*

When problems were created in the church in Antioch by some members of the church in Jerusalem, the issue was taken up directly with the leaders of that assembly.
> *Acts 15:1,2 And certain men which came down from Judea taught the brethren, and said, "Except you be circumcised after the manner of Moses, you cannot be saved." When therefore Paul and Barnabas had no small dissension and disputation with them, they determined that Paul and Barnabas, and certain other of them, should go up to Jerusalem unto the apostles and **elders** about this question.*
>
> *v4 And when they were come to Jerusalem, they were received by the church, and by the apostles and **elders**...*
>
> *v6 And the apostles and **elders** came together for to consider of this matter.*
>
> *v22 Then pleased it the apostles and **elders**...*
>
> *v23 And they wrote letters by them after this manner: "The apostles and **elders** and brethren send greeting..."*

We will not discuss the problem with which they were dealing. We only point out <u>who</u> dealt with the situation.

The elders of each local assembly were responsible for watching over, caring for, nurturing, and teaching their flocks.
> *Acts 20:17,28 ... (Paul) called the **elders** of the church...."Take heed therefore unto yourselves, and to all the flock, over the which the Holy Ghost has made you overseers to <u>feed</u> the church of God."*

There were many elders (also called "bishops," "overseers," or "shepherds"). The particular thing is that they were multiple.
> *Acts 21:18 And the day following Paul went in with us unto James; and ALL the **elderS** were present.*
>
> *Titus 1:5 ...ordain **elders** in every city...*
>
> *James 5:14 Is any sick among you? let him call for the **elders** of the church.*

There were other servants of the church beside the pastor/shepherds; there were those who were ordained by the laying-on-of-hands to serve the church in other natural and spiritual matters. They were called "deacons." This title comes from the *Greek* word meaning "to serve." On the one hand, ALL members of the church are called to serve. But, some are called upon to serve in a particular matter: it may be serving tables, taking care of the church's monies, or ordering a certain situation. Deacons may be ordained for long-term service or for a one-time stint, as we have stated previously. While all Christians serve, ordained deacons assist the ministry in the orchestration of the church.
> *Philippians 1:1 Paul and Timotheus, the servants of Jesus Christ, to all the saints in Christ Jesus which are at*

*Philippi, with the **bishops** and **deacons**...*

The elders and also the deacons are chosen from those in the church who have good reputations and are highly moral and whose family-life is exemplary.

An "elder, an overseer, and a bishop" refer to the same person, who "shepherds, pastors, and feeds" the church.
> *1 Peter 5:1,2 The **elders** which are among you I exhort, who am also an elder, and a witness of the sufferings of Christ, and also a partaker of the glory that shall be revealed: **Feed** the flock of God which is among you, taking the **oversight** thereof...*

This is the feeding-pattern of the early church in the *Bible*. Shouldn't it still apply today?

Authority and Submission

Many people desire to have authority in the church. One principle we learn from the Roman centurion is: To have authority, one must be under authority. A corollary principal is: If you are under authority, you have authority.
> *Luke 7:7,8 I (the Roman centurion) did not think myself worthy to come to you (Jesus): but, say in a Word, and my servant shall be healed. (I know this, because) I also am a man set **under authority**, having under me soldiers, and I say unto one, "Go," and he goes; and to another, "Come," and he comes; and to my servant, "Do this," and he does it.*

The centurion knew what authority he had. He was licensed by the Senate of Rome. He was in submission to the Senate. He operated in the name of Caesar. He had authority, because he was under authority. He perhaps did not know by Whom Jesus was authorized, but he knew beyond doubt from all that Jesus had done that he, too, was under authority.

Many ministers have sent themselves out into the ministry; they called themselves. Others, their family gave them ministerial position. But, they are NOT under authority.

In a local church, it is soon pointed out by the holy ghost that certain individuals have the anointing of God upon them in a certain way. The spirit directs the elders to ordain these men for different works of ministry. They might be prophets, teachers, or evangelists. It is obvious what their office is by their behavior and manner. Unlike pastors, they are NOT restricted to their locality, but may move about the world ministering in other assemblies or even among the heathen.

There is yet a further office that is raised up in the local church, the apostle, one who is "sent out" from the church for the specific purpose of planting new churches. All of these ministers have something in common: they are all "under authority." For example, when Barnabas and Saul were sent out as apostles from the church at Antioch, Syria, they ultimately returned to give account to that assembly what they had done.
> *Acts 14:25-28 Now when they had preached the word in Perga, they went down to Attalia. From there they sailed to Antioch, where they had been commended to the grace of God for the work which they had completed. Now when they had come and gathered the church together, they reported all that God had done*

with them, and that He had opened the door of faith to the gentiles.

As great as had been their success, and as great as had been their spiritual manifestations, yet they were in submission to the church that had ordained them. In this we see how spiritual authority is different from worldly authority. Church authority emanates from meekness and lowliness.

> *Matthew 20:25-28 But Jesus called them unto him, and said, "You know that the princes of the gentiles exercise dominion (lordship) over them, and they that are great exercise authority upon them. But, it shall not be so among you: but, whoever will be great among you, let him be your minister (servant); and whoever will be chief among you, let him be your servant. Even as the Son of Man came not to be ministered to, but to minister, and to give His life a ransom for many."*

The word "submit" means to bow, to defer, to place under. It is an amazing thing that God makes the ministers of the church from the lowest members, and then He expects the rest to place themselves UNDER them. Nothing in the Kingdom is more opposite from the world than this principle. Paul explains that the lowly ministers are God's "higher power" in the church.

> *Romans 13:1-6 Let every soul be subject unto the **higher powers**. For there is no power but of God: the powers that be are ordained of God.*

Authority in the church is granted by those who submit to this God-ordained supervisor. If the individual saint does not submit to the pastor, then the pastor has NO authority. But, where it is granted, the ministry has the responsibility to correct the saints.

> *Whosoever therefore resists the power, resists the ordinance of God: and they that resist shall receive to themselves damnation. For rulers are not a terror to good works, but to the evil. Will you then not be afraid of the power? Do that which is good, and you shall have praise of the same, for he is the minister of God to you for good. But if you do that which is evil, be afraid, for he bears not the Sword (the Bible) in vain, for he is the minister of God, a revenger to execute wrath upon him that does evil. Therefore, you need to be subject, not only for (fearing God's) wrath, but also for conscience sake. For this cause pay tribute also, for they are God's ministers, attending continually upon <u>this very thing</u>.*

The service of the ministry is: KEEPING THE CHURCH STRAIGHT.

Not only are Christians called upon to submit themselves to the ministry, but they are also to place themselves UNDER everyone else in the congregation.

> *Philippians 2:3 In lowliness of mind let each esteem other better than themselves.*

> *Ephesians 5:21 Submitting yourselves one to another in the fear of God.*

> *1 Peter 5:5 ...all of you be subject one to another, and be clothed with humility...*

When God raised Jesus from the dead, at that moment, He gave Jesus authority forever. Jesus declared:

Matthew 28:18 All power is given unto me in heaven and in earth.

Then Paul explained:
Ephesians 1:20-23 (God's power) was wrought in Christ, when (God) raised him from the dead, and set him at His own Right Hand in the heavenly places, far above all principality, and power, and might, and dominion, and every name that is named, not only in this world, but also in that which is to come, and has put all things under (Jesus') feet, and made him to be the head over all things to the Church, Which is his body, the fullness of him that fills all in all.

How lowly is the Christian! He places himself under the ministry, as well as everyone else.

Yeshua Has Delegated His Authority

Jesus has distributed his authority to His Church and its ministers. He said:
Matthew 10:40 He that receives you receives Me, and he that receives Me receives Him that sent Me.

John 13:20 Verily, verily, I say unto you, "He that receives whomsoever I send receives Me; and he that receives Me receives Him that sent Me."

John 20:21 As my Father has sent me, even so send I you.

The goal of God for every saint of God is that he become like Jesus. Therefore, what the ministers receive from God, they pass on to those in their charge. This is the very essence of <u>discipleship</u>.

*2 Timothy 2:2 The things that 1) you have heard from 2) me among many witnesses, commit these to 3) faithful men who will be able to **teach** 4) **others** also.*

Safeguards in the Abuse of Authority

Of all the helps that the Almighty has provided for His people, the most-sure guidance is the *Word of God*. Everything that happens in the church can be gauged by what the *Bible* says. Every Christian worker can measure his life-style, his attitude, and his labor by the *Holy Scriptures*.
2 Timothy 3:16,17 All scripture is given by inspiration of God, and is profitable for doctrine, for reproof, for correction, for instruction in righteousness: That the man of God may be perfect, throughly furnished unto all good works.

There are numerous accounts in the *Bible* where those in authority did not act in obedience to the *Word*. They did immoral things, they fractured the church, they stole saints, they taught false doctrine. We should not be shocked when those kinds of things happen in our day. But, the church is not left defense-less against corruption within the congregation's leadership. However, it is to be exercised in the most tender, careful, and judicious way. For one thing, an allegation against a minister by only one person is not acceptable.
1 Timothy 5:19,20 Against an elder receive not an accusation, but before <u>two or three</u> witnesses. Them that sin rebuke before all, that others also may fear.

So many times when a minister errs, the action that is taken is nothing. It simply doesn't get dealt with. It gets swept under the rug. It gets overlooked. Dealing with a minister's sin is often undone out of respect for the man's office. It is more often undone in fear of the man's person. This is such a tragedy for two reasons: 1) the minister may possibly lose his soul, because he was not confronted with his misdeed; and 2) the structure of the church is undermined by inaction.

Jesus, himself, was quite specific regarding individual church members in dealing with offenses. There is no reason this ought to apply any less to those in authority.

> *Matthew 18:15-18 If your brother sins against you, go and tell him his fault between you and him alone. If he hears you, you have gained your brother. But if he will not hear, take with you one or two more, that "by the mouth of two or three witnesses every word may be established." And if he refuses to hear them, tell it to the church. But if he refuses even to hear the church, let him be to you like a heathen and a tax collector. Assuredly, I say to you, whatever you bind on earth will be bound in heaven, and whatever you loose on earth will be loosed in heaven.*

Peter cites three errors ministers may commonly make: 1) growing lethargic and complacent in serving the church, feeling that one is being forced to manage or to discharge his duties; 2) being corrupted by money; and 3) becoming dictatorial over the church.

> *1 Peter 5:1-3 The elders who are among you I exhort, I who am a fellow elder and a witness of the sufferings of Christ, and also a partaker of the glory that will be revealed: Shepherd the flock of God which is among you, serving as overseers, not by compulsion but willingly, not for dishonest gain but eagerly; nor as being lords over those entrusted to you, but **being examples** to the flock.*

Peter's admonitions are very serious. They are guidelines regarding traps a minister might avoid. The church is greatly damaged when these flaws are unchecked by the other ordained ministers. Herein we also see one great value for the multiplicity of elders in the local church; they can be a check on one another.

Because of the authority bestowed by God upon the ministry, a man might be tempted to become exalted or arrogant or think himself a bigwig, a major player, a notable personage. God knew just how to afflict the apostle to help him to remain humble. He knows just what you, Brother Minister, needs, too.

It may help to remember this adage (which we stated earlier) when you sense your pride is rising up: God chooses His ministers from among the lowliest members of the assembly, raises them up, and then expects everyone else to honor and to obey them.

So, God does not choose the cream of the crop; He does not choose many wise; He does not go for good looks (Remember He did not select David's handsome brothers.); He does not choose the smartest or the best-educated; He is not looking for the wealthy, the strong, the influential, the near-kin. Always remember that God selects from the lowliest. Keep this in mind when pride arises.

We must note that of the men Jesus, himself, selected, he chose men who had been passed over by all the other rabbis. This brings all the more glory to God.

Qualifications for Leadership

Leaders are raised up in the local congregation, not trained in some external institution. Nor, are ministers to be rotated from parish to parish as has been the practice of the *Methodist Church*, which custom has been employed by many other Christian groups. It may not be impossible for a transplanted pastor to feel a burden for the new saints under his charge, but it is exceedingly difficult. The *Bible* is clear that, while apostles, prophets, teachers, and evangelists may be mobile, elder/shepherds serve in the local assembly. That they may rise to another ministerial office and minister elsewhere does negate the truth that elders are strictly local.

Acts 14:23 And when they had ordained elders in every church, and had prayed with fasting, they commended them to the Lord, on Whom they believed.

The ordination of elders or any others ministers of the Gospel should be undertaken with the utmost gravity, surely with prayer and fasting.

It is a fact that the many blessings God bestows upon those He loves, can, after a while, turn around and be a trap. One of the most insidious and potentially corrupting blessings is godly knowledge. How many men of God have been poisoned by the great understanding the Almighty has bestowed upon them! If a minister is not constantly humbling himself before God and majoring in charity, he is doomed. If I may paraphrase Paul:

1 Corinthians 8:1 Knowledge puffs up, but charity builds up.

A great help in avoiding the "big head" is for the minister to remember Jesus wants him to be a servant.

Matthew 20:27 And whosoever will be chief among you, let him be your servant.

We must see how lowly Jesus intends for the ministry to behave. At the last supper Jesus demonstrated the utter humility of ministering, which we earlier quoted:

John 13:12-15 So after he had washed their feet, and had taken his garments, and was set down again, he said to them, "Do you know what I have done to you? You call me Master and Lord: and you say well; for so I am. If I then, your Lord and Master, have washed your feet; you also ought to wash one another's feet. For I have given you an example, that you should do as I have done to you.

Humility is one quality of a minister of the *Gospel*. Another would be faith-fullness. Ministers of God are faithful to details; they play close attention to the small matters. Then, the Lord will promote them to greater and greater responsibility. Dealing with money is always a test of faithfulness, because it can be such a tempting thing. Jesus said:

Luke 16:10-12 He that is faithful in that which is least is faithful also in much: and he that is unjust in the least is unjust also in much. If therefore you have not been faithful in the unrighteous mammon, who will commit to your trust the true riches? And if you have not been faithful in that which is another man's, who shall give you that which is your own?

2 Timothy 2:2 (Teach these truths) to faithful men who will be able to teach others.

Let us itemize the list of qualifications in *1 Timothy* 3 regarding leaders:
1. a good man whose life cannot spoken against
2. married to one wife
3. alert
4. not violent
5. not covetous
6. not an alcohol drinker
7. hospitable
8. inclined to teaching
9. not quarrelsome
10. gentle and kind
11. not avaricious
12. his children and wife also live orderly and holy
13. experienced in church matters
14. a good reputation with non-church members
15. serious-minded
16. a whole-hearted follower of Christ
17. tested

Shepherds/Pastors

The *Greek* word *poimen* appears nineteen times in the *Bible*, eighteen times translated "shepherd" once translated "*pas-tor*," (*Ephesians* 4:11). "*Pas-tor*" is the *Latin* word for shepherd, which has come to mean rather "a preacher." It would be well to call these men what God intended them to be, "shepherds," those who care for sheep. Actually, Jesus Christ, Himself, is the "chief" shepherd, (*1 Peter* 5:4) and all the rest are, you might say, "under-shepherds," acknowledging that all the saints belong to the Lord.

In the tenth chapter of *John*, Jesus lists his own qualifications of shepherdship, which also ought to apply to an under-shepherd. The shepherd:
1. knows the sheep
2. calls them by name
3. leads them
4. provides pasture
5. protects against thief and robber
6. lays down his life for the sheep.

The sheep:
1. know the shepherd
2. recognize his voice
3. follow him.

In the twenty third *Psalm* there are a number of listed duties of a good shepherd in making disciples. He
1. makes full provision for his sheep
2. leads them in paths of righteousness
3. leads them to good pasture (the *Bible*) and water (the holy spirit) and around poisonous, stagnant water
4. walks with them through "the valley of the shadow of death"
5. provides discipline (rod) and support (staff). (Please consider Chapter 16.)

And yet, there are more duties itemized in *Ezekiel* 34:1-10. A shepherd
1. strengthens the diseased
2. heals the sick
3. binds up the broken
4. brings again those who have been driven away
5. seeks that which is lost
6. keeps the sheep from becoming scattered.

Brother Shepherd/Pastor, would you please re-read the above lists.

The Goal of Discipling

<u>The goal of discipleship is to make the pupil AS the teacher.</u>
>   *Matthew 10:25 It is enough for the disciple that he be **as** his master, and the servant be **as** his lord.*

*Luke 6:40 The disciple is not above his master: but every one that is perfect shall be **as** his master.*

There is no other way to make disciples then for teacher and student to be in contact with one another. Jesus' disciples
*Mark 16:10 had been **with** him.*

Disciples are to emulate their masters. Paul said to his disciples:
Philippians 4:9 The things which you have 1) learned and 2) received and 3) heard and 4) seen in me, 5) DO.

They learned, received, heard, saw, DID.

Farrar defines Jesus' DISCIPLE as: "one who believes His doctrines, rests upon His sacrifice, imbibes His spirit, and imitates His example."

Discipleship existed among rabbinic students in Roman Israel and also long before that time in the days of the Prophets. So, we hear Isaiah's prediction about the coming Christ and His disciples:
*Isaiah 50:4 The Lord God has given Me the tongue of **disciples**, that I may know how to sustain the weary one with a word. He awakens Me morning by morning; He awakens My ear to listen as a **disciple**.*

Having been discipled and disciplined, having listened, observed, and learned, the disciple may <u>himself</u> now be qualified to be a discipler.

Isaiah 54:13,14 All your children shall be taught by the Lord, and great shall be the peace of your children. In righteousness you shall be established. You shall be far from oppression, for you shall not fear, and from terror, for it shall not come near you.

When you are taught, you shall have peace, righteousness, free from oppression and fear.

It is a sad truth that "discipleship" is NOT practiced in the modern Church of Christ. <u>It is the Church's greatest weakness</u>. There are many great teachers and preachers in the church world, but discipleship can only be accomplished in the trenches, where men live and deal in life. Preaching from the pulpit cannot substitute for hands-on guidance and tutelage.

Pulpit pronouncements of the most important and serious nature will fall upon forgetful and inattentive ears.

Today's churches are not like a flock of sheep, rather they are a collection of saints, a bunch of church attenders. "Where do you go to church?" is not an expression found in the *Bible*, is it? How can today's pastor possibly know what is going on the lives of the saints without frequently being personally in contact with them?

As long as the Church has one foot in Babylon, She will never want to give up Her pulpit-to-pew ministry. Thus, the Babylonious church will NEVER make disciples.

What a Church Meeting Might Have Looked Like Nineteen Hundred Years Ago

Chapter 12. Rabbinic Discipleship in Jesus' Day

A nation will come to extinction without educating and indoctrinating its youth. There is a Jewish saying: "The world continues on by the breath of school children." Because of this fervent desire to educate the next generation, there were academies in every town and village in ancient Israel.

There were three stages of Jewish education, the first being *bet se-fer'* taught in the local synagogue. On the first day of school the rabbi would put honey (symbol of God's favor) on the students' slates. "Lick the honey," the rabbi would say. "May you never forget that the *Words of God* are the most enjoyable thing you may ever have. May you be like Ezekiel who ate the scroll which was like honey in his mouth." This studying began with *Leviticus* at age six and continued till age 10, by which time the students had memorized the first five books of the *Bible*, the *Torah*, the *Law*.

The second stage was *bet Talmud* for ages ten to fourteen for the advanced students, during which the rest of the *Holy Scriptures*, the *Writings* and the *Prophets* would be memorized. Paul commented to Timothy that

> *2 Timothy 3:15 from a child you have known the* Holy Scriptures, *which are able to make you wise for salvation...*

Timothy well knew the *Bible*. In the *bet Talmud* academies the students (*tal-mi-dim'*) would also learn the technique of "Jewish response," that is, answering a question by asking a question. For example: "What is two times two?" The answer might be given: "What is twelve divided by three?" Thus, the children were grilled in both "Logic" and in *The Word of God*.

We should not be surprised that Mary, at age fifteen or so, responded to her cousin Elizabeth's prophetic utterance. Her remarks in *Luke* 1:46-55 (known in the *Catholic Church* as the *Magnificat*) are in the manner of a *bet Talmud* student, although, as a girl, she was not. Speaking under the influence of the holy spirit, her brief statement touched on over seventy *Old-Testament* passages. Mary responded with *scriptures*, because THEY were her life learned in her home.

The *scriptures* tell us that Yeshua, himself, did NOT attend the academies.
> *John 7:14,15 Now about the middle of the feast Jesus went up into the temple and taught. And the Jews marveled, saying, "How does this man know letters, having never studied?"*

Jesus was but twelve years of age. By what means the crowd discerned that Jesus had not attended the academy we are not told. But, we do know that his wisdom was not acquired from human sources, albeit there was plenty of bible discussion going on in the home.
> *Luke 2:40,46,47,52 And the Child grew and became strong in spirit, filled with wisdom; and the grace of God was upon Him...Sitting in the midst of the doctors, both hearing them, and asking them questions. And all that heard him were astonished at his understanding and answers...And Jesus increased in wisdom and stature, and in favor with God and men.*

It would have been unlikely that any rabbi would have invited a child of such advanced knowledge and understanding. But, what need had he of formal letters, when the spirit of the Living God was touching his young mind? The *Psalms* predicted his quick wit:

> *Palms 45:2-4 You are fairer than the sons of men; Grace is poured upon Your lips; Therefore God has blessed You forever. Gird Your sword* (the Word) *upon Your thigh, O Mighty One, with Your glory and Your majesty. And in Your majesty ride prosperously because of truth, humility, and righteousness; And Your right hand shall teach You awesome things.*

> *Psalm 22:10 I was cast upon You from birth. From My mother's womb You have been My God.*

We could not imagine youngsters in our day who would plead with their teacher to allow them to please get to read the next *scripture*, but they did in those days.

Tal-mi-dim' were students who were disciples of a rabbi. The rabbi would grill a disciple with a question like: "What are the seventeen references from *Deuteronomy* in the book of *Habakkuk*?" These students were sharp.

A technique taught in the academies that became part of every-day life in Israel was the *re-mez'*, which was a method of discussing a *scripture* by not using that *scripture*, but using the one before or after it. A student would respond to the rabbi regarding that verse, but actually using the one after or before it. So, a *scripture* would be discussed without ever quoting it.

There are numerous *re-mez-im* in Jesus' discussions with the Jews. This is why they wanted to kill Jesus for his responses, which, on the surface, do not seem so disturbing to us. However, they understood his *remez* (hint). What he was meaning was very agonizing to them. It was not WHAT he said, but what he did NOT say. Here is an example: The night Jesus was arrested he was questioned by the High Priest about the false charges that had been made, but Jesus did not respond until he was forced under oath to respond:

> *Matthew 26:63 But Jesus held his peace. And the high priest answered and said to him, "**I adjure you** by the Living God, that you tell us whether you are the Christ, the Son of God."*

This cunning question was therefore proposed. The difficulty of the question consisted in this: If he CONFESSED that he was the Son of God, they stood ready to condemn him for "blasphemy;" if he denied it, they were prepared to condemn him for being an impostor, and for deluding the people under the pretence of being the Messiah.

The scripture with which he responded was:
> *Daniel 7:13 I saw in the night visions, and, behold, one like the Son of man came with the clouds of heaven, and came to the Ancient of days.*

Thus, did Jesus respond:
> *Matthew 26:64 "You have said it yourself; nevertheless I tell you, hereafter you shall see the Son of Man **[sitting at the right hand of Power]**, and coming in the clouds of heaven."*

Jesus had quoted part of *Psalm* 110:1, inserting it into *Daniel* 7:13. Remember, what he <u>omitted</u> was the answer to the priest's question. Here is the entire verse:
> *Psalm 110:1 The Lord said to my Lord, "Sit at my **right hand**, until I make your enemies your footstool."*

Jesus had not spoken all the text. The Jews were ready to automatically finish the quotation in their trained minds. So what Jesus did not say was what he was really saying. What had Jesus omitted? It was:
> *Psalm* 110:1 The Lord said to my Lord...

By that un-quote, "The Lord said to my Lord," Jesus was acknowledging that he was indeed the Lord. What Jesus had NOT said infuriated the High Priest:
> *Matthew 26:65,66 Then the high priest tore his clothes, saying, "He has <u>spoken</u> blasphemy! What further need do we have of witnesses? Look, now you have heard His blasphemy! What do you think?" They answered and said, "He is deserving of death."*

Jesus' actual blasphemy was what he had <u>not</u> even said. But they heard:
> *"The Lord said to my Lord..."*

They said that he had spoken blasphemy. They had heard what he had NOT said. And, upon this admission, our Lord was convicted. Had he not inserted, "sitting at the right hand of power," he would only have admitted to being the Christ. But, by deliberately adding the words from *Psalm* 110:1, Yeshua deliberately insured his own death penalty.

In the first teaching of his ministry at the synagogue in Nazareth Jesus was assigned the text in *Isaiah* 61 stating that God's spirit would be on the Messiah, who would declare deliverance for the people, and that he would
> *Luke 4:19,20 preach the acceptable year of the Lord. And he closed the book...*

Jesus did not complete his assigned reading. But, it wasn't the passage that Jesus read that upset the people; it was the next passage that he DID NOT read.
> *Isaiah 61:2 ...and the Day of Vengeance of our God...*

These trained, self-righteous people heard what Jesus did NOT say; he was claiming to be God!!!!! They heard in their trained mind what he did <u>not</u> say.
> *Luke 4:28 And all they in the synagogue, when they **heard** these things, were filled with wrath.*

After a few more choice comments, they attempted to execute Jesus by throwing him over a cliff. Such is the affect of the *re-mez'* taught at the *bet tal-mud'* academy.

The third phase of education was *bet mid-rash'*, for age fourteen and up. These boys would become rabbis; they were the best of the best. It took the invitation of a rabbi to get into *bet mi-drash'*.

These students would leave their parents' home and move in with the rabbi's family. They were not just going to be taught the *Word*, they were going to be taught "life."

The call to discipleship was: Come, follow me!

Rabbis had their own continuing "insight" into the *Word*, which was called the rabbi's "yoke." Students acquired the yoke of their rabbi. A rabbi could trace his yoke back through a series of rabbis. The rabbi might say, for example, "I teach the yoke of Rabbi Simon, which was the yoke of Rabbi Zacheus, which was…"

When Jesus said:
> *Matthew 11:29,30 "Take MY **yoke** upon you, and learn of me; for I am meek and lowly in heart: and you shall find rest unto your souls. For*

*my **yoke** is easy, and my burden is light,"*

he was announcing that he had a <u>new</u> yoke, a new teaching, a new line of thought, a new insight. He said that it would be "easy." Unlike the burdensome rules of the other rabbis, Jesus' teaching was to be "easy."

A rabbi wanted to perpetuate his yoke. He grilled his students to find the ones who had what it took. When he found one, he would utter, "Come, follow me." The student would leave his family and devote himself to becoming like his rabbi. He would study and talk and walk and live like his rabbi. This was *bet midrash*.

Rabbis were so fired up about the *Word of God*. They would dance around the synagogue holding a *Torah* scroll. The men would kiss their fringe and touch it to the scroll passing by.

There is a saying in the *Mish-nah*: "May you be covered in the dust of your rabbi," meaning, "May you be like him." Students wanted to be covered in their rabbi's dust, to become like him.

As they walked down the road accompanying their rabbi, the dust would kick up from his sandals, thus the expression: may you be covered in your rabbi's dust.

Jesus was a rabbi with a new yoke, calling to himself his own disciples:

*Matthew 4:18-20 And Jesus, walking by the sea of Galilee, saw two brothers, Simon, called Peter, and Andrew, his brother, casting a net into the sea: for they were fishers. And he said to them, "**Follow me**, and I will make you fishers of men." And they straightway left their nets, and followed him.*

They were thrilled. Here was a rabbi that believed they could do it! They eagerly followed him.

*Matthew 4:21,22 And going on from there, he saw two other brothers, James, the son of Zebedee, and John, his brother, in a ship with Zebedee their father, mending their nets; and **he called them**. And they immediately left the ship and their father, and **followed** him.*

Was Zebedee upset? No, he was not upset that his sons left him. He was actually greatly honored. Up till then, every great rabbi had overlooked his sons.

There was a rich, young ruler, a quality man. Jesus called him to discipleship:

Luke 18:22,23 Sell all that you have and distribute to the poor, and you will have treasure in heaven; and come, follow Me." But when he heard this, he became very sorrowful, for he was very rich.

When once in a great while a rabbi taught a "new" yoke, not the one of his predecessor, that rabbi spoke with *shmi-ha*, authority. He would say, "You have heard it said,..." He's got a new yoke. For a rabbi to have *shmi-ha*, he would have to have hands laid upon him by two rabbis who, themselves, had *shmi-ha*. One who laid hands upon Jesus and who had *shmi-ha* was John, the Baptist, who witnessed:

John 1:29 "Behold! The Lamb of God who takes away the sin of the world!"

Who was the second witness to Jesus' authority? God was the other.

Luke 9:35 "This is My beloved Son: hear him!"

John 5:31,32 If I bear witness of Myself, My witness is not true. There is another who bears witness of Me, and I know that the witness which He witnesses of Me is true.

The priests questioned Jesus about his authority. You will note that Jesus answered their question with a question:
Matthew 21:23-27 By what authority do you these things? and who gave you this authority? And Jesus answered..., "I also will ask you one thing, which if you tell me, I in like wise will tell you by what authority I do these things: The baptism of John, from where was it? from heaven, or of men?"

And they reasoned with themselves, saying, "If we shall say, 'From heaven;' he will say to us, 'Why did you not then believe him?' But if we shall say, 'Of men;' we fear the people; for all hold John as a prophet."

And they answered Jesus, and said, "We cannot tell." And he said them, "Neither do I tell you by what authority I do these things."

Rabbinic disciples believed that they could become just like their masters. They had faith in themselves that they could be just like him.
Matthew 14:25-31 And in the fourth watch of the night Jesus went to them, walking on the sea. And when the disciples saw him walking on the sea, they were troubled, saying, 'It is a spirit." and they cried out for fear. But straightway Jesus spoke to them, saying, "Be of good cheer; it is I; be not afraid." And Peter answered him and said, "Lord, if it IS You, bid me come to you on the water." And he said, "Come." And when Peter was come down out of the ship, he walked on the water, to go to Jesus. But when he saw the wind boisterous, he was afraid; and beginning to sink, he cried, saying, "Lord, save me." And immediately Jesus stretched forth his hand, and caught him, and said unto him, "O you of little faith, why did you doubt?

Whom did Peter doubt? In whom did Peter lose faith? He lost faith in himself. He lost the faith that he could become like his rabbi, who was walking on the water. The entire rabbinical system was based on the premise: "You can do it!" Jesus knew Peter could walk on water. So could we!

Think about this: Jesus called you. He said to you, "Follow me." Since he called you, he believes that YOU can do it. Believe it! Do you see that Jesus had faith in Peter? He believed in Peter. Jesus believes in you and me. Are you having trouble in some area of your life? Are you struggling with that diet? Are you thinking about giving up on a relationship, a marriage? Are things not working out like they should? Fear not! Rabbi Yeshua has called you; he has empowered you. He believes you can do it. He believes in you. Say this aloud:
Philippians 4:13 I can do all things through Christ who strengthens me.

God could have brought forth His Son at any time and any place. It was at this place and this time and this system that the son of God was manifested, this rabbinic system. God could have chosen any nation, any culture for His Son to reside, any time, any community. But, there never was a civilization like first-century Palestine. Never were there an enlightened people like these. Never was a society so devoted, so edified, so polished, a people whose very nostrils inhaled thoughts of the Divine. It was at this time and in this place that the **Almighty chose to bring forth His only-begotten Son.**

And look whom Jesus chose! These disciples were young (except Peter, who had a mother-in-law). Jesus changed the world by equipping a group of young men whom no other rabbi had taken. They were the "B" team. He thought that they could be like him. They could do it!
> *John 1:43 The day following Jesus would go forth into Galilee, and finding Philip, said to him, "**Follow me**."*

Philip did not choose Jesus. Jesus chose him. Jesus thought that Philip could become like him. Jesus believes you can be like him. God, the Father, has set in motion a special plan, just for you, to make you become just like His Son. God has a plan to re-form you, to make you like Yeshua:
> *Romans 8:29 For whom God foreknew, He also predestined to become **conformed** to the image of His Son.*

Thus, the apostle Paul could also say to his disciples,
> *1 Corinthians 11:1 "Be imitators of me, just as I also am of Christ."*

When a rabbi would conclude a day's teaching he would pronounce the Aaronic benediction over his students:
> *Numbers 6:24-26 "The Lord bless you and keep you;*
>
> *The Lord make His Face shine upon you and be gracious to you;*
>
> *The Lord lift up His Countenance upon you and give you peace."*

His students believed that the rabbi was covering them with this blessing. They believed they were being "covered in his dust."

May you be covered in the dust of your rabbi Jesus from this day on. May you touch the hem of his garment and be made whole. May you be His disciple. May you become Him, as you
> *Romans 13:14 put on the Lord Jesus Christ.*

Then you will say:
> *Isaiah 61:10 "I delight greatly in the Lord. My soul rejoices in my God, for He has clothed me with garments of salvation and covered me in a robe of righteousness."*

Jesus Christ came forth from God, the Father, to the land of Israel just at that historical time when rabbinical discipleship was being practiced. He did not reject it, nor change it, but he used it. Like other rabbis, Jesus worked with a small group of mostly-young men. He ordained twelve
> *Mark 3:14 that they should BE WITH HIM.*

<u>Discipleship cannot be practiced from the pulpit.</u> No. It requires the intensity of a close relationship with the teacher. All the apostles and elders of the early church practiced this kind of discipleship. Thus, Paul said,
> *Philippians 4:9 "Those things, which you have both 1) **learned**, and 2) **received**, and 3) **heard**, and 4) **seen** in me, DO."*

Rabbi Jesus might just as well have said that, himself. The rabbis of his day discipled that way. "Do what I do, son. What you have learned and received and observed and heard from me, do; put that into practice."

For a shepherd/pastor to disciple a handful of disciples is far more labor-intensive then pulpit-preaching, which happens to come to us from the synagogue Martin Luther, not from Jesus of Nazareth!

We shall leave one parting thought: the apostles and elders of the latter day will practice this same intimate mentor-student relationship. This is the master plan of evangelism for our world at the end of this age. The disciples will be covered in their shepherd's dust!

Some Supporting *Scriptures* on Which to Meditate

1 Samuel 2:1 And Hannah prayed, and said, "My heart rejoices in the Lord, my horn is exalted in the Lord: my mouth is enlarged over mine enemies; because I rejoice in Thy salvation."

The Magnificat: *Luke 1:46-55 And Mary said: "My soul MAGNIFIES the Lord, and my spirit has rejoiced in God, my Savior. For He has regarded the low estate of His handmaiden: for, behold, from henceforth all generations shall call me blessed. For He that is mighty has done great things to me, and 'Holy' is His Name. And His Mercy is on them that fear Him from generation to generation. He has shown strength with His Arm; He has scattered the proud in the imagination of their hearts. He has put down the mighty from their seats, and exalted them of low degree. He hath filled the hungry with good things; and the rich he has sent empty away. He has helped His servant Israel, in remembrance of His Mercy. As He spoke to our fathers, to Abraham, and to his seed for ever."*

Isaiah 52:1 Awake, awake; put on your strength, O Zion; put on your beautiful garments, O Jerusalem, the holy city: for henceforth there shall no more come into You the uncircumcised and the unclean.

Luke 15:22 But the father said to his servants, "Bring forth the best robe, and put it on him; and put a ring on his hand, and shoes on his feet"

Galatians 3:27 For as many of you as have been baptized into Christ have put on Christ.

Malachi 2:7 The priest's lips should keep knowledge, and they should seek the Law *at his mouth: for he is the messenger of the Lord of hosts.*

1 Timothy 4:6 If you put the brethren in remembrance of these things, you shall be a good minister of Jesus Christ, nourished up in the words of faith and of good doctrine, which you have followed.

2 Timothy 2:2 And the things that (1) you have heard from (2) me among many witnesses, commit these to (3) faithful men who will be able to (4) teach others also.

It seems to me that pulpit-to-pew discipling is not only unsuccessful, it is also a Babylonious calf-path. I am strongly in favor of Biblical discipleship. Leave the pulpit-preaching to the prophets, teachers, and evangelists.

Home Church Meeting, Singapore

Chapter 13. IN FAVOR OF HOME CHURCHES

The fact that the pastor did not have time to meet with a brother at the parsonage for just an hour or so illustrates a point: we need numerous shepherds tending the flock; one man cannot do the job alone--it's too enormous a load. Even Jesus limited himself intimately to only twelve.

You retort: "That's why we have recognized these other leaders and have them sit up front...." But they are not powerful; if they have not been ordained as elders, then power has not been laid upon their heads; they have NO ordained authority; most of the people would not recognize their power; in fact, they are powerless. They're just sitting on a platform a little higher than the pew-people.

Recently a dinner was hosted in someone's home for the pastor and six of these "leading men." It was a great opportunity for the pastor to give himself to a few good men (which was the host's intention). But, the pastor had to run out in 90 minutes and attend to an important circumstance, perhaps "put out a fire." One would think the Almighty would have rather this pastor had invested his time and energy in a few leading men then to being a fireman.

Our churches are run according to the Babylonious tradition of the church-world, not according to *Bible* example, not often enough by the holy spirit. It is the custom of the church-world to have a CHURCH building, to meet once or twice or four times a week, to preach, to sing, to testify. People go to church out of habit, which is why the church-world is ineffective and devoid of power--it is inert. If they met seven times a week, they would not be served any better.

Most of Christendom is withering on the vine. The flocks are not healthy. The forty or fifty core, "Wednesday-night people" are not even healthy--they attend the meetings out of inertia, out of routine. But they are not powerful like they could be. And what about the fringe members--who cares about them? Who cares about them? Who is there to go after these strays? Who is there to lead them back into greener pastures? Who is there to go through their wool and pluck out the burrs? Who is there to apply salve to their thorny scratches acquired by daily wandering through the world?

I notice Mrs. White saying she has been discouraged, crying out for help. Who is there to minister to her needs on a daily basis? I heard Bro. Jones wrecked his marriage by NOT knowing truly how to love his wife and minister to her needs. Where was the pastor who was ready to counsel them, who was close enough and had an eye to see that trouble was brewing in the Jones family? I see the Smith family with all kinds of problems--health, financial, moral, etc. Their house had deteriorated into a frightful, discouraging wreck. No one even knew. Where was the pastor who could have brought a hundred salvations to their lives instead of leaving them to become diseased and demonized?

I see another member, struggling to make ends meet, needing help with his children, fighting discouragement. Where is his shepherd unto whom he can unburden his soul? Who is there to counsel him day-by-day?

There's John Doe being lost to the church-world? Why? What happened to his connection to the church? Who was that <u>one</u> who cared?

Say, where's Bro. So-And-So? I don't know; he doesn't come around much anymore. What's he doing? I don't know.

Say, I haven't seen the Williams teen lately? What's he doing? I don't know. It cannot be pleasing to God to lose ninety percent of the youth to the devil! **There's got to be a better way to "build the wall."**

Oh, you say that the men of the church are going to meet Saturday to discuss "doctrines." Nothing wrong with that! But it will do little good, because that is not the immediate need of the flock. These people have sores, wounds, and maladies amassed from years of neglect. There are homes not in order; there are wives and children abused; there is immorality undealt with; there are saints ill-educated in the precepts of Christian living. There are no shepherds close to the flock to tend these serious needs. The church boasts of an order of liberty, but deep down, the saints are spiritually impoverished and weak--because the order is wrong--it is church-world order; it is Babylonian; it is pagan.

Just imagine a group within the church: let's say that it has six or seven couples, some with children, plus a few single people, a couple of widows, and a brother in a nursing home. This group crosses the boundaries of familial relationships within the general body. One man is the ordained shepherd (elder) of the group. When they meet, everyone feels the burden of the meeting; spiritual gifts are frequently manifested; this one has a song; another has a banjo; this one has a testimony; that one has a problem to bare; another has the answer; this one has a gift of praying earnestly, simply, piously, who can touch heaven for the whole group; that sister encourages; this one brings a couple of friends to enjoy the fellowship. (They're not the type to be easily evangelized in a large crowd, but they're convicted by the love and simplicity, care and mutual concern of this little Christian church.) This group meets approximately once a week, but they're in <u>constant touch throughout the week</u>. They eat occasionally at one another's homes; they frequently visit the one in the nursing home; the teen-agers hear and recognize the wisdom of the elderly ones in the group, and are benefited thereby; the elderly are thrilled to be able to have a meaningful opportunity to dispense some of their hard-earned wisdom and a lifetime of experience; the children, just a handful, are disciplined and receive care from all the adults. The group has a bond of love; they have a care and concern one for another, even a sense of responsibility that they do not feel for the general body; they are frequently in one another's homes; they share housekeeping chores, baby-sitting, shopping, home repairing.

The one who has the gift of giving can easily see and know the needs, and quietly take care of them; the one who has the gift of organizing is often called upon to help plan the picnic, the joint-community project of re-roofing a house, and setting up the prayer chain; the one who has the gift of giving mercy has ample opportunities during the week to soothe others' troubles; the ones who serve have a special care for this little group, and are not often called upon by the general body; thus they are not always worn out from being overworked; they are busily involved with their little church family. The sister gifted in teaching has frequent opportunity to illuminate the other ladies. The one with the gift of a prophet is called upon for vision for the group; he is respected and also ministered to, himself, because he sometimes gets down in the dumps. There are two having the gift of encouraging, and what a blessing they are; they always can see the bright side. In the big congregation their talents are rarely manifested or used.

Imagine the strength of this church; imagine the strength of seven or ten or fifteen more of them. Do you think this might be a better order than the church-world has? Do you see that it is Biblical? Do you think it would revitalize the whole congregation? Do you think it would energize? And, if it is the mind of Christ for this day, as it was in the early days of the church, then the holy spirit will aid and abet its implementation. (Note our examples in Chapter 4.)

Now, where does this church meet? In different homes. But every month or two or three all the home churches in town meet together in an auditorium, hotel ballroom, tent, or field, etc.
> *1 Corinthians 14:23,26 If therefore the whole church be come together into one place...How is it then, brethren? **When** you come **together**, **everyone** of you has a psalm, has a doctrine, has a tongue, has a revelation, has an interpretation. Let all things be done unto edifying.*

What happens at this "altogether" meeting? Sometimes it is to receive instruction, sometimes to rejoice and celebrate, sometimes to discuss a problem requiring the entire Body's attention, sometimes to read a letter from a distant minister, sometimes to hear the teacher expound on a pressing matter, sometimes to receive correction or encouragement from a prophet.

You might wonder how the same teaching and doctrine and information is administered in all the homes? The elder/shepherds meet together during the week for prayer, fellowship, and discussion, developing a strong bond and camaraderie; they pass this information and doctrine to their individual home churches; the pastors in each of these homes take the same information and pass it on to their groups. This relationship may be likened to a vine, where all the branches receive the same nourishment, since they are all connected to the same root.

Is there a danger that someone may abuse this trust and teach something different in their home? Yes. But, this then becomes a matter of trusting the Work of God to God.
> *2 Timothy 2:19 The Lord knows them that are His.*

Paul exhorted Timothy:
> *2 Timothy 1:13-16 Hold fast the form of sound words, which you have heard from me, in the faith and love which is in Christ Jesus; that good thing which was committed unto you keep by the holy ghost which dwells in us. Be aware that there are those in Asia that turned away from me, among them Phygellus and Hermogenes. (But), the Lord give mercy to the **house** of Onesiphorus; for he often refreshed me, and was not ashamed of my chain.*

> *2 Timothy 4:14,15 Alexander.. has greatly withstood our words.*

John told of troubling news:
> *3 John 9 I wrote to the church: but Diotrephes, who loves to have the preeminence among them, receives us not.*

Paul sadly warned:
> *Acts 20:29,30 For I know this, that after my departing shall grievous wolves enter in among you, not sparing the flock. Also of your own*

selves shall men arise, speaking perverse things, to draw away disciples after them.

So, there will probably be problem elders and renegades. It's nothing new. God uses these things for **His Purposes**.

How does the whole church keep informed about what's going on in the other divers homeses? The shepherds bring news and information up the "vine," which gets re-dispensed down the vine. So, eventually, everyone is "in the know."

What are the problems with having a church building? Firstly, the people think of the building as the church when, in the divine reality, the people are the church. We say: "I like to go to church," which clearly illustrates this ingrained misconception. But, the small church group can be the church all week long, wherever the saints are. There is no limit to how close they can be.

Secondly, the growth of the congregation is limited by the size of the church building. The true church is like an organism that can keep growing and never be crowded, not being limited by four walls. How big is your vision? Is it fifty people? How many pews do we need for three hundred people? Maybe we build a church with nine thousand one hundred theater-style seats (as we have one such in Louisville, Kentucky). Would that be big enough?

Finally, there is a great expense in constructing and up-keeping big buildings, which the home-church system eliminates; there is a comparatively small cost of home meetings and then occasionally renting facilities for the "altogether" meetings. The people are drained of finances to maintain a big church structure. If the air conditioning in the big church goes out, there's going to be huge expense. If it goes out in one home, the group can pick up and meet elsewhere.

One should note that the pulpit-to-pew system did not originate in the early church, but, rather, by the Jewish elders during the Babylonian captivity. But, didn't the early church meet in large synagogues? There are at least fifteen references in *Acts* of the preaching of Christ in the synagogues, but it was impossible to have established Christian meetings therein. Paul always left the synagogue.

> *Acts 13:42-44 And when the Jews were gone out of the synagogue, the gentiles besought that these words might be preached to them the next sabbath. Now when the congregation was broken up, many of the Jews and religious proselytes followed Paul and Barnabas. who, speaking to them, persuaded them to continue in the grace of God. And the next sabbath day came almost the whole city together to hear the Word of God.*

Do you think that they were able to meet in the synagogue? No. Paul always left the synagogue.

> *Acts 19:9 But when different ones were hardened, and believed not, but spoke evil of that Way before the multitude, Paul departed from them, and **separated the disciples**, disputing daily in the school of one Tyrannus.*

Actually, it was the emperor Constantine, who in 325 AD ordered the construction of church buildings. He also paved the way for the conversion of many pagan temples into church buildings. Not until this time were their special buildings devoted to Christian worship.

As a matter of fact, as we have stated: Christianity was the world's first non-temple-based religion.

Is there any scriptural example of the church meeting in homes? Yes, a number of them:

*Acts 5:42 And daily in the temple, and in every **house**, they ceased not to teach and preach Jesus Christ.*

*Acts 12:12 He (Peter) came to the **house** of Mary, the mother of John whose surname was Mark, where many were gathered together praying.*

Acts 20:8 And there were many lights in the upper chamber, where they were gathered together.

*Acts 20:20 I (Paul) have taught you publicly, and **from house to house**.*

*Acts 21:8 ...We entered into the **house** of Philip (where Agabus prophesied regarding the fate of Paul).*

*Romans 16:5 Likewise greet the church that is in their **house**.*

*Romans 16:10,11 Salute them which are of Aristobulus' **household**....Greet them that be of the **household** of Narcissus...*

*1 Corinthians 16:19 Aquila and Priscilla salute you much in the Lord, with **the church that is in their house**.*

*Colossians 4:15 Salute the brethren which are in Laodicea, and Nymphas, and **the church which is in his house**.*

*Philemon 2 ...and to our beloved Apphia, and Archippus our fellowsoldier, and to **the church in your house**.*

Didn't the early church have to meet in homes, because of persecution? No. In none of the above illustrations, did the saints meet in homes because of persecution or the fear thereof. Thus, persecution was not a motivating factor in their origination. However, it is known, for instance, that the movement of the holy spirit in China in the 1920's and 1930's resulted in home churches, and that after the communist revolution, Christians were persecuted, but that movement survives and flourishes to this day "underground," if you please, because of this home-church structure. The government only permits meetings up to twenty five; that's the law. Guess what? They are growing by the millions!

Likewise, no doubt, when such persecution comes in the latter days, the home churches would continue to propagate the faith and to "occupy" until He comes again.

When the Church began to fade in the early days, foreign customs and practices began to seep in. These things drained the power of the Church. Then the Church was filtered through Rome and picked up all kinds of pagan practices for over a thousand years. The Protestant Reformation began a process of restoration. However, the Reformation added many things which were not Biblical including new musical customs, pastoral sermons, and building structures. Many of our present-day practices which we cherish and to which we are so accustomed have come down to us from our forefathers, not from the Jerusalem apostles, but from Rome and Protestantism and the Charismatic Renewal.

Some people argue that this is a different day then the early churches in Jerusalem,

Judea, Antioch, and Ephesus: customs have changed; life-styles have changed; ways and means have changed. You cannot completely go back to a by-gone era.

No, we cannot restore first-century life-styles. But, we <u>can</u> strive to be church in the first-century-style. We can seek the guidance of the holy spirit to fill in the blanks, so to speak, of the many details with which the *scriptures* do not deal.

Furthermore, how can the Church of Jesus Christ be restored to its early glory, and not employ the early-day pattern??? Could the latter-day Church possibly dare to think She could be as powerful as the early-day Church? Could the latter-day Church be the potent witness of charity, grace, resurrection power, over-coming, and mutual care as our predecessors?

Finally, one of the main purposes for the saints congregating is to experience the manifestations of the spiritual gifts. There can be nothing more exhilarating then to hear from Heaven. How did it come? Tongues and interpretation? Prophecy? A word of knowledge? A message for the Eternal One with guidance, correction, encouragement, warning! The atmosphere is charged. The Lord has spoken through clay lips. Was it God, or was it the good intentions of the flesh? The brethren must decide.

It is a great occasion for the saints to assemble; it is a time for the manifestation of power. It is a time for *elohym* to speak to and through His saints. I said "power." Can you imagine anything more powerful than God speaking through His people?!!

What precipitates the elders to call for a meeting? What brings about an assemblage? It is the holy ghost.

This is not to be like some kind of game; this is serious business. Herein are the saints being trained to be sensitive to the "still, small Voice" from another world. Perhaps not today will the particular word be critical. But, in due season all the saints are going to have to be responsive to, receptive to, aware of, perceptive of the leading of the holy spirit when they are not in the group, but all alone.

It seems most amazing that human beings could possibly hear God's Voice in their hearts, but that is His design. The home church setting is the primary place for the saints to be trained and skilled and qualified and disciplined for the tasks of the latter days.

It is very likely that the suggestions put forth in this book will not be widely practiced. It is likely that these words will fall upon deaf ears. Some precepts herein will be rejected by-and-large. There is really only one thing that will encourage assemblies to make the bold moves proposed and recommended: observing in a few widely scattered cases how home groups are so successful. The proof will be in the pudding, as they say.

If you think these words might be meritorious, why not give it a try in your local assembly? Suggestions: replace a regular week-night service with a men's get-together; observe which men seem to have leadership and who support others; target them as home-group leaders; meet with them personally; notice to whom others gravitate; replace another regular service (possibly Sunday morning) with home meetings; observe life flowing from the vine through the branches!

Chapter 14. LAY HANDS SUDDENLY ON NO MAN

Surely our fathers have inherited lies! Jeremiah 16:19

It should be with great care, caution, and concern that the minister's of the church function in their divinely ordained offices, leading, organizing, and administrating the House of God, and feeding God's flock.

The subject of this chapter is not the Doctrine of Laying on of Hands (Chapter 14), but we will touch it in establishing our point of view by giving a very few examples. The following items are not an exhaustive list on this topic.

1) Jesus iterated one of the purposes of laying-on of hands just before he went to heaven: healing. He said healing was among the signs that would follow his disciples.
> *Mark 16:18 They shall take up serpents; and if they drink any deadly thing, it shall not hurt them; they shall **lay hands on** the sick, and they shall **recover**.*

in his life. By installing him in an office of the church you might inadvertently and carelessly be concurring with and participating in his sin.

2) In another instance Peter and John imparted the gift of the holy spirit at Samaria.
> *Acts 8:17 Then they **laid their hands on** them, and they **received the holy ghost**.*

3) Later on, the church at Antioch ordained Barnabas and Paul as apostles with the laying-on of hands before sending them away. They were being ordained to another office of the ministry than what they presently held.
> *Acts 13:3 And when they had fasted and prayed, and **laid their hands on** them, they **sent them away**.*

4) Spiritual gifts were bestowed on Timothy by laying on of hands.
> *1 Timothy 4:14 Neglect not the **gift** that is in you, which was given you by prophecy, with the **laying on of the hands** of the presbytery.*

We will observe that some churches around the world to practice these four points in varying degrees.

These *scriptures* here have illustrated different purposes of laying on of hands:

Let us now consider our focus verse:
> *1 Timothy 5:22 **Lay hands** suddenly **on** no man, neither be partaker of other men's sins: keep thyself pure.*

Almost everyone is in agreement that the sense of this passage is:

There are four occasions for laying on of hands:
>for physical healing
>for the receiving of spirit baptism
>for ministerial ordination
>for the bestowing of spiritual gifts.

***

Do not be too hasty in ordaining elders.

1 Timothy 5:22 Do not lay hands on anyone hastily...

The thought would be that in being too quick to ordain a man to the ministry you might not yet know all the negative things

Another consideration would be that by ordaining an inexperienced man you might inconsiderately and accidentally cause him to get an exalted attitude. Paul had earlier cautioned Timothy on this very point.
> *1 Timothy 3:6 Not a novice, lest being lifted up with pride he fall into the condemnation of the devil.*

He further instructed:
> *1 Timothy 3:10 And let these also first be proved.*

Before ordaining a man, first let him be seasoned and tested. I find this explanation of these *scriptures* absolutely consistent with the rest of the *Bible*.

In the *Bible* there is another completely different usage of this expression of "laying on of hands," and, again, I'd like to give several examples thereof. The first one is found in the parable of the unjust servant.
> *Matthew 18:28 But the same servant went out, and found one of his fellow-servants, which owed him an hundred pence: and he **laid hands on** him, and took him by the throat, saying, "Pay me what you owe."*

When he laid lands on him, it was NOT to impart a blessing; this man <u>grabbed</u> his fellow-servant. The next two examples regard the plotting of the priests and the Pharisees to arrest Jesus.
> *Matthew 21:46 But when they sought to **lay hands on** him, they feared the multitude, because they took him for a prophet.*

> *John 7:30 Then they sought to take him: but no man **laid hands on** him, because (Jesus') hour was not yet come.*

When he was betraying Jesus, Judas Iscariot gave instructions to the priests on how they would know whom to arrest.
> *Matthew 26:48 Now he that betrayed him gave them a sign, saying, "Whomsoever I shall kiss, that same is he: **hold him fast**."*

> *Mark 14:45,46 And as soon as he was come, he went straight to him, and said, "Master, Master," and kissed him. And they **laid their hands on him**, and took him.*

> *Matthew 26:57 And they that had **laid hold on** Jesus led him away to Caiaphas the high priest, where the scribes and the elders were assembled.*

Jesus had prophesied and warned the disciples that they would be arrested and persecuted as he himself would be. Jesus said:
> *Luke 21:12 "But before all these, they shall **lay their hands on** you, and persecute you, delivering you up to the synagogues, and into prisons, being brought before kings and rulers for my name's sake."*

And it was not long after the church began that Peter and John were indeed arrested.
> *Acts 4:3 And they **laid hands on** them, and put them in hold unto the next day: for it was now eventide.*

> *Acts 5:18 And **laid their hands on** the apostles, and put them in the common prison.*

This also happened to the apostle Paul on more than one occasion.

Acts 21:2 The Jews which were of Asia, when they saw him in the temple, stirred up all the people, and **laid hands on Paul…**

***

Some synonyms for this usage of the laying of hands would be:

arrest	detain	confine
apprehend	seize	delay
capture	rebuke	correct
imprison	stop	accuse
grab	constrain	check
catch		

***

Laying-on-hands might mean in a "blessing-kind-of way." Or it might mean to "stop" someone. Having given here the two very different ways the *scriptures* use this expression, let's reconsider out focus scripture:

1 Timothy 5:22 **Lay hands suddenly on no man…**

Encil Edmonds has stated that this passage refers to the ministry dealing with the ministry. It cannot be that there are <u>no</u> built-in cross-checks in the church for errors among the ministry. We'd be foolish to believe they might not slip in the face of so many passages in the *New Testament* which confront waywardness in the clergy. Paul explained to Timothy how these things are to be handled:

1) don't even deal with allegation, complaints, and insinuations against a minister by only one accuser.

2) like anyone else in the church, preachers and their sins may need to be publicly dealt with. Paul declares that this kind of order would bring the fear of God into the congregation

Let us hypothesize that an elder has a child with a serious disability requiring much expensive medical attention. The minister, in his pride, unwisely keeps his worsening financial situation to himself. He doesn't make it known that the bills are mounting, and that now the bank is threatening foreclosure. To stave off disaster, he stealthily takes some funds from the church treasury. This diabolic scheme works, and then he does it again and again.

Finally, his intrigue is discovered by another elder. When confronted he denies at first, but the evidence is obvious. He becomes irate and storms out. The other elder then goes to another minister of the church, and the two of them return to him. Because of their love and compassion, the man breaks down and confesses all.

All the elders are now brought into the matter. They chastise their brother preacher. He expresses his anguish and sorrow. He repents to them, and they quickly and lovingly forgive him.

A plan is worked out to help this elder in his financial distress. He also agrees to cease much of his pastoral oversight for a season of testing. The church is to be made aware that the stress of family and the financial situation has rendered their minister unable to serve in this capacity for a while for which the prayers of all are appealed. The congregation is moved to compassion. It is agreed that for the season the minister's embezzlement be withheld from the assembly.

Shepherds Rising Up

One might think that when the Church is restored, there will be no conflict within her hallowed halls. One might think that discontent will not exist in the flocks. Since everyone will see alike, there will be no disputes. If everyone is "in Christ," that is, walking in His Way, how could there ever again be an quarrel, a note of discord, a contradiction, tension, struggle for power, a clash? But, we foolishly forget that we are yet walking around in human flesh. It will yet be the responsibility of the ministry to continually strive to keep the church straight (*Romans* 13:6). We apply this passage, not to civil authority, but to the ecclesiastical.

> *Romans 13:3-5 For rulers hold no terror for those who do right, but for those who do wrong. Do you want to be free from fear of the one in authority? Then do what is right and he will commend you. For **he is God's servant** to do you good. But if you do wrong, be afraid, for he does not bear the **sword** for nothing. He is God's servant, an agent of wrath to bring punishment on the wrongdoer. Therefore, it is necessary to submit to the authorities, not only because of possible punishment but also because of conscience* (NIV).

The sword he bears is the *Word of God*.

One of the purposes for baptizing us "into" the Body of Christ is to present opportunities for the saints to interact. Living amongst those with whom we are committed, we will have opportunities to show acts of kindess, to help, to comfort, to share, to sacrifice. We will also have occasions to offend and to be offended. We will rub against one another, whereby we will cause each other to become smooth stones.

It will also be possible for us to go astray; after all, no shackles bind us to the Body of Christ. It will be possible for us to wander away from the truth or even be deceived. We can wound and be wounded; we can slander and be slandered; we can ignore and also be ignored. But, all the hurts work for our good when we receive them rightly.

It will even be possible for the leaders to fall into these errors. They might misjudge; they might slip up. Paul gave a dire prediction:

> *Acts 20:30,31 Also of your own selves shall men **arise**, distorting the truth in order to draw a following. Remember that for three years I did not cease to warn everyone night and day with tears.*

> *2 Timothy 2:16-18 Avoid godless, foolish discussions that lead to more and more ungodliness. This kind of talk spreads like cancer. Hymenaeus and Philetus are examples of this. They have left the path of truth, preaching the lie that the resurrection of the dead has already occurred; and they have undermined the faith of some.*

Paul had already given instructions where accusations might be brought forth.

> *1 Timothy 5:19,20 Do not receive an accusation against an elder except from two or three witnesses. Those who are sinning rebuke in the presence of all, that the rest also may fear.*

Are they any safe-guards against ministerial abuse of power and false teaching? There are. The local church is composed of a number of individual home churches, each led by a shepherd-pastor. All of them are under the authority of another minister; none are leaderless. All the ministers might be under the oversight of the most senior pastor. Or, like a vine, they might be branches of one of the older brothers, who is under someone else. There might be an out-of-town pastor to whom the most senior brother looks. The out-of-towner has not authority in this local church, but he has spiritual responsibility for the man he oversees.

All of the ministers of a local church and their wives frequently interact socially. The men also meet often to pray and study together. They are charged with the responsibility of hearing the directions of the holy spirit for the assembly. They call the meeting times; they invite other saints to speak, even those not local; they determine actions to be taken regarding wayward saints; they advise and correct one another, both doctrinally and personally; as I have previously said, their decisions are unanimous, because they are all receiving from the same Head.

So, if a shepherd were to rise up with a strange doctrine, if a home church leader were to abuse his saints or mislead them, if he were to lead some in another direction, the other brothers are there to correct him, to help him, to step in and assist. Since everyone is under authority, and since the elders are all submissive one to another, the damage can be minimized. Sometimes ministers can cause great harm (*1 Timothy 1:19,20*). But, the checks-and-balance system I have outlined are God's ways of dealing with the recalcitrant.

Some will fear governing-the-local-assembly in this way; they will point out that there will be men of who split off and start their own church, and that the more pastors there are, the greater the possibilities of schisms. My answer to this criticism is to agree with it. Wolves <u>will</u> enter the flock unawares; there will be splits; lives will be lost. These tragedies will occur. And, listen to this: the Holy One has already foreseen who will do what, when, and where to hurt the Great Congregation. But, the spread of heresy is minimized by this manner and order.

Here is something YOU do not know: you do not know what other ministers might do; you do not know which are wheat and which are the tares. The Sower has been very generous in sowing His seed; some of it falls on rocky or thorny or wayside places. He wants as many invited as can be found *Matthew 22:9,10,14 both BAD and good...For, many are called, but few are chosen.*

But, <u>you</u> do not know which are which. What must you do: be wise as a serpent, but harmless as a dove. Love everybody. Loooooove everybody. Give, serve, care, love everybody.

The church with a single pastor is Babylonious; it is not biblical; it is following the calf path. It is an "order," but God did not author it.

***

(Some *Scriptures* Dealing with Waywardness in the Ministry)

Matthew 7:15 Beware of false prophets, which come to you in sheep's clothing, but inwardly they are ravening wolves.

2 Peter 2:1 But there were false prophets also among the people, even as there shall be false teachers among you, who privily shall bring in damnable heresies...

Jude 4,12,17,18 For there are certain men crept in unawares, who were before of old ordained to this condemnation, ungodly men, turning the grace of our God into lasciviousness, and denying the only Lord God, and our Lord Jesus Christ...These are spots in your feasts of charity, when they feast with you, feeding themselves without fear: clouds they are without water, carried about of winds; trees whose fruit withers, without fruit, twice dead, plucked up by the roots...remember the words which were spoken before of the apostles of our Lord Jesus Christ; How that they told you there should be mockers in the last time, who should walk after their own ungodly lusts.

1 Timothy 4:1 In the latter times some shall depart from the faith, giving heed to seducing spirits, and doctrines of devils...

2 Timothy 4:3 For the time will come when they will not endure sound doctrine; but after their own lusts shall they heap to themselves teachers, having itching ears...)

***

Jesus' motive is first and foremost "redemption," and the wise and charitable handling of that above dreadful pastoral situation would likely lead to a happy end. But, so often, sins of ministers are brushed aside and never confronted. Those who might have been offended by the minister are left in dismay and discouragement. Usually, wayward pastors are shuffled off to another congregation of unsuspecting parishioners. Please consider the gross negligence of the *Roman Catholic Church* in this regard. By disregarding reports of sexual sins of some of its ministers, it appears that hundreds, even thousands of youngsters were unnecessarily and savagely abused.

I also would like to expand this correct usage of our key *scripture* to apply it also to the entire congregation: could we enlarge the scope of 5:22 to this:

exhorting ministers to <u>not be hasty</u> in rebuking or stopping a lay member of the church?

1 Timothy 5:22 Lay hands suddenly on no man...

You might wonder why we would want to discourage hasty judgment upon a <u>saint</u> whom we knew was doing something wrong? It would be the same as hastily rebuking a fellow minister. Could it be advisable to delay pointing out a person's fault to give his Lord a chance to do it? We have examples in *scripture* where people were convicted by their own conscience and completely altered their own courses of action. Consider those who were accusing the woman of adultery. But they,

*John 8:9 being **convicted by their own conscience,** (departed).*

Would you think that the conviction placed on us by the spirit of God might be more durable, more effective than, if a mere mortal told us to quit sinning? John put it like this:

1 John 3:20 For if our heart condemn us, God is greater than our heart, and knows all things.

Before moving on, please re-read:

1 John 3:20 For if our heart condemn us, God is greater than our heart, and knows all things.

1 John 3:19,20 This then is how we know that we belong to the truth, and how we set our hearts at rest in his presence whenever our hearts condemn us. For God is greater than our hearts, and He knows everything.

To enlarge upon Paul's thought in *1 Timothy 5:22*: don't be hasty in correcting a minister or church member; let the heavenly Father have His opportunity to speak to his heart first. Let's say that a husband was ill-treating his wife. Or, another brother was too talkative. Or he was a busy-body; or, maybe using foul language; or, perchance cheating on his taxes. How about the pastor or elder, when he becomes aware of this or that problem, at first committing that situation to prayer? Perhaps he will be greatly burdened for the person in his oversight who is sinning or being carnal. So, he prays. And, he prays. And, he prays. He tells it to God. He makes intercession. He asks God to reveal this and that to the person. He waits for the Lord. And

*Luke 8:15 on the good ground are they, which in an honest and good heart, having **heard the Word**, keep it, and bring forth fruit with patience.*

Isn't it marvelous when we can "hear the *Word*" often without a human word being uttered? So, with patience the shepherd also waits for the Lord to speak the *Word* to the saint's heart; he doesn't quickly lay hands on him and stop his erroneous ways, hoping and praying that the person will "hear the *Word* and keep it."

But, but, but, but, he cannot wait forever, either. You see, the shepherd knows about it. He gives God the first chance. The saint

1) knows what he's doing, but doesn't realize it's displeasing to the Lord; or
2) he is blind to his wrong-doing, doesn't realize it's wrong; or,
3) he has hardened his heart to his sin.

The pastor cannot wait too long. Paul says that, if he doesn't do something about it eventually, then the pastor, himself, will be a "partaker" of his sin.

*1 Timothy 5:22 Lay hands suddenly on no man; neither **be partaker** of other men's sins: keep thyself pure.*

What do you mean? How could one man's sins also become the pastor's sins? Here are excerpts from *Ezekiel* about the responsibility of "watchmen," which speaks directly to the New-Covenant minister's accountability to God.

Ezekiel 33:6 If the watchman see the sword come, and blow not the trumpet, and the people be not warned; if the sword come, and take any person from among them, he is taken away in his iniquity; but his blood will I require at the watchman's hand.

Ezekiel 3:18 When I say to the wicked, "You shall surely die," and you (the watchman) give him no warning, nor speak to warn the wicked from his wicked way, to save his life, that same wicked man shall die in his iniquity; but his blood I will require at your hand.

In the church there are also times when the ministry must "lay hands on" one of the members or an elder of the church in this, shall I say, negative way--not for the imparting of a blessing or an ordination--but to STOP a brother or sister from doing something wrong. It becomes necessary for the watchman-shepherd to sound out a warning.

But, and if, he does NOT sound out a warning, and the preacher, brother, or sister continue their blunder, fault, indiscretion, misdeed, then that thing will fall upon the head of the pastor as well. He will be accounted guilty, too. The church member will continue in his or her error and maybe even die with the error; and the pastor will also, because he uttered no warning.

For example, there was a terrible sin occurring in the Corinthian church--a man was having an affair with his father's wife. The problem didn't end there. The elders of the church did nothing, said nothing. This really grieved the apostle Paul. He boldly instructed how they were to deal with such a situation:
> *1 Corinthians 5:5 Deliver such an one unto satan for the destruction of the flesh, that the spirit may be saved in the day of the Lord Jesus.*

He further charged
> *v7 Purge out the old leaven.*

He meant: "Don't let wickedness remain in the church." Paul took the initiative to charge the ministry, who then took this to heart and dealt appropriately with this situation at last. In Paul's next recorded letter he rehearses what a good affect their actions had accomplished:
> *2 Corinthians 7:11 See what this godly sorrow has produced in you: what earnestness, what eagerness to clear yourselves, what indignation, what alarm, what longing, what concern, what readiness to see justice done. At every point you have proved yourselves to be innocent in this matter.*

And, the sinning brother had repented and was able to be restored to fellowship. By acting, the ministry also proved themselves "to be innocent in this matter." This was the blessed result of proper handling by the elders.

In other words, ALL church problems must be dealt with either by
1) the person with the problem, or
2) by the ministry.

It should be of paramount importance for the ministry to teach the church the importance of individual saints completely and righteously dealing with and judging their own issues. In this regard Paul says:
> *1 Corinthians 11:31,32 For if we would judge ourselves, we should not be judged.*

If we can only see our problems and deal with them, neither the pastor nor the Lord will need to judge us

And, when the Lord deals with us, it may be while we're still living, which although unpleasant, we'll still have opportunity to straighten things out. On the other hand, we may carry our sins with us beyond this life. So Paul stated what a merciful blessing it is when God deals with us here and now:
> *v32 But when we are judged, we are chastened of the Lord, that we **should not be condemned with the world**.*

When Paul stated, "not be condemned with the world," he referred to the condemnation of the world on the Day of Judgment; he was hoping that the members of the church would not carry their iniquity to that Day. In the same vein he instructed Timothy:
> *1 Timothy 5:24 Some men's sins are <u>open</u> beforehand, going before to judgment; and some men they follow after.*

1 Timothy 5:24 Remember that some men, even pastors, lead sinful lives, and everyone knows it. In such situations you can do something about it. But in other cases only the judgment day will reveal the terrible truth (TLB).

Some see this as meaning that "some men's sins are obvious." I think, however, that the word "open" here means "exposed," which would render the verse:
Some men's sins are exposed before the Day of Judgment; and some men's sins follow after them right up to the Judgment Day.

How blessed we would be, if our sins were exposed and revealed, not on Judgment Day, but while we were still living, either by
  1) conviction of conscience or
  2) intervention of a wise and caring shepherd.

The marvelous result is that we won't have to face them on the Day of Wrath.

Matthew Henry commented on this passage, saying:
  Ministers have need of a great deal of wisdom, to know how to accommodate themselves to the variety of offenses and offenders that they have occasion to deal with.

He added:
  The effects of church-censures are very different; some are thereby humbled and brought to repentance, so that their good works are manifest, while it is quite otherwise with others.

The Wycliffe Bible Commentary offers another incite on our subject, one I thought well-worth consideration:
  Paul is offering another caution regarding Timothy's dealing with men who were to be rebuked: he should use <u>no partiality</u>, no violent measures, or unnecessary severity, nor, on the other hand, undue leniency, so as to be a partaker of their sins.

With regard to "no partiality," ministers should take their example from God, Himself, Who
  Acts 10:34 is no respecter of persons.

We may have in our midst one who has wealth or one who is kin to a number of other church members, in which situations a pastor might be tempted to alter his good judgment. Don't let that happen. Just because one is a generous giver or has a large family and close friends is no reason to overlook his erroneous ways. The shepherd is responsible to God.

Regarding "no violent measures or unnecessary severity," ministers are not to forget Whose sheep with whom they are dealing. You might regard people's sins as so vile that you might be tempted to speak loudly or harshly to them; you might deem someone's acts as potentially subversive to the health of the whole congregation and be tempted to fierce retaliation.

Dushon Petrovic cautions:
  "Do not bombard him right away."

Leviticus 19:16 ...Do not do anything that endangers your neighbor...I am the Lord.

Encil Edmonds admonishes:
  "God's people do not put others to shame."

The minister must not lose sight of the nature of the Chief Shepherd who is meek and mild. Some pastors would counter that Jesus on two occasions was quite violent when he overturned the money-changers tables and used whips:
> *John 2:15 And when he had made a scourge of small cords, he drove them all out of the temple, and the sheep, and the oxen; and poured out the changers' money, and overthrew the tables.*

Please do not think you are authorized to do any such thing. Jesus, who is Lord, has such authority. On the other hand,
> *2 Timothy 2:24 a servant of the Lord must not quarrel but be gentle to all...*

Ministers must be gentle. They must remember that shepherds "lead on softly." Bear in mind that they are NOT exalted, but they serve as the lowliest members of the church, as Jesus demonstrated by washing the disciples' feet. With that attitude let us consider the rest of this passage:
> *2 Timothy 2:24-26 And a servant of the Lord must not quarrel but **be gentle** to all, able to teach, patient, **in humility** correcting those who are in opposition, if God perhaps will grant them repentance, so that they may know the truth, and that they may come to their senses and escape the snare of the devil, having been taken captive by him to do his will.*

Ministers are to correct "in humility," praying that the wandering saint "may come to his senses" and resist the devil. The motive and purpose is always: redemption. The object should never be to destroy the offending brother or sister, but to win them back to the Way of Christ. To tell a saint, "I'm sorry, we cannot help you here," is to admit your failure Jesus' worker.

It is an awesome responsibility given to pastor/shepherds. One who truly has the Office of Pastor is thrilled in seeing one sinner come to repentance. Such similar instructions were given to Titus:
> *Titus 1:7-9 For a bishop must be blameless, as a **steward of God**, not self-willed, not quick-tempered, not given to wine, not violent, not greedy for money, but hospitable, a lover of what is good, sober-minded, just, holy, self-controlled, holding fast the faithful* Word *as he has been taught, that he may be able, by sound doctrine, both to exhort and convict those who contradict.*

Ministers are God's "stewards" in the church; it is an enormous task, seeing that, if they are negligent in keeping the church straight, they will have to face their own carelessness and laxity on Judgment Day. Some ministers don't deal with a situation, counting on the fire to go out; they leave it "undealt" with. But, God will not forget.

We are going to consider a passage from one of Paul's epistles which has been incorrectly interpreted by most scholars to be an exhortation to obey the civil law and to pay one's taxes. In other places like *1 Peter* 2:13-15 this very thing is commanded us: obeying the civil law and authorities. But in *Romans*, which we have already quoted, the reference is to the assembly honoring and obeying the ministry:
> *Romans 13:1-6 Let every soul be subject unto the higher powers (the church authorities). For there is no power but of God: the powers that be are ordained of God. Whosoever resists the power (the ministry), resists the ordinance of God: and they*

that resist shall receive to themselves damnation. For rulers (the ministry) are not a terror to good works, but to the evil. Will you then not be afraid of the power? do that which is good, and you shall have praise of the same, for he is the minister of God to you for good.

But if you do that which is evil, be afraid; for he bears not the sword (the Word of God) in vain: for he is the minister of God, a revenger to execute wrath upon him that does evil. Therefore you need to be subject, not only for (the fear of God's) Wrath, but also for conscience sake. For this reason pay tribute (tithe) also: for they are God's ministers, devoting themselves continually upon this very thing.

God Almighty has ordained His servants. Their responsibility is awesome. To resist them is to bring condemnation on oneself. Ministers are to be fully armed with God's *Word* which is to be used effectively and impartially. To be instructed by the Man of God and to reject his counsel could lead to your damnation. That's a heavy statement, but the truth. And, the ministers of God must execute the *Word*; they must! They can't leave things undone to be "politically correct."

The lives of the ordained ministers are not their own; they are the most imprisoned by Christ of all the church members. Since their lives are consumed in serving the Lord, their families, and the saints, they ought to be entirely financially supported by the people.

And, Paul concluded:

*Romans 13:6 they are God's ministers, attending continually upon this **very thing**.*

Upon what "very things" are they devoted to and "attending continually?" It is: keeping the saints in order. They are to be devoted to correcting the church. Jesus has ordained them to feed the sheep and to keep the church straight, the flock over which the holy ghost has made them overseers.

*Acts 20:28 Take heed to yourselves and to all the flock, among which the holy ghost has made you **overseers**, to shepherd (feed) the church of God which He purchased with His own blood.*

In "keeping the church straight" we must note that the authority of "elders" does not go beyond their local assembly. They have not authority in dealing with ministers in another church, nor with those saints. The Church has no Sanhedrin Court. Only when there exists a problem between saints of different cities should the ministers be involved trans-locally or if they might pastor a pastor in another city.

One of the worst weaknesses I have seen in the ministry is in their <u>not</u> dealing with people who have quit attending church services. "Well, they don't come around anymore!" is argued. This is entirely contrary to the intention of Jesus.

Matthew 18:12-14 If a man have an hundred sheep, and one of them be gone astray, does he not leave the ninety and nine, and go into the mountains, and seek that which is gone astray?...Even so it is not the will of your Father which is in heaven, that one of these little ones should perish.

Alas, I have seen people leave the church and little is done to reach out to them. The problem is that the church is so building-oriented that we cannot see beyond its four walls. People can't be dealt with because they "don't come around anymore." But, note how thrilled Jesus is when one is restored:

> *Luke 15:6,7 Rejoice with me; for I have found my sheep which was lost. I say unto you, that likewise joy shall be in heaven over one sinner that repents, more than over ninety and nine just persons, which need no repentance.*

In Jesus' example the shepherd was caring. The sad truth is that many church pastors are not really "pastors," so they have not the kind of shepherd's heart Jesus needs in tending the church. They like to preach and evangelize and teach and exhort and prophesy, and they may even like the offerings.

> *John 10:12,13 But he that is an hireling, and not the shepherd, whose own the sheep are not, sees the wolf coming, and leaves the sheep, and flees: and the wolf catches them, and scatters the sheep. The hireling flees, because he is an hireling, and cares not for the sheep.*

If you are a preacher or a teacher or an evangelist or a prophet, but not a true pastor, raise up some who are, and let them shepherd the flock. Pastors, true shepherds, care deeply, empathetically, and sympathetically for the welfare of the saints. Whatever your office, hear Paul's exhortation:

> *Romans 12:8 He that rules (do it) with diligence.*

(I have observed men who were other offices of the ministry but trying to pastor a church. Herein is a fault exposed: evangelists, eager to get people saved are apt to not deal at all with people's problems and faults; prophets are apt to be too severe, bringing condemnation; and teachers are apt to give lessons on the situation teaching it to death. Only true shepherds are equipped by God with the heart, the stamina, the insight, the tenderness, and the wisdom to get down to the nitty-gritty.)

Be persistent in your devotion to the saints' welfare. Let us conclude by noting the motive of redemption in Jesus, and also his severity:

> *Matthew 18:15-17 Moreover, if your brother shall trespass against you, go and tell him his fault between you and him alone: if he shall hear you, you have gained your brother. But, if he will not hear you, then take with you one or two more, that in the mouth of two or three witnesses every word may be established. And if he shall neglect to hear them, tell it unto the church: but if he neglects to hear the church, let him be unto you as an heathen man and a publican.*

This is the sum of the lesson: wait on the spirit; first let God work on people's consciences. But, if they yet "oppose themselves," do not fail to <u>lay hands on</u> them, whether saint or minister, lest you be judged with <u>their</u> sins. Rule with diligence. Keep the church straight.

Surely our fathers have inherited lies! Jeremiah 16:19

Chapter 15. LAYING ON OF HANDS

In the laying on of hands there is no magical power in the hands themselves, but it is an act of faith in God. There are three basic reasons for performing this act: 1) pronouncing a blessing, 2) ordaining ministry, and 3) imparting a spiritual gift. The laying on of hands is one of the elementary teachings about the Christ (*Hebrews* 6:2) and a basic foundation stone of His Church. Without this practice, as well as repentance, baptisms, resurrection for the dead, and eternal judgment, being taught and performed, the Church cannot be built. Therefore, let us devote ourselves herein to study one of our foundation doctrines--the laying on of hands.

As Practiced In Israel

When Israel was on his death bed, he spoke a blessing upon his children. In his blessing for Joseph's sons, Israel reached one hand over the other, crossing his hands:

*Genesis 48:14 And Israel stretched out **his right hand**, and laid it upon Ephraim's head, who was the younger, and his left hand upon Manasseh's head, guiding his hands wittingly; for Manasseh was the firstborn.*

Jacob assured Joseph that he had not erred in crossing his hands, and then proceeded to pronounce a blessing on the two boys. This passage shows that it was an accepted practice to transmit a blessing by the laying on of hands, and further, that the greater blessing was transmitted by the right hand.

Later on, in the Wilderness, the sons of the eleven tribes of Israel laid their hands upon the twelfth tribe, the Levites, ordaining them to minister to God in their behalf.

*Numbers 8:6-13 Take the Levites from among the children of Israel, and cleanse them...Sprinkle water of purifying upon them, and let them shave all their flesh, and let them wash their clothes, and so make themselves clean...Then let them take a young bullock with his meat offering...and another young bullock shall you take for a sin offering. And you shall bring the Levites before the tabernacle of the congregation: and you shall gather the whole assembly of the children of Israel together. And you shall bring the Levites before the Lord: and the children of Israel shall **put their hands** upon the Levites. And Aaron shall offer the Levites before the Lord for an offering of the children of Israel, that they may execute the service of the Lord. And the Levites **shall lay their hands** upon the heads of the bullocks...And you shall set the Levites before Aaron, and before his sons, and offer them for an offering unto the Lord.*

The people were putting their trust upon the Levites. They were acknowledging this trust. The Levites were Israel's offering to God.

Late in his life Moses was instructed by God to lay his hand upon Joshua:
> *Numbers 27:18-23 And the Lord said unto Moses, "Take Joshua the son of Nun, a man in whom is the spirit, and **lay your hand** upon him, and set him before Eleazar the priest, and before all the congregation; and give him a charge in their sight. And you shall put some of your honor upon him, that all the congregation of the children of Israel may be obedient...And he laid his hands upon him, and gave him a charge, as the Lord commanded by the hand of Moses.*

It is further recorded:
*Deuteronomy 34:9 And Joshua the son of Nun was full of the spirit of wisdom; for Moses had **laid his hands** upon him...*

And secondly that, as a result of Moses' public acknowledgment of God's appointment, the whole congregation "hearkened" unto Joshua.
> *...and the children of Israel hearkened unto him.*

Another account of divine confirmation is the blessing of King Joash by the prophet Elisha:
> *2 Kings 13:15-17 And Elisha said unto him, "Take bow and arrows." And he took unto him bow and arrows. And he said to the king of Israel, "Put your hand upon the bow." And he put his hand upon it: and Elisha **put his hands** upon the king's hands. And he said, "Open the window eastward." And he opened it. Then Elisha said, "Shoot." And he shot. And he said, "The arrow of the Lord's deliverance, and the arrow of deliverance from Syria: for you shall smite the Syrians in Aphek, till you have consumed them.*

Elisha was transmitting wisdom and authority to the King in delivering God's people from the Syrians.

Many of the sacrifices under the *Law* included the laying on of hands. One instance regards the sacrifice of the scape goat.
> *Leviticus 16:21 Aaron shall **lay both his hands** on the head of the live goat, confess over it all the iniquities of the children of Israel, and all their transgressions, concerning all their sins, putting them on the head of the goat.*

In the first century there came to prominence a class of men called "rabbis." They called men to follow them by laying on of hands, to be their disciples, to learn their insights, and to become like them. Jesus of Nazareth was such.

Ordaining New Testament Ministers

Hands are to be laid on Christian workers being sent out from a local church, and also in the appointment to service administrators in a local church.

When the holy spirit called upon Barnabas and Saul they "laid their hands on them, and sent them away."
> *Acts 13:2-4 The holy ghost said, "Separate to Me Barnabas and Saul for the work whereunto I have called them. And when they had **fasted** and **prayed**, and **laid their hands** on them, they sent them away. So they, being sent forth by the holy ghost, departed unto Seleucia.*

We should note three things here: 1) and 2) the corporate fasting <u>and</u> praying of the church leadership, and 3) the resultant prophetic utterance directing them in the Will and Purpose of the holy spirit. These three things, prayer, fasting, and prophecy, preceded the laying on of hands. We should further note the close parallel to the earlier account where Moses laid hands upon Joshua publicly acknowledging God's choice for a God-appointed task.

There are two other closely related purposes for which church leaders lay on hands which we will see in the account of the result of the first missionary journey of Paul and Barnabas:

> *Acts 14:26,27 From there they sailed to Antioch, where they had been **commended to the grace of God** for the work which they had completed. Now when they had come and gathered the church together, they reported all that God had done with them, and that He had opened the door of faith to the gentiles.*

The laying on of hands constitutes a means by which Christian ministers may be recommended to God's grace to fulfill their God-given work.

A similar account is given in the ordaining of seven men to "serve tables."

> *Acts 6:1-7 Now in those days, when the number of the disciples was multiplying, there arose a complaint against the Hebrews (traditional Jews) by the Hellenists (Jews who had adopted the Greek life-style), because their widows were neglected in the daily distribution. Then the twelve summoned the multitude of the disciples and said, "It is not desirable that we should leave the Word of God and serve tables. Therefore, brethren, seek out from among you seven men of good reputation, full of the holy spirit and wisdom, whom we may appoint over this business; but we will give ourselves continually to prayer and to the ministry of the Word."*

> *And the saying pleased the whole multitude. And they chose Stephen,...Philip, Prochorus, Nicanor, Timon, Parmenas, and Nicholas, ...whom they set before the apostles; and when they had prayed, they **laid hands** on them. Then the word of God spread, and the number of the disciples multiplied greatly in Jerusalem.*

We will make several observations from this passage:
1) The elders of the church delegated to the whole congregation the choosing of these men;
2) Then they prayed for those selected;
3) They publicly acknowledged that they accepted these men by the laying on of their hands;
4) They made a public commitment for these men to perform this assigned task;
5) They commended the men to God's anointing power to do the work; and
6) They transmitted to them a measure of their own spiritual grace and wisdom needed for the job.

We have seen illustrated in *Scripture* that elders, pastors, deacons, and apostles were ordained to the ministry with the confirmation of the laying on of hands. Although the ordinations of prophets, teachers, and evangelists are not detailed in the *Bible*, it is undoubtedly the divinely designated means of their anointing and public recognition.

We might add here, that although the Church eliminated these offices of the ministry late in the first century, it is our belief that they shall be reestablished in the Church before the coming of our Lord, that their functions are vital to the restoration of the Church, and that prophets, teachers, and evangelists will be acknowledged and ordained to their offices by the laying on of hands.

Imparting Spiritual Gifts

There is an unspecified gift in Timothy's life we would first like to consider. We should note here the exact similarity to the aforementioned act of ordination. Paul writes to Timothy:

> *1 Timothy 4:14-15 Do not neglect the gift that is in you, which was given to you by prophecy with the **laying on of the hands** of the presbytery.*

> *1 Timothy 1:18 This charge I commit to you, son Timothy, according to the prophecies previously made concerning you, that by them you may wage the good warfare.*

> *2 Timothy 1:6 I remind you to stir up the gift of God which is in you through **the laying on of MY hands**.*

Now let us make some observations about these passages:
1) Timothy received some definite spiritual gift;
2) The gift was imparted in the act of laying on of hands;
3) Paul, along with local elders, performed this action;
4) The laying on of hands was carried out in association with prophetic utterance;
5) These prophecies (advance revelations) were to enable Timothy to wage good warfare, i.e., to fulfill the ministry committed to him; they weren't extraneous, irrelevant, or ostentatious, but vitally necessary for his success;
6) By the laying on of hands with the gift of prophecy, Timothy was given direction;
7) He was encouraged; and
8) He was also strengthened thereby.

I have seen it happen many times that when a man was designated for a service to the Lord, there came an anointing upon him that changed the man.

It is like what happened to Saul after the prophet Samuel ordained him. Samuel said:
> *1 Samuel 10:6 And the spirit of the Lord will come upon you...and you shall **be turned into another man**.*

Baptism

About half the accounts of people receiving the gift of the holy spirit in the *New Testament* were accomplished by the laying on of hands. One time, believers in Ephesus were spirit-baptized:
> *Acts 19:5,6 When they heard this, they were baptized in the Name of the Lord Jesus. And when Paul had **laid his hands** upon them, the holy ghost came on them; and they spoke with tongues, and prophesied.*

Earlier, there were people in Samaria who came to believe that Jesus was the Christ. Peter and John came down from Jerusalem and ministered to them.
> *Acts 8:17 Then they **laid their hands** on them, and they received the holy ghost.*

Healing

There are numerous accounts in the *Bible* of healing by the laying on of hands. Jesus did it, himself:

*Mark 6:5,6 And Jesus could do no mighty work (in Nazareth), except that he **laid his hands** upon a few sick folk, and healed them. And he marveled because of their unbelief.*

(Poor Nazareth! By unbelief and contempt of Christ, men stopped the flow of God's favors to them.)

Yet another time Jesus healed a deaf man:

*Mark 7:32-35 They brought to Him one who was deaf and had an impediment in his speech, and they begged Him to **put His hand** on him. And He took him aside from the multitude, and put His fingers in his ears, and He spat and **touched** his tongue. Then, looking up to heaven, He sighed, and said to him, "Eph-pha-tha," (the Aramaic for, "Be opened.") Immediately his ears were opened, and the impediment of his tongue was loosed, and he spoke plainly.*

Although it was expected that Jesus would actually put his hand on the man, he rather stuck his fingers in the man's ears, and then spat and touched the man's tongue. Sometimes the conventional way is NOT the way of the spirit. Usually isn't!

On another occasion Jesus healed a blind man at Bethsaida unconventionally:

*Mark 8:22-25 Then He came to Bethsaida; and they brought a blind man to Him, and begged Him to touch him. So He took the blind man by the hand and led him out of the town. And when He had spit on his eyes and **put His hands** on him, He asked him if he saw anything. And he looked up and said, "I see men like trees, walking."*

*Then He **put His hands** on his eyes **again** and made him look up. And he was restored and saw everyone clearly.*

Not only did Jesus spit on the man's eyes before laying hands on him, but the healing was not complete until Jesus laid his hands on his eyes <u>two</u> times.

Many times Jesus healed, and some were delivered of evil spirits:

*Luke 4:40,41 Now when the sun was setting, all they that had any sick with divers diseases brought them unto him; and he **laid his hands** on every one of them, and healed them. And demons also came out of many.*

He further raised from the dead the daughter of the synagogue official:

*Mark 5:23,41,42 "My little daughter lies at the point of death. Come and **lay Your hands** on her, that she may be healed, and she will live."...Then He **took the child by the hand**, and said to her, "Talitha, cumi," Aramaic for: "Little girl, I say to you, arise." Immediately the girl arose and walked, for she was twelve years of age. And they were overcome with great amazement.*

And he cast out a demon of sickness from a woman by the laying on of his hands:

*Luke 13:10-13 Now He was teaching in one of the synagogues on the Sabbath. And, there was a woman who had a spirit of infirmity eighteen years, and was bent over and could in no way raise herself up. But when Jesus saw her, He called her to Him and said to her, "Woman, you are loosed from your infirmity." And He **laid His hands** on her, and* *immediately she was made straight, and glorified God.*

Not only did Jesus heal by this means, but we find others in the *scriptures* did as well. And, not all of them were prominent ministers, either. Ananias, who is referred to as "a certain disciple," laid hands on Saul who regained his eyesight and was filled with the holy spirit all at the same time.

Acts 9:10-12,17,18 There was a certain disciple at Damascus named Ananias; and to him the Lord said in a vision, "Ananias." And he said, "Here I am, Lord."

*So the Lord said to him, "Arise and go to the street called Straight, and inquire at the house of Judas for one called Saul of Tarsus, for behold, he is praying, and in a vision he has seen a man named Ananias coming in and **putting his hand** on him, so that he might receive his sight."*

*And Ananias went his way and entered the house; and **laying his hands** on him he said, "Brother Saul, the Lord Jesus, who appeared to you on the road as you came, has sent me that you may receive your sight and be filled with the holy spirit." Immediately there fell from his eyes something like scales, and he received his sight at once; and he arose and was baptized.*

Paul, himself, laid on his hands in ministry many times. On one occasion Paul, himself, laid his hands on Publius' father in Malta and healed him.

*Acts 28:8-10 And it happened that the father of Publius lay sick of a fever and dysentery. Paul went in to him and prayed, and he **laid his hands** on him and healed him.*

This healing brought much fame and glory to Jesus Christ and His *Word*, which, after all, was God's intention for these healings.

We, of course, expect Jesus' disciples to do this, because it is one of the signs He said would accompany those who have believed:

*Mark 16:18 They shall take up serpents; and if they drink any deadly thing, it shall not hurt them; they shall **lay hands** on the sick, and they shall recover.*

We must mention that in these illustrations, the healings were sometimes instantaneous, sometimes gradual, sometimes with the sensation of power, other times, not.

In every case, however, whether the pronouncement of blessings, recognizing ministry, the imparting of special gifts, the giving of holy spirit baptism, or healing, the laying on of hands is/was simply an act of naked faith, of obedience to *God's Word*. If there is genuine faith, the intended result will operate.

Laying-on-of-hands is utterly important in the Church for it strengthens it in three ways: spiritually, by equipping the members through the imparting of spiritual gifts; and practically, through the appointment of ministers; and thirdly, by the public recognition they bring.

Prayer Lines

Some years ago I witnessed a "healing service" led by Kathryn Kuhlman (1907-1976). Since then, I have observed many church services and evangelistic meetings where people received prayer for healing. I believe in the yearning quest to experience that which we have read in the *Bible*, our exuberance has caused us sometimes to practice manifestations of the flesh, rather than of the holy ghost. Ms. Kuhlman pushed the people in the head with such force that they fell backward on the floor, and some pretended (they later confessed) to have been "slain in the spirit," a thing she had truly experienced in earlier and simpler days. I have seen even wilder excesses of human exhibition.

I admit that in my Christian youth I behaved bizarrely in church on occasion. When some brethren complained about my woolly displays, my good Pastor, James Sowders, responded: "I'd rather have to tame a wild fire, than to have no fire at all." I was so caught up in the emotion of it all, it was not until many years later that I realized he had actually been referring to me.

I'm sure that I had been wanting to show how much I was rejoicing in the Lord and how spiritual I really was. But, as I have lived in the Church of Christ for many years, I have experienced and observed both carnal and fake displays and genuine, heart-felt, deep-down, holy moments. I've seen wonderful times of rejoicing, great roars of high praises, tears of tenderness, divine touches, moments of holy joy and hilarity, and times of intense quiet, stillness, and godly reflection.

I've also seen things dressed up to look like the real article. I have seen gross mockeries of divine things. I'm reminded of that time in Babylon:

Daniel 5:3,4 Then they brought the golden vessels that were taken out of the temple of the house of God which was at Jerusalem; and the king, and his princes, his wives, and his concubines, drank in them. They drank wine, and praised the gods of gold, and of silver, of brass, of iron, of wood, and of stone.

They took the holy things of God and profaned them. They were having this wild, regal orgy in the palace, and they used God's vessels for their debauchery. I don't want to play games with the sacred things of Jesus.

I have been in services where there were prayer lines. But, after a while, instead of just the <u>ministers</u> laying hands upon the people, everybody was doing that. The laying-on-of-hands became a play-thing. It prompts me to think of James' wise words:

James 5:14-15 Is any sick among you? Let him call for the elders of the church; and LET THEM pray over him, anointing him with oil in the name of the Lord. And the prayer of faith shall save the sick, and the Lord shall raise him up; and if he have committed sins, they shall be forgiven him.

It is the elders' job to do this. When in a meeting, never lay hands on anyone, unless an elder authorizes you to do so. Then, you know that you are in God's order to lay hands on the sick; you know that it has been endorsed in heaven. However, at your home with family, this is always in order.

In an effort, and I mean a HUMAN effort, to produce divine results, we sometimes resort to great, excessive manifestations of the flesh in praying for people, pushing, shoving, poking, yelling, messaging. It finally borders on the savage. Do you remember the contest the prophet Elijah had with the priests and prophets of Baal? All day long the pagans screamed to their God, they whirled in the dervish, they cut themselves, they bled, they perspired, they

hollered some more. Elijah chided them about Baal Melkart, their God:
> *1 Kings 18:27-28 It was, at noon, that Elijah mocked them and said, "Cry aloud, for he is a god; either he is meditating, or he is busy, or he is on a journey, or perhaps he is sleeping and must be awakened." So they cried aloud, and cut themselves, as was their custom, with knives and lances, until the blood gushed out on them.*

Then, after he had prepared his own sacrifice,
> *1 Kings 18:36,38 Elijah the prophet came near, and said, "Lord God of Abraham, Isaac, and of Israel, let it be known this day that You are God in Israel"...Then the fire of the Lord fell, and consumed the burnt sacrifice, and the wood, and the stones, and the dust, and licked up the water that was in the trench.*

We do not have a God that must be yelled at.
> *Psalm 20:6 Now, I know that the Lord saves His anointed; He **will hear** him from His holy heaven with the saving strength of His Right Hand.*

> *1 John 5:14,15 Now this is the confidence that we have in Him, that if we ask anything according to His Will, **He hears** us. And if we know that He hears us, whatever we ask, we know that we have the petitions that we have asked of Him.*

We do not need to go through bodily exercises and gyrations to provoke our God. We do not need to shake people with our hands. Just a gentle touch of our hand is a symbol of the mighty Hand of the great God of Heaven. He has given us much authority; let us not exceed our duty to Him. Let us not play holy games in His Church. There is such simplicity and tenderness in Christ. We are not speaking against prayer lines, just against excesses. Paul advises the Church:
> *1 Corinthians 14:40 Let all things be done decently and in order.*

Often I have seen during a time of praise or worship or rejoicing in a church meeting one or more will come forward for prayer. That there was not at that moment a spirit present for healing mattered not. It seems that we ought to wait on the Lord.
> *Luke 5:17 And the power of the Lord was present to heal them.*

It is necessary to wait till the proper time to ask for personal prayer. If, however, we are more concerned about self then what is the order of the moment, we will bull right ahead with our petition. I have sometimes seen wise ministers politely suggest to that person to either wait for the right time or to recommend that they fervently join in the present worship.

Some purposes of laying on of hands: ordination to serve or be a minister; public acknowledgment of what God has already affirmed; the impartation of spiritual gifts; healing of diseases and evil spirits; raising the dead; the transmission of a blessing; and the baptism of the holy ghost. The laying on of hands is such an important service of the Church, one of Its major doctrines.

It is most regrettable that the Church has gotten on the "calf path" of prayer lines and outrageous emotional displays that are a mockery of true faith. They would be more at home in the practice of Hinduism. Here is another Babylonious area out of which the Church must come.

Chapter 16. The Ministry of Melchizedek Today

When the children of Israel were in the Wilderness, God consecrated them to Himself and set them apart. His love for them was magnanimous, and His calling upon them was sure.

> *Exodus 19:5,6 You shall be a peculiar treasure unto Me above all people: for all the earth is Mine: And you shall be unto Me a kingdom of priests, and an holy nation...*

Sadly the people of God failed Him and have been cut off from His Presence for these last two thousand years. Another people, the Gentiles, were grafted into the Jewish tree and have been given custody of the ministry of the Holy Word of God. The very same thing that God had authorized for Israel has now been bestowed upon the Christian Church composed today mainly of "former" gentiles. Peter uses very similar words to describe the Church that Moses had used to describe Israel:

> *1 Peter 2:9 You are a chosen generation, a royal priesthood, an holy nation, a **peculiar** people; that you should show forth the praises of Him who has called you out of darkness into His Marvelous Light.*

Paul also uses the word "peculiar" in referring to the church. He said that Jesus

> *Titus 2:14 gave himself for us, that he might redeem us from all iniquity, and purify unto himself a **peculiar** people, zealous of good works.*

We, the church, are Jesus' peculiar people.

A King and a Priest

There are numerous scriptures that attest to the fact that Jesus is both a king and a priest, that both offices are met in this one person. Other people have attempted to combine these rolls in their own persons. But, Jesus was called before time began to hold these offices.

> *Zechariah 6:13 He...shall sit and rule upon his throne; and he shall be a **priest** upon his throne:*

> *Psalms 110:4 Thou art a **priest** forever...*

> *Hebrews 3:1 Consider the apostle and **high priest** of our profession, Yeshua haMashiakh.*

> *Hebrews 4:14 Seeing then that we have a great **high priest**, that is passed into the heavens, Jesus the Son of God...*

> *Revelation 17:14 He is Lord of lords, and **King of kings**: and they that are with him are called, and chosen, and faithful.*

The *Bible* says that King Jesus' followers are "called, chosen and faithful." By virtue of having come into Christ, His attributes have passed on to them by endowment. His followers are becoming like Him, even to the extent that they have entered into Jesus' very own ministry and sphere of responsibility. Those who are the believers in this Yeshua, who, Himself, has gone into heaven, have taken up His work here on the earth. His work is now being done by them.

*1 Peter 2:5 You also, as lively stones, are built up a spiritual house, an holy **priesthood**, to offer up spiritual sacrifices, acceptable to God by Jesus Christ.*

We, the church, have become priests "by Jesus Christ;" he has ordained us to share in his office and his ministry, to serve and minister spiritual sacrifices.

*Revelation 20:6 They shall be **priests** of God and of Christ, and shall reign with Him a thousand years.*

Not only are the members of that holy congregation to be priests, but they shall reign as kings, too. Jesus

*Revelation 1:6 has made us **kings** and **priests** unto God and his Father; to Him be glory and dominion forever and ever.*

We have many scriptures that demonstrate the royal priesthood of the believer, don't we? We look forward to the day when our voices ring out praises:

*Revelation 5:9,10 "(You) have redeemed us to God by your blood out of every kindred, and tongue, and people, and nation, and has made us unto our God **kings** and **priests**: and we shall reign on the earth."*

The Three Offices of Jesus:

Proofs That He Is a Prophet

Yeshua/Jesus is a prophet and a priest and a king. During his brief three-year ministration he was a prophet. He prophesied about himself. He was the messenger, and he was the message. He was the preacher, and he was the sermon. For three years and six months he functioned as a prophet. This was foreseen by Moses:

*Deuteronomy 18:15 The Lord, your God, will raise up unto you **a prophet** from the midst of you, of your brethren, like unto me; unto him you shall hearken.*

Moses told the people that God would raise up a prophet who would be like Moses. This prophet the people were to obey. God, Himself, told Moses about Jesus:

*Deuteronomy 18:18 I will raise them up a **prophet** from among their brethren, like unto you, and will put My Words in his mouth; and he shall speak unto them all that I shall command him.*

John, the Baptist, spoke of Jesus, saying

John 3:34 he whom God has sent speaks the Words of God.

Speaking God's Words is what prophets do. By the holy spirit Jesus was able to speak, here on earth, Words from another world. He spoke God's Words.

*Acts 3:22,23 For Moses truly said unto the fathers, "A **prophet** shall the Lord your God raise up unto you of your brethren, like unto me; him shall you hear in all things whatsoever he shall say unto you." And it shall come to pass, that every soul, which will not hear that prophet, shall be destroyed from among the people.*

Proofs that Jesus is King

We shall shortly demonstrate the priesthood of Jesus. But first, let us confirm that he is king. David had a covenant promise from God that his child would be an eternal king:
> *Psalms 89:3,4,35,36 I have made a covenant with my chosen, I have sworn unto David my servant, "Thy seed will I establish forever, and build up your throne to all generations."... Once have I sworn by My Holiness that I will not lie unto David. His **seed** shall endure forever, and his throne as the sun before me.*

This is a prophecy that David's messianic descendant will be king forever.
> *Psalms 132:11 The Lord has sworn in truth unto David; He will not turn from it; "Of the fruit of your body will I set upon your throne."*

David's offspring will inherit an eternal throne.
> *Isaiah 9:6,7 For unto us a child is born...Upon the throne of David, and upon his kingdom, to order it, and to establish it with judgment and with justice from henceforth even forever.*

A child will be born. He will justly rule the world forever. This man would often be labeled as "the Branch of David," or, as the Jews designated: "The Branch."
> *Jeremiah 23:5 "Behold, the days come," says the Lord, "that I will raise unto David a Righteous **Branch**, and a king shall reign and prosper, and shall execute judgment and justice in the earth.*

For hundreds of years the Jews looked for the Christ to come, this "Branch" of David, the one the people often referred to as "The Branch." He was even more popularly referred to as the Christ, or Messiah:
> *Daniel 9:25 The **Messiah**, the Prince.*

We are demonstrating that Jesus is king by descent from King David:
> *Ezekiel 37:24 And **David**, My servant, shall be king over them; and they all shall have one shepherd: they shall also walk in My Judgments, and observe My Statutes, and do Them.*

Now, let's consider verses that declare Jesus to be, not only king, but also LORD:
> *Hosea 3:5 Afterward shall the children of Israel return, and seek the **Lord** their God, and David their **king**; and shall fear the Lord and his goodness in the latter days.*

This passage clearly identifies this descendant of David as "the Lord." And then, our Lord, himself, declares:
> *Psalm 110:1 The Lord said unto my Lord, Sit thou at my right hand, until I make thine enemies thy footstool.*

Jesus is saying that, not only is he the descendant of David, he also was David's source, his "root," in that Jesus was the Creator of the universe, the "root" of all.

The angel Gabriel had declared to Mary that her son was, in fact, that very descendant of David and also the Lord:
> *Luke 1:32,33 "He shall be great, and shall be called the Son of the Highest: and the Lord God shall give unto him the throne of his father **David**: And he shall reign over the house of Jacob for ever; and of his kingdom there shall be no end.*

The apostle Paul further stated:
> *2 Timothy 2:8 Remember that Jesus Christ of the seed of **David** was raised from the dead.*

*Romans 1:3 Concerning his Son Jesus Christ our Lord, which was made of the seed of **David** according to the flesh...*

All these passages confirm that Jesus of Nazareth is the rightful heir to David's throne. Yet, he's also to be the eternal king of the universe, but NOT by David.

The *Bible* tells us that there is another royal dynasty that is NOT Davidic. There is a scripture in *Genesis* (we shall look at it again when considering the priesthood of Jesus) that shows us the name of this other dynasty.

Genesis 14:18 And Melchizedek, KING of Salem, brought forth bread and wine.

In the next section we shall spell out the priestly side of the Melchizedek. We shall show clearly that Melchizedek is one of the several *OT* manifestations of Jesus.

Melchizedek, we are told, was king of Salem. So Salem was his location. But, see that this Melchizedek appeared centuries before David. Jesus posed this question to the Pharisees in reference to *Psalm* 110: 4 (which we will also consider again later):

*Matthew 22:42-45 "What do you think of Christ? whose son is he?" They say unto him, "The Son of **David**." He said to them, "How then does **David** in the spirit call him 'Lord,' saying* (Psalm 110:4): *'The Lord said unto my Lord, Sit thou on my right hand, till I make your enemies your footstool?' If **David** then called him Lord, how is he his son?"*

David was referring to Jesus, the messiah, as "MY Lord." He refers to God, the Father, as "THE Lord." How could David be the SON of this messiah before the messiah was ever born? Of course, they were unable to answer, because they would have had to have admitted that although Christ was to come from David, yet Christ was eternal as God, the Father, and therefore, BEFORE David. "The Lord said to my Lord!"

King David's father was named Jesse. The following passage speaks of Christ being from Jesse's stem.

*Isaiah 11:1 And there shall come forth a rod out of the **stem of Jesse**, and a Branch shall grow out of his roots.*

When the scripture speaks of a "rod," we are to see the rod of a ruler. But, this passage also says that the Christ will be a "branch" from Jesse's roots. Christ will come from someone who is BEFORE Jesse, from Jesse's roots.

*Revelation 5:5 And one of the elders said to me, "Weep not: behold, the Lion of the tribe of Judah, the **Root of David**, has prevailed to open the Book, and to loose the seven seals thereof.*

*Revelation 22:16 I, Jesus, have sent my angel to testify unto you these things in the churches. I am the root AND the **offspring of David**, and the bright and morning star.*

An Everlasting Dynasty

The fact that Jesus is the "offspring of David" is very important, especially to the Jews. The *scriptures* made it very obvious to them the Messiah must be the "offspring of David." As a matter of fact, it is more important to the Jews then it is to the Church. Why? Because there is this other dynasty that has meaning to the church. Jesus said, "I am the root...of David," that is, he is before David. He is NOT just king by descent from David, but he is king because he IS Melchizedek. Melchizedek was before the *Law*. I repeat: Melchizedek existed long before the *Law of Moses*. He appeared to Abraham, but existed long before; he is eternal. His throne is eternal. It is, not only the throne of David from which Jesus will

Luke 1:33 reign over the house of Jacob forever,...

but, it is the eternal throne of Melchizedek from which he will reign over the church for ever. Jesus (of David) will reign over Israel forever, AND Jesus (of Melchizedek) will also reign over his church, his holy congregation, forever.

There is but one throne. To the Jews it's critical that it is David's throne. But, it is also Melchizedek's throne, which is eternal, and this is vitally important to the redeemed children of Israel AND to the redeemed children of the gentiles, that is, to the Church of Jesus Christ.

We are so very grateful for the harmony of the *Holy Scriptures*, how everything so beautifully meshes together. We all rejoice to bear witness that the child conceived by the seed of David has become Lord and King. We bow in awe that he is the ancient creator and king of the universe. We shall, with the Jews, proclaim him: Yeshua ha-mel-khi-zedek, "Jesus, the king of righteousness."

Isaiah had this amazing prophecy:

Isaiah 9:6,7 For unto us a child is born, unto us a son is given: and the government shall be upon his shoulder: and his name shall be called Wonderful, Counselor, The Mighty God, The Everlasting Father, The Prince of Peace. Of the increase of his government and peace there shall be no end, upon the throne of David, and upon his kingdom, to order it, and to establish it with judgment and with justice from henceforth even forever. The zeal of the Lord of hosts will perform this.

Look at those magnificent titles by which our Lord will be called when he sits upon His throne:
Wonderful
Counselor
Mighty God
Everlasting Father
Prince of Peace

Please consider that these titles are NOT, however, by virtue of Jesus' descent from David, but by the everlasting dynasty of Melchizedek.

The dynasty of David counted twenty-one kings. The dynasty of Melchizedek counts but one king. The prophetic *Word* proclaims Jesus to be a king. To be sure, his disciples acknowledge him to be the Lord and the King of their lives right now, today. But, the rest of the world regards him as an impostor, a fake, an illegitimate child. The time is not yet

Philippians 2:10,11 that at the name of Jesus every knee should bow, of things in heaven, and things in earth, and things under the earth, and that every tongue should confess that Jesus Christ is Lord, to the glory of God the Father.

The following prophecy precisely declared that the time of Jesus' acknowledged monarchy will be AFTER the Battle of Armageddon. He told us:

Zechariah 14:16 And it shall come to pass, that every one that is left of all

the nations which came against Jerusalem shall even go up from year to year to worship the King, the Lord of hosts...

For a thousand years the saints shall go to Jerusalem each year to celebrate the coronation of their king and to pay homage to Him and thank Him that they are part of the great harvest of souls.

Jesus has been a prophet, and he will be proclaimed King forever. Firstly prophet, lastly king. But, what role does He hold today?

Proofs that Jesus is Priest

When the Israelites were in the Wilderness God ordained the family of Moses' brother Aaron to become priests to serve the nation. The Aaronites were of the tribe of Levy, which tribe was set apart to serve the other tribes. They were to be solely supported by the tithes of the other tribes. The tithes were to be their only means of support. Then the Levites took one tenth of their income and tithed it to their brethren, the Cohens, that is, the sons of Aaron, the priests. The *Bible* refers to them as "the Levitical priesthood."

We have seen how Jesus was the descendant of David, who was of the tribe of Judah, and not Levi. Therefore, Jesus cannot be an heir to the Levite priesthood. Indeed, we shall see that he is, in fact, a priest after a different order. Paul reasons:
> *Hebrews 7:11 If therefore perfection were by the Levitical priesthood, (for under it the people received the Law,) what further need was there that another priest should rise?*

Indeed, had the priesthood of Aaron made the people perfect, there would have been no further need for another kind of priest. But, the truth is that the people never could be perfect; they never could keep the *Levitical Law*. They needed yet another priest--Jesus.

What was the name of this new order? Or was it a "new order?" As a matter of fact, we discover that Yeshua's priesthood does not come from a "new order" of priests, but from one that is far more ancient then the Levitical Order. We find a brief mention of it early in the *Bible*. This scene immediately follows that where Abram had defeated the confederacy of kings. This short passage ensues:
> *Genesis 14:18-20 And Melchizedek, king of Salem brought forth bread and wine: and He was the PRIEST of the Most High God. And he blessed him, and said, "Blessed be Abram of the Most High God, Possessor of heaven and earth: And blessed be the Most High God, which has delivered your enemies into your hand. And (Abram) gave (Melchizedek) tithes of all.*

Melchizedek is priest of the Most High God, that is, He is the priest of God, the Father. Who is God's priest? It is Melchizedek.
> *Hebrews 7:1,2 This Melchisedec, king of Salem, priest of the most high God, who met Abraham returning from the slaughter of the kings, and blessed him; To Whom also Abraham gave a tenth part of all; first being by interpretation King of Righteousness, and after that also King of Salem* [shalom], *which is, King of Peace.*

The *Hebrew* word *Me-lek'*, means "king." The word *ze-dek'* mean "righteousness." When you put *me-lek* and *ze-dek* together in

Hebrew, it becomes *Melkhi-zedek*, which means "king of righteousness." When Paul tells us in the foregoing verse that this man is also the king of "Salem," which is a form of the *Hebrew* word *sha-lom'*, meaning "peace," he is telling us that he is both the king of righteousness AND the king of peace. You should note that the word "Salem" is part of the name of the city of Jeru-salem. This ancient site is where Abram met Melchizedek. It is also the site where later Abraham took Isaac to offer him as a sacrifice on Mount Moriah. It was later the site of the threshing floor of Ornan, the Jebusite, which David purchased as the location of the Holy Temple in Jerusalem.

We should observe that Abram gave a tenth to this priest-king. Later on, Jacob, Abraham's grandson, had an unusual dream of a ladder that reached to heaven with the Lord standing above it pronouncing a great promise to Jacob and his offspring. Jacob named the place this vision occurred "Beth-el", meaning "house of God." To the "Lord," (*Genesis* 28:22) Jacob gave a "tenth." I point out that Abraham tithed to the "priest-king," and that Jacob tithed to the eternal "Lord," and also that the "priest-king" is also the Lord God. Abram and Jacob tithed to the same person. This is saying that this King of Righteousness, this Melchizedek, also known as the King of Salem (Sha-lom', peace) was Yeshua, the Lord (YHVH) (יהוה), appearing in the *Old Testament*. [Some believe this refers to the Father, which in many cases *Yah* is the Father.]

Paul speaks of this person saying that He is
*Hebrews 7:3,4 without father, without mother, without descent, having **neither beginning of days**, nor end of life; but made like unto the Son of God; abides a priest continually. Now consider how great this man was, unto whom even the patriarch Abraham gave the tenth of the spoils.*

Paul has just described Jesus. He did not have a father on earth since the holy ghost placed the seed that impregnated his mother Mary. Jesus did not have a mother in heaven. He has no end of life, because he is eternal. He had no beginning of days since he was with God from the beginning.
Proverbs 8:23 I was set up from everlasting, from the beginning, or ever the earth was.

Here is Jesus speaking through the pen of Solomon. "I'm everlasting; I'm eternal; I am from the beginning." Jesus referred to himself as:
*Revelation 3:14 the Amen, the faithful and true Witness, the **beginning** of the creation of God.*

The very first thing the Almighty God did in the beginning of creation was to make His own son Jesus. He is the beginning of God's creation. Paul says he "abides a priest continually," meaning he is "eternal." Paul also says Melchizedek was made like unto the son of God and called him a "man."

To be such an important doctrine, it is remarkable that it is only mentioned in *Hebrews* and *Genesis* and one other passage. Let's consider it now:
Psalms 110:4 The Lord has sworn, and will not repent, "You are a priest for ever after the order of Melchizedek."

There it is: the Levitical priests inherited their priesthood generation after generation, and then they died. Jesus is a priest forever; He ever lives.

And, another point: the priests of Aaron were born to their role; Jesus received his priesthood by an oath from God.
> *The Lord has **sworn**, and will not repent, "You are a priest forever after the order of Melchizedek."*

Before going further I'd like to rest here in the 110th *Psalm* for a moment. The first verse has a remarkable statement. This is a *Psalm* of David, referring to God, the father, as "THE Lord" and to Jesus as "MY Lord."
> *Psalms 110:1* **The** *Lord said unto* **my** *Lord, "Sit thou at My Right Hand, until I make your enemies your footstool."*

David is saying, "The Lord God said to David's Lord...," that is, "God, the Father, said to God, the son..."

God is telling His son to sit at the right hand of His Throne until God has crushed the son's enemies.

And, this expression "sit at My right hand" of God's throne is another word demonstrating the "kingship" of the son. And then in *v4* we have the eternal priesthood sworn to and proclaimed:
> *You are a priest forever...*

Paul makes much of the importance of this. He demonstrates that Melchizedek, who has no ancestry, received tithes from, and gave blessings to Abraham.
> *Hebrews 7:6 But he (Melchizedek) whose descent is not counted from (Levi) received tithes from Abraham, and blessed him...*

Melchizedek received Abraham's tithes, and blessed him. Abraham gave to and received ministry from someone other than the one whom Abraham's descendants obtained. Paul tell us that Jesus, whose descent is not from Levi, has now become our priest, that is, there has been a change in the priesthood; we no longer have the sons of Aaron as priests, but we have Jesus. And, this change in priesthood also means there is a change of laws.
> *Hebrews 7:12 For the priesthood being changed, there is made of necessity a change also of the Law.*

What is the change of Law? It is this: no longer must we perform the rituals of the *Law of Moses*, but now Jesus has brought us to a new law, the "*Law of Grace*." This means that we don't have to keep sacrificing animals for our sins; this means we no longer have to struggle in ourselves to do what is right. This means that we no longer have to die because of our sins. This means that we can have power from Heaven to walk righteously. And this is because Almighty God has sworn
> *Hebrews 7:21 Because of God's oath, Christ can guarantee forever the success of this new and better arrangement* (TLB).

Because Jesus is everlasting, he can assure us of our own triumph. The priests of Israel executed their office until they died. But, Yeshua is eternal.
> *Hebrews 7:24,25 But (Jesus), because he continues **forever**, has an unchangeable priesthood. Therefore, he is also able to save to the uttermost those who come to God through him, since he **always** lives to make intercession for them.*

1. Intercession

Here is one of the functions of our high priest: intercession. Here is what Jesus did to procure this ministry--He poured out his life.

*Isaiah 53:12 He has **poured out his soul** unto death: and he was numbered with the transgressors; and he bare the sin of many, and made intercession for the transgressors.*

We are the transgressors. Jesus stands between us and the Holy God. He is an intercessor, a mediator.

*1 Timothy 2:5 For there is one God, and one **mediator** between God and men, the man Christ Jesus.*

Hebrews 9:24 For Christ is not entered into the holy places made with hands, which are the figures of the true; but into heaven itself, now to appear in the presence of God for us.

*1 John 2:1 If any man sin, we have an **advocate** with the Father, Jesus Christ the righteous.*

John 17:9 I pray for them: I pray not for the world, but for them which You have given me; for they are Yours.

Jesus is a mediator; he appears in God's presence in our behalf; when we are guilty, he is our advocate; he is our only hope; he prays for us; he makes intercession for us.

*Romans 8:34 Who is he who condemns? It is Christ who died, and furthermore is also risen, who is even at the right hand of God, who also makes **intercession** for us.*

No one can condemn you, even your own self. No one can judge you except Christ. And God has given to him such power and authority.

John 16:23 Whatsoever you shall ask the Father in my name, He will give it to you.

What a mighty intercessor we have!

We have already noted that since Jesus is a priest, and that when we come INTO Christ, we take on his attributes. If he is a priest, we are to be priests. One of the functions of priests is intercessory prayer. <u>We</u> are to be pray-ers.

Revelation 8:3,4 Then another angel, having a golden censer, came and stood at the altar. And he was given much incense that he should offer it with the prayers of all the saints upon the golden altar which was before the throne. And the smoke of the incense, with the prayers of the saints, ascended before God from the angel's hand.

Psalms 141:2 Let my prayer be set forth before You as incense; and the lifting up of my hands as the evening sacrifice.

It is our priest Jesus' ministry to pray for us; then, as priests ourselves, we are to give ourselves to prayer, too.

Acts 1:14 These all continued with one accord in prayer and supplication, with the women, and Mary the mother of Jesus, and with his brethren.

Before the church began, the saints were giving themselves to prayer, and afterward:

Acts 6:4 But we will give ourselves continually to prayer...

James 5:16 Pray for one another.

Romans 12:12 Continuing instant in prayer...

This is a function of the Melchizedekal priesthood: intercessory prayer. This ministry is not just for the ordained ministers, but all the saints. We are all to be prayer warriors.

> *Ephesians 6:18,19 Praying always with all prayer and supplication in the spirit, and watching thereunto with all perseverance and supplication for all saints and for me...*

What do you make of that: "praying always with all prayer"? Think about that a moment. Here are a few more quotes proving that part of every saint's Melchizedekal ministry is prayer:

> *Philippians 4:6 In everything by **prayer** and supplication with thanksgiving let your requests be made known unto God.*

> *Colossians 4:2,3 Continue earnestly in **prayer**, being vigilant in it with thanksgiving; meanwhile praying also for us...*

> *1 Peter 4:7 But the end of all things is at hand: be therefore sober, and watch unto prayer.*

Without question, our priestly order of Melchizedek has the function of praying and interceding!

2. Comforting

Yeshua of Nazareth is the great shepherd of the church. It is the shepherd's job to console and pacify his sheep. The Lord is our shepherd.

> *Psalms 23:4 Your rod and your staff they **comfort** me.*

This is one of the priestly functions of Jesus. This *Psalm* clearly outlines the provision that he is to bring to us, comfort. Jesus will comfort us. Following is a prophetic passage looking forward both to John, the Baptist, and to the coming Savior.

> *Isaiah 40:3 The voice of him that cries in the wilderness: "Prepare ye the way of the **Lord**; make straight in the desert a highway for our God."*

None could doubt that "the Lord" about whom Isaiah prophecies is Jesus.
Prepare ye the way of the Lord.

The Baptist is told here to make a straight path for our YHVH (יהוה), that is, for Jesus. But, listen how Isaiah introduces this coming Jesus. He begins with a command from the Father, to His son:

> *Isaiah 40:1 "**Comfort** ye, comfort ye My people," says your God.*

What are the instructions??? "Comfort My people." This is God's mandate for Jesus.

> *Isaiah 51:3 For the Lord shall **comfort** Zion...*

Yeshua, himself, speaking through Isaiah proclaims his priestly ministry. He says he is

> *Isaiah 61:2,3 to **comfort** all that mourn, to appoint unto them that mourn in Zion, to give unto them beauty for ashes, the oil of joy for mourning, the garment of praise for the spirit of heaviness...*

> *Isaiah 66:13 As one whom his mother **comforts**, so will I comfort you.*

Can you imagine such language? Jesus compares his comfort to that of a "mother." How marvelous! "So I will comfort you."

Do you think God's people need comforting? Just think of all the terrible things from your past life that need and have needed to be healed. Think of all the griefs we bare. We need the priestly comfort of Jesus. The *Bible* tells us that's just what he'll do.

> *Jeremiah 31:13,14 "I will turn their mourning into joy, and will **comfort** them, and make them rejoice from their sorrow. And I will satiate the soul of the priests with fatness, and my people shall be satisfied with my goodness," says the Lord.*

> *Psalms 85:8 I will hear what God, the Lord, will speak: for he will **speak peace** unto his people.*

Jesus, himself, before he was crucified told the disciples that he would not abandon them:

> *John 14:18 I will not leave you **comfortless**: I will come to you.*

And this he did by the holy ghost on the Day of Pentecost. He declared that he would be right there with them to comfort them, to give them peace of mind.

Paul attests to this pacific ministry of Jesus:

> *2 Corinthians 1:3,4 Our Lord Jesus Christ, the father of mercies, and the God of all comfort, who **comforts** us in all our tribulation...*

Paul tells, however, that this comfort from the Lord is not just for our own personal benefit, but he

> *2 Corinthians 1:4-6 **comforts** us in all our tribulation, (so) that WE may be able to **comfort** them which are in any trouble, by the **comfort** which we ourselves are **comforted** by God.*

Just as the Melchizedekal service of "comforting" is ministered to us, we are to comfort others. We are priests of the order of Melchizedek, and one of our functions is to be comforters. Just as Jesus received much affliction and received comfort and consolation from the Father, we, too, receive comfort in our trials from our high priest. The mature child of God has come to a place in his life where he trusts everything in it to Jesus. He may not understand at the moment why something awful has just happened, but he is confident that Jesus has a purpose in it. He knows that he will finally be comforted through the trial. He knows that whatever the day's events bring his way, whether affliction or joy, it is not only for his well-being, but that it will also be a benefit to all those who come into contact with him. He knows that he, as a priest of God, will minister comfort to someone else.

> *2 Corinthians 1:5,6 For as the sufferings of Christ abound in us, so our consolation also abounds by Christ. And whether we be afflicted, it is for your consolation and salvation, which produces in you patient endurance of the same sufferings we suffer; or whether we be **comforted**, it is for your consolation and salvation.*

We are to see in Paul's use of his own personal example that in trusting Christ for whatever may happen we can pass on to others the comfort of Jesus.

> *1 Thessalonians 2:7 I was gentle among you, even as a (nursing **mother**) cherishes her children.*

Consider the following how much Paul was blessed by Titus. And, then he was overjoyed to know the marvelous, mature attitude of the saints.

> *2 Corinthians 7:6,7 God, Who **comforts** those that are cast down, **comforted** me by the coming of Titus, and not by his coming only, but by the consolation wherewith he was comforted in you, when he told us your earnest desire, your mourning,*

your fervent mind toward me; so that I rejoiced the more.

What good news Titus had brought to Paul! He was so thrilled. The saints didn't think at the time when they were so worried about Paul that he would someday hear about it and be so blessed. The church didn't think at the time when they were expressing their fervent concerns and their love for Paul that someday he'd hear about it and be greatly cheered.

All of us can look back on our lives and recall the times when we have been comforted by others. Jesus said that he would comfort his people. But, Jesus has given a large part of that priestly ministry to us.

I remember the day that I was absolutely grief-stricken. My wife had left me and taken our three children. I did not know where she had hidden them. I don't say this lightly: "I was devastated." I was crying and crying, walking through that empty house. I actually could not stop sobbing. I thought I must have lost my mind. I couldn't quit crying. I was feeling so sorry for myself.

I said, "Oh God, I'm all alone in the world. Would you please put it on someone's heart to call me right now."

That very moment the phone rang. It was Morris and Phyllis King, Christians whom I had just recently met. I could barely say, "hello."

They wanted to take me to dinner, which I really didn't think I could handle at that moment. But, they insisted and persisted. That evening they helped me get somewhat glued back together. Numerous times after that they reached out to me with Jesus' love.

They inconvenienced themselves to comfort me. They were not the only ones whom God used to save me, either.

Ultimately, I survived this tragedy in my life. I'm sure at the time I could not see any good thing in this wrecking of a marriage and a family.

I stand back now somewhat amazed at the good things that Jesus has wrought out of it all. I had thought that my children would turn out to be "basket cases," but, in fact they're all doing well.

I can't count the number of people that I, myself, have been able to console in their tragedies by my testimony. And, the comfort I received, I have been able to pass on to them. I am so thankful to Jesus for providing the right people and the right things at the right time. I thank him for letting me pass on this wonderful consolation. After all, this is our priestly service, which we are exhorted to minister to one another.

*1 Thessalonians 5:11 Therefore **comfort** each other and edify one another.*

It is our purpose to console and to build up others.
Hebrews 12:12 Lift up the hands which hang down, and the feeble knees...

I can guarantee you that you will not find a shortage of people to help, especially as we move closer and closer to the end of this age.

3. Serving

Interceding. Comforting. And now, another function of a priest: serving. Jesus is a servant. God has ordained him for that role. The prophets repeatedly proclaimed Yeshua to be God's servant. Not only is he servant of God, but he has made himself servant to us. Jesus has been anointed by God's spirit to serve:

*Isaiah 42:1 Behold my **servant**, whom I uphold, Mine elect, in whom My soul delights; I have put My spirit upon him.*

*Isaiah 52:13-15 Behold, My **servant** shall deal prudently. He shall be exalted and extolled and be very high. Just as many were astonished at you, so his visage (appearance) was marred more than any man and his form more than the sons of men. So shall he sprinkle many nations.*

It is remarkable what Jesus had to go through to achieve the role of servant. This verse predicts the horrible beatings Jesus received on the way to Calvary. His appearance was so marred, tradition says, that his own mom did not recognize him.

And, then the blood he shed on the cross sprinkled and continues to sprinkle to this day...

As we had pointed out earlier, we also know Jesus as "the Branch:"

*Zechariah 3:8 Behold, I will bring forth My **servant** the Branch*

Jesus is God's "Branch." This next prophecy speaks of Jesus as a shepherd. It refers to him by the name "David," but you know that is Jesus' name by descent:

*Ezekiel 34:23,24 I will establish one shepherd over them, and he shall feed them -- My **servant David**. He shall feed them and be their shepherd.*

Above, God said that Jesus "shall feed them." Look what Jesus then said to Peter:

*John 21:15 When they had dined, Jesus said to Simon Peter, "Simon, son of Jonas, do you love me more than these?" (Peter answered) him, "Yes, Lord; you know that I love you." (Jesus) said to him, "**Feed** my lambs."*

How is God's servant Jesus feeding today? How is he serving? Through us. His ministry has passed on to us. This is the ministry of Melchizedek today: we feed.

Serving is one of the great signs of our priesthood. Jesus said:

*John 12:26 if any man **serve** me, let him follow me; and where I am, there shall also my **servant** be: if any man **serve** me, him will my Father honor.*

We are always serving Jesus when we are serving others. It is as though we are doing it in his behalf.

*2 Corinthians 4:5 For we preach not ourselves, but Christ Jesus the Lord; and ourselves your **servants** for Jesus' sake.*

Colossians 3:23,24 Whatsoever you do, do it heartily, as to the Lord, and not unto men, knowing that from the Lord you shall receive the reward of the inheritance: for you serve the Lord Christ.

John 13:4,5,12-17 He rose from supper, and laid aside his garments; and took a towel, and girded himself. After that he poured water into a bason, and began to wash the disciples' feet, and to wipe them with the towel with which he was girded...After he had washed their feet, and had taken his garments, and was set down again, he said unto *them, "Do you know what I have done to you? You call me Master and Lord: and you say well; for so I am. If I then, your Lord and Master, have washed your feet; you also ought to wash one another's feet. For I have given you an example, that you should do as I have done to you. Verily, verily, I say unto you, "The **servant** is not greater than his lord; neither he that is sent greater than He that sent him." If you know these things, happy are you if you DO them.*

Jesus is not telling his disciples that they are to have ritual foot-washings. He said, "I have given you an example." This was perhaps his ultimate lesson in giving of self. How much more lowly could one serve then to be at his neighbor's feet? Jesus was passing on his Melchizedekal priesthood to the twelve. What is the ministry of Melchizedek today? Serving.

Later on, during this last supper, he served them bread. And, then after the meal he served them wine. This is so significant that it is one of the few events recorded in all four *Gospels* plus Paul's account in *1 Corinthians*.

Luke 22:19,20 And he took bread, and gave thanks, and brake it, and gave unto them, saying, "This is my body which is given for you: this do in remembrance of me." Likewise also the cup after supper, saying, "This cup is the new testament in my blood, which is shed for you."

When Jesus said, "This do in remembrance of me," what was he wanting them to remember? Did he want them to remember the bread? No. Did he want them to remember the Passover seder? No. Did he want them to remember his broken body upon the cross? Well, could it be referring to Jesus' broken (?) body upon the cross?:

John 19:33,36 But when they came to Jesus, and saw that he was dead already, they did NOT break his legs...For these things were done, that the scripture (Psalm 34:20) should be fulfilled, "A bone of him shall not be broken."

Jesus' body was not broken on the cross. Then what did the broken bread represent? It does refer to "broken**ness**." Jesus was broken all of his life, not just at the very end. Had he not gone through many experiences of heartache, rejection, and want, he could never have agreed to his crucifixion.

Luke 22:42 Father, if You are willing, remove this cup from me: nevertheless not my will, but Thine, be done.

These are the words of brokenness. He is exhorting the disciples to be that way also. He says that every time their bread was broken, that is, every time things didn't go the way they would have wanted, that is, every time they lost their own will, they were remembering his brokenness.

Similarly for the wine. The wine represents Jesus' blood, in fact his life which he poured out, not just on the cross, but all of his life. Jesus was always giving, always helping, always healing, always serving, always pouring himself out. Jesus poured himself out entirely. He gave himself completely. He held nothing back. This is his example to us. That is why he said:

Matthew 26:27 Drink ye all of it.

Isaiah 53:10-12 Yet it pleased the Lord to bruise him; (God) has put him (Jesus) to grief: when You (God, the Father) shall make (Jesus') soul an *offering for sin...(God) shall see of the travail of (Jesus') soul, and shall be satisfied: by his knowledge shall My righteous servant justify many; for he shall bear their iniquities...He has **poured out his soul** unto death.*

Jesus made himself a drink offering; he poured out the wine of his life--all of it.

Now here is your priestly lesson: if you are serving and pouring yourself out, and you save some back, all you'll have left to give the next time is what you reserved. But, if you pour yourself out entirely, He fills you back up completely. Now, you can give it all again. How different from the world! If we give all, we have yet more.

There is much more to be said about this bread and wine at the last supper and all of its meaning. But, I would like to point out that "bread and wine" is the emblem of the Melchizedekal priesthood. You will remember that Abram tithed to Melchizedek. But, Melchizedek gave something to Abram. Do you recall what it was? What did the priest of the most high God serve to Abram?
*Genesis 14:18 Melchizedek king of Salem brought forth **bread and wine**: and he was the priest of the most high God.*

At that "last supper" the Nazarene brought forth bread and wine to his disciples, just as he, himself, had done nineteen centuries before when he served their great, great, great......grandfather Abraham bread and wine. By this act at that dinner table, Jesus was proclaiming his eternal priesthood. "Eat my bread; drink my wine."
Psalms 110:4 Thou art a priest for ever after the order of Merchizedek.

"Bread and wine" are the signs, symbol, emblems of this priestly order.

"Serving" is the ministry of Melchizedek today, and it is very extensive. We have much work to do.
Mark 16:15-18 Go ye into all the world, and preach the gospel to every creature...Cast out devils...Lay hands on the sick, and they shall recover.

Matthew 28:19-20 Go ye therefore, and teach all nations, baptizing them in the name of the father, and of the son, and of the holy ghost, teaching them to observe all things whatsoever I have commanded you:

4. Delivering

Interceding. Comforting. Serving...When people come out of the world and into the wonderful Kingdom of Heaven, they bring with them all their garbage. I mistakenly thought that when I got saved that I had suddenly become perfect. After all, those wonderful, loving people around me surely were. I was absolutely dumb-founded the first time as a Christian that I slipped. I couldn't believe it. I thought there must be something wrong with my salvation. What was even more stunning was when I discovered that those "perfect" people in the church weren't...........They weren't perfect after all. They still had lots of flaws.

So, my first lesson was this: salvation is an ongoing process in each saint's life; salvation didn't make me suddenly angelic. There was still a bunch of rubbish there. I had these wounds; I had these hurts; I had these offenses; I was selfish; I was conceited; I was stingy; I was arrogant; I was bull-headed; I was a liar; I was lustful; I was a glutton........................I needed deliverance. I was saved, yet I still had these problems.

When Jesus began his ministry at the age of thirty his first public proclamation was in the synagogue in his home-town, Nazareth. In synagogues all over the world that day, one of the passages to be read in the service was the first three verses of *Isaiah* 61. Jesus was called to the *bema*, the platform, to be one of the day's scripture readers. Of all things, it was assigned to him to read that very portion. When he stopped reading the *Hebrew* words, he ceremoniously rolled up the scroll; he tied a cord around it; he slipped over it the cover which had two holes in the top where the rollers protruded; he draped a chain over the rollers to which was attached a silver, reading pointer; and he handed it to the minister.

> *Luke 4:20,21 And the eyes of all them that were in the synagogue were fastened on him. And he began to say unto them, "This day is this scripture fulfilled in your ears."*

There was no doubt; they understood that by this *scripture*, which they very-well knew was a messianic prophesy, he was claiming to be the fulfillment. Let us take a look at this entire passage that Jesus had been appointed to read.

> *Isaiah 61:1-3 The spirit of the Lord God is upon me; because the Lord has anointed me to preach good tidings unto the meek; he has sent me to bind up the brokenhearted, to proclaim liberty to the captives, and the opening of the prison to them that are bound; to proclaim the acceptable year of the Lord, and the day of vengeance of our God; to comfort all that mourn;*
>
> *to appoint unto them that mourn in Zion, to give unto them beauty for ashes, the oil of joy for mourning, the garment of praise for the spirit of heaviness; that they might be called trees of righteousness, the planting of the Lord, that He might be glorified.*

This is the quotation as it appears in Luke:
> *Luke 4:18 to preach the gospel to the poor; he has sent me to heal the brokenhearted, to preach deliverance to the captives, and recovering of sight to the blind, to set at liberty them that are bruised...*

This passage is the defining description of the priestly ministry of deliverance. Jesus said: "This day this *scripture* is fulfilled in your ears."

Let us look at it more closely. He will:
1) declare good news to the meek;
2) bind up and heal the broken-hearted;
3) set the captives free;
4) open the prison to those who are bound;
5) set free those who are bruised;
6) comfort those who mourn;
7) substitute joy in the place of heaviness; and
8) make God's people to be righteous.

The result of this priestly ministry will bring glory to God by the marvelous transformation that comes upon us.

> *Psalms 79:9 Help us, O God of our salvation, for the glory of Your Name: and **deliver** us, and **purge** away our sins, for Your Name's sake.*

> *Romans 7:24 O wretched man that I am! who shall **deliver** me from the body of this death?*

> *Hebrews 2:15 ...And **deliver** them who through fear of death were all their lifetime subject to **bondage**.*

God's people have these problems in their lives: they are in bondage to phobias and character flaws and bad habits; they're in bondage to "family problems;" they're in bondage to things they have mistakenly said or done in the past, how they've been abused, gossiped about.......

The following passage shows that we don't need to be saved just one time from our bondages, but "oftentimes."

> *Job 33:27-30 (God) looks upon men, and if any say, "I have sinned, and perverted that which was right, and it did not profit me," He will **deliver** his soul from going into the pit, and his life shall see the Light. Lo, all these things God works **often-times** with man, to bring back his soul from the pit, to be enlightened with the Light of the living.*

God wants to bring our soul back from whatever pit it's in. He wants us to see His Light. God will deliver us from death, AND He keeps on delivering us--"often-times"--bringing us out of our pits, our bondages. Notice how David expressed this:

> *Psalms 56:13 For You have **delivered** my soul from death: will You not (also) **deliver** my feet from falling?*

God saved, and He has to keep delivering our feet from falling. Paul tells us that God delivers and "does deliver."

> *2 Corinthians 1:10 Who **delivered** us from so great a death, and **does deliver**: in Whom we trust that He **will** yet **deliver** us.*

Paul was trusting that everything that was not right in his life God would "yet deliver" him. He did not just want to be saved, he wanted to be all-the-way saved. He knew he could count on Jesus to finish the job.

> *Philippians 1:6 Being confident of this very thing: that He which has begun a good work in you will perform it until the day of Jesus Christ.*

We're not worried about these troublesome things still in our lives; we know it will all get worked out of us in due time for His Good Pleasure. Jesus will help us. He is our Rock of Help. The *Hebrew* word for "Rock of Help" is *Eben-ezer*. If you'd like another name for Jesus, here it is: *Ebenezer*. Notice what the prophet Samuel thought about the delivering virtue of his Ebenezer, his "Rock of Help."

> *1 Samuel 7:10-13 And as Samuel was offering up the burnt offering, the Philistines drew near to battle against Israel: but the Lord thundered with a great thunder on that day upon the Philistines, and discomfited them; and they were smitten before Israel. And the men of Israel went out of Mizpeh, and pursued the Philistines, and smote them...Then Samuel took a stone, and set it between Mizpeh and Shen, and called the name of it* Ebenezer, *saying, "(Up to this point) has the Lord helped us." So the Philistines were subdued, and they came no more into the coast of Israel: and the Hand of the Lord was against the Philistines all the days of Samuel.*

Later, when young David went out confidently to face Goliath, he said

> *1 Samuel 17:37 "The Lord that **delivered** me out of the paw of the lion, and out of the paw of the bear **will deliver** me out of the hand of this Philistine."*

> *Job 5:19 He shall **deliver** you in six troubles: yea, in seven there shall no evil touch you.*

*Psalms 34:19 Many are the afflictions of the righteous: but the Lord **delivers** him out of them all.*

*2 Timothy 4:16,17 At my first answer no man stood with me (Paul), but all men forsook me...Notwithstanding the Lord stood with me, and strengthened me,...and I was **delivered** out of the mouth of the lion.*

*2 Peter 2:9 The Lord knows how to **deliver** the godly out of temptations.*

Deliverance is the stated ministry of Yeshua/Melchizedek

*John 8:31-34,36 Then said Jesus to those Jews which believed on him, "If you continue in my Word, then you are my disciples indeed. And you shall know the truth, and the truth shall **make you free**." They answered him, "We are Abraham's seed, and were never in bondage to any man: how can you say, 'You shall be **made free**'?" Jesus answered them, "Verily, verily, I say unto you, Whosoever commits sin is the servant of sin....If the Son therefore shall **make you free**, you shall be free indeed."*

It is not only Jesus' ministry to set us free from our bondages, but the ministry with which he has ordained US has this function, as well. Are there, for example, those in your church who have fears? They need to be helped. They need to know that they can open up to their minister those deep troubling things in their lives: I was abused as a child; I went through a period of time when I was very hungry: Once I was shut up in a dark room all by myself; We were tree climbing, and I slipped; I've been afraid of heights ever since; One time they dunked me in the pool; Dad hit me in public; My parents were always yelling. They need you, dear Christian, to be their Ebenezer, a rock of help!

These wounds and hurts need to be exposed to the Light. It is the job of the shepherds to probe and discover these dark spots in the lives of their flock. These fearful bondages have got to go! Melchizedek will deliver us.

2 Timothy 1:7 For God has not given us the spirit of fear; but of power, and of love, and of a sound mind.

Romans 8:15 For you have not received the spirit of bondage again to fear.

Jesus is Love. Let his love work on you personally to deliver you. If you retain "fears," you will not have perfect love. Open up your heart to the elders; study God's *Word*; pray, and get healed.

*1 John 4:18 There is no fear in love; but perfect love **casts out** fear: because fear has torment. He that fears is not made perfect in love.*

Jesus has come to "set at liberty them that are bound."

Let's consider once more this passage:
Isaiah 61:3 To appoint unto them that mourn in Zion, to give unto them beauty for ashes...
which we have said earlier was Melchizedek's ministry of deliverance. Here's the question: how does he give us beauty for ashes?

The ashes speak of the altar of burnt sacrifice. After the fire had consumed the offering, the ashes fell down under the altar grate. We Christians have been exhorted to:
Romans 12:1 present your bodies a living sacrifice, holy, acceptable unto

God, which is your reasonable service.

Unlike the sacrifices of the Temple, which were killed before being placed upon the altar, we are told that it is reasonable service to God to present ourselves, while yet alive, to be dealt with by circumstances and God, to be burnt up till there is nothing left of us but ashes. It seems that there is not too much of us that is really useful to God, maybe just a few of our ashes. That's what Jesus is looking for: ashes. And then he promises
to give them beauty for ashes.

Let's get all this junk delivered out of our lives by placing them upon the flames. Keep putting your problems there until they are totally consumed. I know this doesn't sound real pleasant, but remember, Jesus has promised to give us
Isaiah 61:3 the oil of joy in the place of mourning.

Psalms 30:11 You have turned for me my mourning into dancing: You have put off my sackcloth, and girded me with gladness.

5. Counseling

Counseling is often necessary, as we have already indicated, to effect deliverance. Jesus is "the Wonderful Counselor (*Isaiah 9:6*),
Psalm 16:7 I will bless the Lord who counsels me; He gives me wisdom in the night. He tells me what to do (TLB).

He has passed this ministry on to his church, also. Paul, for example, knew the wonderful ministry that had been supplied to the churches. He said:

*Romans 15:14 I am persuaded of you, my brethren, that you also are full of goodness, filled with all knowledge, able also to **admonish** one another.*

This word "admonish" is from the Greek word *noutheteo* (noo-thet-eh'-o) meaning: to put in mind, to caution or reprove gently, to counsel, to advise, to warn. (We will look at "counseling" in more detail in Chapter 18.)

Jesus is not going to come down here to Earth to do this, but has enabled us. Paul says that you are "able to admonish one another." Paul proclaimed:
*Colossians 1:28 We preach Jesus, **warning** every man, and **teaching** every man in all wisdom; that we may present every man perfect in Christ Jesus.*

The purpose of counseling is: to present every man perfect in Christ Jesus. By the wisdom the teacher has acquired by 1) having himself been taught by another; 2) having studied the written *Word*; and 3) life's experiences, including divine inspiration; he is able to proclaim the Way of Jesus, warning and teaching.
*Colossians 3:16 Let the Word of Christ dwell in you richly in all wisdom; **teaching** and **admonishing** one another.*

It is obvious from this verse that the "*Word*" must be well-studied and become a part of the minister's life. A man of God must never allow himself to get stale. God has supplied the "*Word*" and will anoint *It* in the hands of the ministry.

It is part of divine order that spiritual teaching is to be supplied to children by their own fathers. We will not say more about that here, except that God has ordained fathers for this ministry, and He will anoint their teaching. It is a great strength to the church when parents do their God-ordained jobs in spiritual ministration to their own off-spring.

> *Ephesians 6:4 Fathers, provoke not your children to wrath: but bring them up in the nurture and **admonition** of the Lord.*

It is often necessary for fathers to counsel (*nou-the-te-o*) and admonish and warn their children. They would do well to consider and teach them the book of *Proverbs*.

Jesus' motive is always redemption. He is able to look past the dreadful, sinful condition of people and see what they can be. This attitude of redemption is always to be foremost in the mind of the people of the church. They must guard themselves against snap-judgments and condemnation when they see a brother or sister in error.

> *2 Thessalonians 3:14,15 And if any man obey not our word by this epistle, note that man, and have no company with him, that he may be ashamed. Yet count him not as an enemy, but **admonish** him as a brother.*

This would be right in line with Jesus' exhortation:

> *Matthew 18:12 Seek that which is gone astray.*

God's people are prone to be wandering sheep. It is necessary for the shepherd to go after them and try to help them get back on track:

> *James 5:19,20 Brethren, if anyone among you wanders from the truth, and someone turns him back, let him know that he who turns a sinner from the error of his way will save a soul from death and cover a multitude of sins.*

> *1 John 5:16 If anyone sees his brother commit a sin that does not lead to death, he should pray and God will give him life.*

> *2 Timothy 2:24-26 The servant of the Lord must not strive; but be gentle unto all men, apt to teach, patient, in meekness **instructing** those that oppose themselves; if God peradventure will give them repentance to the acknowledging of the truth, and that they may recover themselves out of the snare of the devil, who are taken captive by him at his will.*

> *Jude 22,23 ...On some have compassion, making a distinction, but others save with fear, pulling them out of the fire...*

The fire Jude speaks about refers to the judgment of God. What a service it is to pull someone out of the fire of his deadly ways!

> *Galatians 6:1,2 Brethren, if a man be overtaken in a fault, you which are spiritual, **restore** such an one in the spirit of meekness; considering yourself, lest you also be tempted. Bear one another's burdens, and so fulfill the Law of Christ.*

At one point Jesus charged Peter to
> *Luke 22:32 strengthen your brothers.*

If you are strong yourself, you are able to strengthen your brothers. It is absolutely critical that ministers structure their own ways straight, before tending to the flock. If there is something amiss in your own life, you will likely mislead those whom you

counsel. But, if you're in good shape, you may be able to pull them out of the fire, you may be able to admonish, you may be able to warn, you may be able to heal.
> *Hebrews 12:13 And make straight paths for your feet, lest that which is lame be turned out of the way; but let it rather be healed.*

I believe that every single one of us is damaged in some way or another, mostly by things that happened to us in our earliest years. Even the best parent has a bad day and blows up. The child didn't deserve that treatment, but got it anyway. That child has just experienced rejection, a rejection that will be part of his foundation until he gets deliverance. It is in pastoral counseling that these damages from the past come bubbling up to the surface. If the people of the church today need counseling, just wait till you see what's coming in the future! There will be folks who have such addictions, such perversions, such imprisonments, such captivities. "Pastoral counseling" is a prison ministry. Oh! Help set those captives free.

***

We have earlier referred to the following verses, but I'd like to consider them again:
> *Zechariah 6:12,13 Thus says the Lord of hosts, saying, "Behold **the man** whose name is <u>The Branch</u>; and he shall grow up out of his place, and he shall build <u>the temple</u> of the Lord. Even he shall build the temple of the Lord; and he shall bear the glory, and shall sit and rule upon his throne; and he shall be a priest upon his throne: and the counsel of peace shall be between them **both**.*

The "man" Jesus is "The Branch." Today he is building his temple, which is the church, the house of God. The *scripture* says he will "rule upon his throne," which makes us to know that he is a king. But, then it says that will "be a priest upon his throne." So, Jesus is priest and king. And then it says that "the counsel of PEACE shall be between them both." Between both what? Peace is ministered to us through the two offices of priest and king. That's why he, as a priest, is on a throne.

And remember that Jesus is king, not only by natural descent from King David, but, in particular that he is the King of Righteousness, Melchizedek.
> *Hebrews 7:2 First, his name means "king of righteousness"; then also, "king of Salem (Hebrew - shalom)" meaning "king of PEACE."*

> *Hebrews 7:15-17 Jesus is the priest who has come, not according to the Law of a fleshly commandment (The Law of Moses), but according to the power of an endless life. For (God) testifies:*
>> *"You are a priest forever according to the order of Melchizedek."*

> *Hebrews 7:23-25 There were many priests, because they were prevented by death from continuing. But...HE is able to save to the uttermost those who come to God through Him, since HE ever lives.*

Our priest-king is bringing us to Salem, shalom. And, then remember that Jesus
> *Revelations 1:5,6;5:10 has loved us, and washed us from our sins in his own blood, AND has made US **kings and priests** unto God and his Father...He has made us unto our God **kings and priests**: and we shall reign on the earth.*

Jesus has left the earth. He has given his authority to the church.

> *Mark 13:34 For the son of man (i.e., Jesus) is as a man taking a far journey (to heaven), who left his house, and gave authority to his servants.*

What power and authority Jesus has, he has bestowed upon us, his servants. The ministry of Melchizedek did not die two thousand years ago, nor vanish into heaven. We are to be doing it. He "gave authority to his servants." He gave us authority.

> *1 Corinthians 3:9 We are **laborers** together with God.*

> *1 Corinthians 15:58 Therefore, my beloved brethren, be steadfast, unmoveable, always abounding in the **work** of the Lord.*

> *Luke 10:2 Pray you therefore the Lord of the harvest, that he would send forth **laborers** into his harvest.*

What is the ministry of Melchizedek today?
1) Interceding
2) Comforting
3) Serving
4) Delivering
5) Counseling

This list is by no means entire. The Lord's work is vast and extensive. These things Jesus did while on earth. These are the things he is still doing in the earth today by the sponsorship and guiding patronage of the holy spirit and also by and through the individual members of his church and its ordained ministers.

What power and authority has Jesus conferred upon the church in these last days?

1) to declare God's plan of salvation to those who want to hear;
2) to bind up and heal the broken-hearted;
3) to help liberate people from the ungodly things that have a hold on their lives;
4) to release people from the spiritual prisons in which they are bound, including false doctrines and false religions;
5) to heal people from the wounds with which life's ordeals have left them;
6) to comfort those who mourn;
7) to substitute joy in the place of heaviness;
8) to "make disciples" and teach them to be righteous.

This is the power and authority and ministry of Melchizedek TODAY:

> *John 14:12 He that believes on me, the works that I do shall he do also.*

> *Matthew 28:18-20 And Jesus came and spoke to them, saying, "All authority has been given to Me in heaven and on earth.*
> > *Go therefore and make disciples of all the nations,*
> > *baptizing them*
> > *teaching them to observe all things that I have commanded you;*
> *and lo, I am with you always, even to the end of the age." Amen.*

Do you think the early saints followed the Master's instructions? Do you think it is possible for the latter-day church to, also? I do.

This ministry of Melchizedek has been very neglected in Jesus' Church. Re-ordering the Church must include its restoration. It is so critical, that I will say it again in Chapter 21.

We must understand that, not only the ordained ministers, but the entire Church of

Jesus is called to serve. We are so used to being pew-sitters, that our true ministry is forgotten.

Revelation 5:10 You have made us unto our God to be kings and priests...

We do not appreciate our role as kings and priests today. All that we have outlined in this chapter is wanting in the Church. She wanders the calf path of Babylon, yet today.

Chapter 17. THE BASQUE SHEEP HERDER AND THE SHEPHERD PSALM

(Condensed from *The National Wool Grower*, December 1949)

Old Fernando D'Alfonso is a Basque herder employed by one of the big Nevada sheep outfits. He is rated as one of the best sheep rangers in the state, and he should be; for back of him are at least twenty generations of Iberian shepherds.

But D'Alfonso is more than a sheepherder; he is a patriarch of his guild, the traditions and secrets of which have been handed down from generation to generation, just as were those of the Damascus steel temperers and other trade guilds of the pre-medieval age. Despite a thirty-year absence from his homeland, he is still full of the legends, the mysteries, the religious fervor of his native hills.

I sat with him one night under the clear, starry skies, his sheep bedded down beside a pool of sparkling water. As we were preparing to curl up in our blankets, he suddenly began a dissertation in a jargon of *Greek* and *Basque*. When he had finished, I asked him what he had said. In reply, he began to quote in *English* the Twenty-Third *Psalm*. There in the desert I learned the shepherd's literal interpretation of this beautiful poem.

"David and his ancestors," said Alfonso, "knew sheep and their ways, and David has translated a sheep's musing into simple words. The daily repetition of this *Psalm* fills the sheepherder with reverence for his calling. Our guild takes this poem as a lodestone to guide us. It is our bulwark when the days are hot or stormy; when the nights are dark; when wild animals surround our bands. Many of its lines are the statements of the simple requirements and actual duties of a Holy Land shepherd, whether he lives today, or followed the same calling six thousand years ago. Phrase by phrase, it has a well-understood meaning for us."

The Lord is my shepherd;
I shall not want.

"Sheep instinctively know," said D'Alfonso, "that ere they have been folded for the night, the shepherd has planned out their grazing for the morrow. It may be that he will take them back over the same range; it may be that he will go to a new grazing ground. They do not worry. His guidance has been good in the past, and they have faith in the future, because they know he has their well-being in view."

He maketh me to lie down in green pastures.

"Sheep graze from around 3:30 o'clock in the morning until about 10:00. They then lie down for three or four hours rest," said D'Alfonso. "When they are contentedly chewing their cuds, the shepherd knows they are putting on fat. Consequently the good shepherd starts his flocks out in the early hours on the rougher herbage, moving on through the morning to the richer, sweeter grasses, and finally coming with the band to a shady place for its forenoon rest in fine green pastures, best grazing of the day. Sheep, while resting in such happy surroundings, feel contentment."

He leadeth me beside the still waters.

"Every shepherd knows," said the Basque, "that sheep will not drink gurgling water. There are many small springs high in the hills of the Holy Land, whose waters run down the valleys only to evaporate in the desert sun. Although the sheep need the water, they will not drink from these fast-flowing streams. The shepherd must find a place where rocks or erosion have made a little pool, or else he fashions with his hands a pocket sufficient to hold at least a bucketful."

He restoreth my soul.
He leadeth me in the paths of righteousness for His Name's sake

"Holy Land sheep exceed in herding instinct the Spanish Merino or the French Rambouillet," went on D'Alfonso. "Each takes his place in the grazing line in the morning, and keeps the same position throughout the day. Once, however, during the day each sheep leaves its place and goes to the shepherd. Whereupon the shepherd stretches out his hand as the sheep approaches with expectant eyes and mild little baas. The shepherd rubs its nose and ears, scratches its chin, whispers affectionately into its ears. The sheep, meanwhile, rubs against his leg or, if the shepherd is sitting down, nibbles at his ear, and rubs its cheek against his face. After a few minutes of this communion with the master, the sheep returns to its place in the feeding line.

Yea, though I walk through the Valley of the Shadow of Death,
I will fear no evil for thou art with me;

Thy rod and Thy staff they comfort, me.

"There is an actual Valley of the Shadow of Death in Palestine, and every sheep-herder from Spain to Dalmatia knows of it. It is south of the Jericho Road, leading from Jerusalem to the Dead Sea, and is a narrow defile through a mountain range. Climatic grazing conditions make it necessary for sheep to be moved through this valley for seasonal feeding each year.

"The valley is four-and-a-half miles long. Its side walls are over a thousand feet high in places, and it is only ten or twelve feet wide at the bottom. Travel through the valley is dangerous, because its floor, badly eroded by cloud bursts, has gullies seven or eight feet deep. Actual footing on solid rock is so narrow that in many places a sheep cannot turn around, and it is an unwritten law of shepherds that flocks must go up the valley in the morning hours, and down toward the eventide, lest flocks meet in the defile. Mules have not been able to make the trip for centuries, but sheep and goat herders from earliest Old-Testament days have maintained passage for their stock.

"About halfway through the valley the walk crosses from one side to the other at a place where the path is cut in two by an eight-foot gully. One section of the path is about eighteen inches higher than the other. The sheep must jump across it. The shepherd stands at this break and coaxes or forces the sheep to make the leap. If a sheep slips and falls in the gully, the shepherd's rod is brought into play. The old-style crook is encircled around a large sheep's neck or a small sheep's chest, and is lifted to safety. If a more-narrow, modern crook is used, the sheep is caught about the hoofs and lifted up to the walk.

"Many wild dogs lurk in the shadows of the valley, looking for prey. After a band of sheep has entered this defile, the leader may come upon such a dog. Unable to retreat, the leader baas a warning. The shepherd, skilled in throwing his staff, hurls it at the dog and knocks the animal into the washed out gully where it is easily killed. Thus the sheep have learned to fear no evil even in the Valley of the Shadow of Death, for their master is there to aid them and protect. them from harm."

Thou preparest a table before me in the presence of mine enemies.

"David's meaning is a simple one," said D'Alfonso, "when conditions on the Holy Land sheep ranges are known. Poisonous plants abound which are fatal to grazing animals. Each spring the shepherd must be constantly alert. When he finds the plants he takes his mattock and goes on ahead of the sheep, grubbing out every stock and root he can see. As he digs out the stocks he lays them upon little stone pyres, some of which were built by shepherds in Old-Testament days, and by the morrow they are dry enough to burn. In the meantime the sheep are led into the newly prepared pasture, which is now free from poisonous plants, and, in the presence of their deadly plant enemies, they eat in peace."

Thou anointest my head with oil; my cup runneth over.

"At every sheepfold there is a big earthen bowl of olive oil and a large stone jar of water. As the sheep come in for the night, they are led to a gate. The shepherd lays his rod across the top of the gateway just higher than the back of his sheep. As each sheep passes in single file, he quickly examines it for briers in the ears, snags in the cheek, or weeping of the eyes from dust or scratches. When such conditions are found, he drops the rod across the sheep's back, and it steps out of line.

"Each sheep's wounds are carefully cleaned. Then the shepherd dips his hand into the olive oil and anoints the injury. A large cup is dipped into the jar of water, kept cool by evaporation in the unglazed pottery, and is brought out--never half-full, but always overflowing. The sheep will sink its nose into the water clear to the eyes, if fevered, and drink until fully refreshed.

"When all the sheep are at rest, the shepherd lays his staff on the ground within reach in case it is needed for protection of the flock during the night, wraps himself in his heavy woolen robe, and lies down cross the gateway, facing the sheep, for his night's repose.

"So," concluded D'Alfonso, "after all the care and protection the shepherd has given it, a sheep may well soliloquize in the twilight, as translated into words by David:

*Surely goodness and mercy shall follow me all the days of my life:
and I will dwell in the house of the Lord forever."*

***

Of the five offices of the ministry, it is that of the shepherd that is most intimate with the saints. This beautiful account of the twenty third *Psalm* has been included, because I believe it portrays the relationship between the ministry and the people and vice versa, close, warm, friendly, personal, confidential. The other offices of the ministry have not this kind of association, connection, affiliation, rapport, bond, liaison with the church. While all the offices of the ministry are absolutely necessary for a complete church, as the position and function of today's "pastor" if so aloof, detached, unapproachable, standoffish, and superior, the personal needs of the congregation are not being met.

In Hannah Hurnard's masterful allegory, "Hinds Feet in High Places," the shepherd impressed Much Afraid, the book's main character, that all she ever needed to do was to cry, "Shepherd, I need you," and He would appear. Since, the ministers of the church carry out the Melchizedekal office and functions today, those men ought to be very available to their flocks. "Shepherd, I need you." How comforting! What solace! Church ought to be such.

May I highly recommend Hurnard's book.

Shepherd Rescuing His Sheep

Marriage Counseling

Chapter 18. Pastoral Counseling (*Noutheteo*)

God has ordained in the organization of the church that all the members grow into mature, healthy Christians. Jesus has given numerous helps to the church, including the indwelling of the holy spirit, the cross, the gifts of the spirit, the fellowship of the saints, and the gift of ministry. We wish to amplify here some points made in Chapter 15, The Ministry of Melchizedek Today.

It is God's purpose that each saint be transformed inwardly to become like His son.
> *Romans 8:29 For whom He did foreknow, He also did predestinate to be conformed to the image of His son...*

Regarding the ministry, it has been designed that they are to serve the rest of the members of the body
> *Ephesians 4:12 for the perfecting (equipping) of the saints, for the work of the ministry (service), for the edifying of the body of Christ:*

The purpose of the ministry is to help the members mature so that each one in turn may learn how to serve the church and build it up. Jesus called this kind of instruction "making disciples."
> *Matthew 28:19 Go therefore, and teach (make disciples of) all nations...*

> *Matthew 13:52 Every scribe which is instructed (that is, discipled) into the kingdom of heaven is like unto a man that is an householder, which brings forth out of his treasure* Word of the Lord *things new and old.*

Barnabas and Saul illustrated Jesus' plan in their first missionary journey:
> *Acts 14:21,22 And when they had preached the gospel to that city and had taught (had discipled) many, they returned again to Lystra, and to Iconium, and Antioch, confirming the souls of the disciples, and exhorting (strengthening and encouraging) them to continue in the faith, and that we must through much tribulation enter into the kingdom of God.*

We see the tender care, diligence and concern they had for the saints. Part of their care was preaching and teaching. These must be very important divine tools in the church. Preaching is mentioned fifty five times in the *New Testament*, and teaching is mentioned ninety eight times.
> *Acts 15:35 Paul also and Barnabas continued in Antioch, teaching and preaching the, with many others also.*

Part of the ministry of discipling and teaching and preaching is "counseling." The *Greek* word for this is *nou-thet-e'-o*, which is usually translated in the *King James* as "warn" and "admonish."

When Paul was near the end of his ministry he called the elders of the church of Ephesus to meet with him, knowing it would be his last opportunity to speak to them. He reminded them that it was the holy spirit that had ordained them to the ministry. He recalled to their attention that they had been given oversight of the flock of God. He commended them to continue to feed the people.
> *Acts 20:28, 31 Take heed therefore unto yourselves, and to all the flock,*

> *over the which the Holy Ghost has made you overseers, to **feed the church** of God, which he (Jesus) has purchased with his own blood.*

He then recounted his own ministry to them (which was far longer than he had given to any other church). He recalled the passion and intensity and devotion he had given to them.
> *Acts 20:31 Therefore watch, and remember, that by the space of three years I ceased not to **warn** every one night and day with tears.*

The word "warn" above is *nou-thet-e'-o*, that is, to counsel or admonish. Paul had likewise used this word in his reprimand of the Corinthian church:
> *1 Corinthians 4:14 I write not these things to shame you, but as my beloved sons I **warn** you.*

He also had told the church in Rome that they, themselves, were capable of counseling and admonishing.
> *Romans 15:14 And I myself also am persuaded of you, my brethren, that you also are full of goodness, filled with all knowledge, able also to **admonish** one another.*

Counseling is one of the most important parts of ministering to people. In my own pastoring experience I have realized that the help of the holy spirit is essential. Often, people are not readily forthcoming with all the truth. Sometimes they don't even know what the facts really are. It is then that a counselor needs divine help.
> *1 Corinthians 12:8 For to one is given by the spirit the word of wisdom; to another the **word of knowledge** by the same spirit;*

> *1 Corinthians 14:6 Now, brethren, if I come unto you speaking with tongues, what shall I profit you, except I shall speak to you either by revelation, or by **knowledge**, or by prophesying, or by doctrine?*

In the foregoing verses, when Paul uses the word "knowledge," I think he is meaning the "gift of the word of knowledge."

Once when I was counseling a young man, he asserted that he felt cut off from God. He couldn't understand why. "What have you been doing?" the spirit prompted me to ask.

"Well," he replied, "I have been misusing a prescription drug for dieting to get high on."

I said, "That's not it."

"What do you mean 'That's not it'?" he retorted.

I responded, "That's not what's cutting you off from God."

"Okay," he said. He mentioned something else he was doing, to which I again returned, "That's not it." He became irate. "What do you want from me? I'm spilling my guts."

"That's not it."

"Why do you say, 'That's not it?"

"The holy ghost tells me 'That's not it'."

"Okay, okay," he whined. "I've been stealing money from my mom's wallet."

"That's it!" I exclaimed.

This was a gift of a word of knowledge. Now, we had gotten to the crux of the problem. Now, we were getting somewhere by the spirit's help. I told him all was not lost; the Lord knew his weakness; Jesus still loved him. He broke down in tears. Now, it was time for words of wisdom from that same holy spirit. This was a serious problem, but not unforeseen by God. There was an attitude of repentance developing. He wanted to make restitution. We were going to be able to work through this predicament. Thanks be to God!

Recently, I was counseling with a couple who had been married for seventeen years. For most of those years the wife had not trusted the husband. When he would go to the bank, she was suspicious why it was taking him so long. When she saw him conversing with a sister in church, she was suspecting there was something going on.

Needless to say, this was causing a repressive relationship in the marriage. The husband admitted that in the army, years back, he had been overly kind to women officers. There had been no improper contact, but he knew there was that intent on these ladies' parts. I saw that it had flattered his ego. But, when they had called him at home, it understandably had provoked the wife.

I felt, in privately meeting with him, that he loved his wife. He realized he was the cause of her indignation. He had discontinued these bad relationships flat out. He acknowledged he had caused his wife's mistrust. But, her attitude would not be dissuaded.

The holy spirit revealed to me that there was something else that was undermining her trust. This is why it is such a blessing for married couples to be able to share their problems with a spirit-filled pastor-shepherd-counselor. It was revealed to me that they had had relations before they were married. This they admitted. I told them that even though they had ultimately married one another, they had transgressed God's law. When they were having these illicit relations, they were well aware that they were sinning, but, they had given in to their lust. Because of that flaw in the foundation of their marriage, mistrust had developed. "If he would sin with me," she was reasoning, "what will keep him from sinning with someone else?"

We dealt with this very simply. Standing, facing one another, they confessed aloud that they had sinned against God AND against one another before their marriage. They acknowledged it was still haunting them. They repented, asking God and one another for forgiveness. The wife has agreed that whenever she might get a suspicious thought she would lay it upon the altar. She would give these notions to Jesus. This is having a marvelous effect with this couple. Again, it was the work of the holy ghost that brought good results.

In marriage advising, the counselor should lift up the husband's reputation in the wife's eyes. He ought not impugn the husband nor denigrate his opinions nor correct him in a humiliating way. He should elevate the husband's standing with his wife. When a man may have severely strayed from righteousness, the shepherd should be careful in denouncing or deprecating him, hoping that they shall once again be restored to marital bliss. He must be cautious in relating to all women, married or otherwise, because he is only the head of one lady, his own wife.

I think one of the most important things for a counselor is to care about people. He must come to a place where his attitude about a person is like what Christ's attitude would be. Good counselors become deeply sensitive, compassionate, and empathetic. Paul said

> *2 Corinthians 11:29 Who is weak, and I am not weak? who is offended, and I burn not?*

> *Galatians 4:19 My little children, of whom I travail in birth again until Christ be formed in you...*

> *1 Thessalonians 2:7,8 But we were gentle among you, even as a nurse cherishes her children: So being affectionately desirous of you, we were willing to have imparted unto you, not the gospel of God only, but also our own souls, because you were dear unto us.*

Do you see how deeply Paul cared? His was not some salaried nine-to-five job; Paul really felt the joy and sorrows of the people in his inner-most being. Without doubt this made him a good "discipler." With all modesty he could tell the people that they might emulate him in living their lives.

And that is precisely how the church grows well.
> *2 Timothy 2:2 And the things you have heard from me among many witnesses, the same commit to faithful men, who shall be able to teach others also.*

Look at the impact of that verse. We have in one sentence the passing-on, through four generations, truth about the Kingdom of God. What you heard from me, commit to faithful men, who will teach others also. This is how the kingdom of God spreads out. This is how an effective church increases: me, you, more faithful men, others also.

This growth is not just numerical; it consists of the substantial increase in the personal lives of all the members.
> *Philippians 4:9 Those things, which you have both learned, and received, and heard, and seen in me, DO...*

Not only what Paul had preached and taught, but the things they had "seen" in his life were worth copying. This was not pulpit-to-pew ministry. Those people saw Paul daily. He could not have exhorted them to imitate his actions and behavior had they not often been with him. I think the more important thing in discipleship is relationship rather than preaching. Let's be very bold and say that a whole lot of preaching, even years of it, isn't worth nearly what seeing it lived in the flesh is. Sometimes, there's a whole lot of counseling done without even one word being spoken. It needn't be spoken; it is lived; it is observed; it is emulated.

If you find it easier to preach to the crowd, raise up some real shepherds while it is still today! Shepherd/counselors are needed!

I've already said that counseling and preaching and teaching were vital. But, association is even moreso. I think there is a real lack in the body of Christ of real, true discipleship. Quite frankly, there are not enough elder/pastors for the numbers of people who need to be served. May I remind you that the Master limited himself to but twelve. Recall the close and constant fellowship he had with those few. Remember how he dealt with them, how he rebuked them, corrected them, advised them, encouraged them. Do you think he could have accomplished that behind a

Babylonious pulpit? Could he have been able to intimately counsel the multitudes?

Let us be quite clear about the ministry: they are God's gift to the church, and their purpose is to produce mature Christians.
> *Colossians 1:27,28 ...Christ in you, the hope of glory: Whom we preach, **warning** (noutheteo) every man, and **teaching** every man in all wisdom; that we may present every man perfect (mature) in Christ Jesus:*

> *Colossians 3:16 Let the word of Christ dwell in you richly in all wisdom; **teaching** and **admonishing** (noutheteo) one another...*

> *1 Thessalonians 5:12-14 Now we exhort you, brethren, **warn** (noutheteo) them that are unruly, comfort the feebleminded, support the weak, be patient toward all men.*

How are the saints to regard this kind of ministry? They are not only to support them, but they are to regard them greatly. After all, these men have given up their own lives to serve Christ and his church.
> *v13 And we beseech you, brethren, to know them which labor among you, and are over you in the Lord, and admonish (noutheteo) you; and to esteem them very highly in love for their work's sake.*

In their day-to-day work among the flock, the shepherds will be confronted with many different situations, some which may seem impossible, others, shocking. They must keep in mind that God is never surprised by the things His people do. They also must know that their oversight comes from on High, and that they are bestowed with much authority.

> *2 Thessalonians 3:14,15 And if any man obey not our word by this epistle, note that man, and have no company with him, that he may be ashamed. Yet count him not as an enemy, but admonish (noutheteo) him as a brother.*

Let's suppose that a man in the congregation is having an affair with his step-mother. The elder confronts him and counsels him, but he will not listen.
> *Matthew 18:16,17 But if he will not hear you, then take with you one or two more, that in the mouth of two or three witnesses every word may be established. And if he shall neglect to hear them, tell it unto the church: but if he neglect to hear the church, let him be unto you as an heathen man and a publican.*

Brother Shepherd, are you bold enough to do that? Is it in your heart to "confront?" Jesus has given the ministry that authority. As Paul put it:
> *1 Corinthians 5:5 Deliver such an one unto Satan for the destruction of the flesh, that the spirit may be saved in the day of the Lord Jesus.*

(Great authority has been given by the Head. Use it wisely.) Now then, the church has "shunned" this person. But, the elder is still willing to get together with him and to admonish him again. This man is not an enemy; he has just yielded himself to obey his carnal nature. However, the protection of God's covering has been removed; it is no telling what might befall him. This, of course, would be the mercy of God, trying to draw him or her back into the fold. The angels would rejoice over such a turn of events.

I have seen some ministers who seemingly had failed for the time being to convince a person of his wrong-doing. They ought to wait; God hasn't finished working in this situation. Give place to God. Sometimes, rather than doing that, the minister may be offended that his advice was not heeded. He may take on a judgmental attitude. He may give up.

There is a saying they teach at the Baptist Seminary in Louisville: If your faith fizzled at the finish, it wasn't fit at the first.

So then, it's okay to give up on the saint. There was a flaw in their foundation to begin with. But, I believe much more pastoral effort should be given to the weak and to the feeble.

There was one sister in our church who I had never seen. I don't know what she had been doing all those years, but she did not appear in church. But then, she got cancer. Immediately, she became a regular attender. She sought out the pastor. She became a prayer-warrior. As the painful cancer spread in her body, she testified in church: "God knows what He's doing." All of the sudden she had become a paragon of faith. She left this life in a blaze of glory.

What might it have been had her name been dropped from the rolls? What might it have been had the pastor ignored her all those wayward years?

The oversight which God has given to the ministry bears awesome responsibility. The man of God must be prepared at any moment's notice to swing into action.

*2 Timothy 3:16 All scripture is given by inspiration of God, and is profitable for doctrine, for reproof, for **correction**, for **instruction** in righteousness:*

*2 Timothy 4:2 Preach the word; be instant in season, out of season; **reprove**, **rebuke**, **exhort** with all long-suffering and doctrine (patience and instruction).*

The pastor/shepherds of the church are to keep watch over the flock. This is not an option. God has given them the grave responsibility of a "watchman."

Ezekiel 33:2-6 Son of man, speak to the children of your people, and say to them, "When I bring the sword upon a land, if the people of the land take a man of their coasts, and set him for their watchman: if when he sees the sword come upon the land, he blow the trumpet, and warn the people; Then whosoever hears the sound of the trumpet, and takes not warning; if the sword come, and take him away, his blood shall be upon his own head. He heard the sound of the trumpet, and took not warning; his blood shall be upon him. But he that takes warning shall deliver his soul. But if the watchman see the sword come, and blow not the trumpet, and the people be not warned; if the sword come, and take any person from among them, he is taken away in his iniquity; but his blood will I require at the watchman's hand."

*1 Timothy 5:20-23 Them that sin **rebuke before all**, that others also may fear. I charge you before God, and the Lord Jesus Christ, and the elect angels, that you observe these things without preferring one before another, doing nothing by partiality. Lay hands suddenly on no man, neither be partaker of other men's sins: keep thyself pure.*

Bro. Pastor, do you do this? Elders are watchmen. They ought not let anything slip between the cracks. They are to be vigilant. This is the very reason that many shepherds are required for each local assembly!

The foregoing verse is often misunderstood, but taken in context, it is obviously dealing with sin in the church, possibly even in the life of one of the fellow-ministers as we discussed in Chapter 14. When Paul says, "Lay hands suddenly on no man," he is using that expression "lay hands on" as if to arrest or stop someone. His instruction is: "Don't be too quick to point out someone's fault." Why would he say that? Paul wants them to give the wayward saint time to receive correction from his conscience and from his holy spirit. It is important that all church members exercise sensitivity to God's spirit, which cannot happen, if the pastor becomes their conscience. So then, if the pastor steps in too quickly, he doesn't give the Lord opportunity to get through.

On the other hand, the pastor ought not let things go on and on, never taking action. Then he will become like Ezekiel's watchman who gave no warning. The sinner died in his sin, and the blood guiltiness fell upon the sinner, as well as the watchman. By allowing sin to go unchecked, the shepherd becomes partaker of the sin, himself. His silence is like tacit approval of the transgression. He is a partaker of the sin, because he gave no counsel.

You may not see the above passages as I have expressed them. Nevertheless, the principle put forth is absolutely right.

Counseling is one of the most serious and important jobs of the man of God. He must always keep himself in good spiritual condition, praying often, fasting, continuously reading the *Word*.

And on top of all that, he must be
1 Timothy 3:2 given to hospitality

> *Titus 1:7-9 For a bishop must be blameless, as the steward of God; not self-willed, not soon angry, not given to wine, no striker, not given to filthy lucre; But a lover of hospitality, a lover of good men, sober, just, holy, temperate; Holding fast the faithful word as he has been taught, that he may be able by sound doctrine both to exhort and to convince the gainsayers.*

All the aforementioned qualifications are obvious except "hospitality." Why must a bishop, that is, an overseer or shepherd/elder, love to be hospitable? It would not do for a pastor to be very private or wrapped up in his own family or in his favorite hobby. He's got to be right in there at many times with those in his oversight. He must enjoy having people in his home. He must be hospitable. His life and his wife's life are not their own. They belong to God.

Therefore, he must be generous, not only with his things, but with himself. God will cause His ministers, even the most pious, shy, backward, meek ones to become open, jolly, social, gregarious, and congenial. I have personally witnessed this miraculous transformation in the demeanor of my own pastor after he was ordained. (There is much to commend the laying-on-of-hands in ordination.)

Another reason for having this hospitable trait is that he may be hosting a church in his home. It would surely take a hospitable person to have an assembly in one's home, wouldn't it?

Furthermore, a shepherd-pastor-counselor should carry himself in somewhat of a "fatherly" manner, kind, benevolent, firm, tender. The following advice to a parent should well-apply to any instructor:

> *Ephesians 6:4 And you, fathers, do not provoke your children to wrath, but bring them up in the training and admonition* (noutheteo) *of the Lord.*

When a parent confronts a child, it is usually unpleasant for the youngster. But, a gentle, pleasant approach softens the blow. The same tactic applies in counseling, especially when the counselee might become agitated, uneasy, disturbed, or shaken.

> *Proverbs 15:1 A soft answer turns away wrath, but a harsh word stirs up anger.*

But, on the other hand, a pastor must not fear offending. Often he must confront wrong "point-blank." He must ask the leading question that brings forth the devastating answer. He may need to probe, to prod, to bare. He may need to peel back layers of "fig leaves" with which we're so prone to cover ourselves.

The sheep have wounds hiding behind wounds, scars of many years past, hurts forgotten except in the subconscious, debilitating bruises, crippling spiritual maladies. God intends for them to all be healed. That is why He put them in the Church. He has provided the office of the shepherd for that purpose. Wounded sheep need not preaching; to them the pulpit is of no avail!!!!! They need to be interrogated, probed, confronted, warned, covered with balm.

Pastors are not preachers per se; if you are a preacher, you may rather be a prophet or an evangelist, but you will not have the aptitude of a pastor/shepherd. Prophets and evangelists do not have the same heart as a shepherd.

Before, concluding, I might insert something else about my pastor: he has the "spirit of counsel," which is one of the things prophesied about Jesus (*Isaiah 11:2*). I think it must be a treasured gift to have the ability at almost any time to say just the right word, utter a warning, give good advice, bring peace, and convey reconciliation. It's a tremendous blessing to have the "spirit of counsel" operating in a church. In associating with him, the other elders will pick up some of that spirit; it will be imparted to them.

All of these things are required of elders: they instruct on the kingdom of heaven; they counsel; they're on the watch; they're given to hospitality; they have diligent, tender care for the saints, as John[*1] would say:

> *3 John 4 I have no greater joy than to hear that my children walk in truth.*

Right there is a shepherd's heart.

<><><>

*1 We have quoted in this book pastoral statements, not from pastors, but from Paul and John, who were apostles. And, within the person of the apostle lays the attributes of the pastor, as well as the prophet, teacher, and evangelist. A great difference between apostles and shepherds is this: apostles are sent from a local church to go out and establish new works; pastors are raised up in the local church, and, as long as they are serving as a shepherd, they are <u>not</u> mobile, but remain bound to their local church; they have not the inclination to travel.

We have principally dealt with the office of shepherd. The other ministerial offices are vitally important to the success of the Body of Christ, which will never accomplish its assigned purpose in the latter day without all their proper functionings. I felt it critical to deal herein with one particular duty of the shepherd.

Chapter 19. Restoring The Ministry of Prophets

Surely our fathers have inherited lies! Jeremiah 16:19

When Jehovah brought out the children of Israel from Egypt, He began to reveal to them His Ways and His Secrets. It was the intention from the beginning that God would raise up a people from this world to rule and reign over the earth with Him. In the end there will be those overcomers who will say: "(Jesus Christ)
> *Revelation 5:10 has made us to be kings and priests unto our God: and we shall reign on the earth."*

Not all at the first understood the God-Plan. But, Moses certainly did:
> *Psalm 103:7 God made known his Ways unto Moses, His Acts unto the children of Israel.*

The Israelites saw the mighty acts of God in Egypt, at the Red Sea, in the Wilderness, at Mount Sinai. They could not help but see the manna He provided them daily, nor the cloud by day nor the fire by night, nor the Rock from which gushed living water for them. They knew God by "His Acts." But, Moses had a deeper revelation: He knew "the Ways" of God. God did not share this intimacy with the rest of the people. God kept His Secrets to Himself. Moses explained that "the secret things belong to the Lord."

However, from time to time the Almighty allows us to peer behind the veil; sometimes He gives us a glimpse.
> *Deuteronomy 29:29 The secret things belong unto the Lord our God: but those things which are revealed belong unto us.*

And, when the Lord DOES reveal things to us, they not only belong to us, but He holds us responsible for them. He expects us to be good stewards of the treasures He shares with us. Jesus says it will be required of us to be good custodians of that with which Heaven blesses us.
> *Luke 12:48 For everyone to whom much is given, from him much will be required.*

Perhaps that which the Almighty has bestowed upon you is not really for your benefit at all, but for that someone or the many with whom you share it. Perhaps you are to be that divine conduit by which others are blessed, are edified, are revealed the things of God, are helped, are consoled.

God is so very desirous to share His vastness with a people who are His. He wants to share His Secrets. In many generations the Lord has raised up prophets to proclaim His Plans. As a matter of fact, the sovereign Lord does nothing without first revealing His Plan to His servants, the prophets.
> *Amos 3:7 Surely the Lord God will do nothing, but He reveals His Secret unto his servants, the **prophets**.*

When Jesus was here on the earth, he functioned for three-and-one-half years in the office of a prophet. John, the Baptist, made this observation of the Christ:
> *John 3:34 For he whom God has sent speaks the Words of God, for God gives the spirit without measure.*

John, the Baptist, was a prophet. And, Jesus himself was a prophet. He spoke the Words of God. He revealed God's secrets to those who had ears to hear him. Although they did not fully understand him at the first, he said:

John 14:29 And now I have told you before it come to pass, that, when it is come to pass, you might believe.

Another time Jesus said:
John 13:19 Now I tell you before it come, that, when it is come to pass, you may believe that I am he.

God revealed to Noah that He would bring the deluge. He revealed to Abraham and Lot that He would destroy the cities of the plain. He showed Joseph the seven years' famine in Egypt. He disclosed to Jonah the destruction of Nineveh that they who heard of the coming punishment, might either avoid it by repentance, or, if they should despise it, might be more justly punished. He showed through Joshua all the chastisements that would befall the people, if they rejected God's Word:
Joshua 24:20 If you forsake the Lord and serve foreign gods, then He will turn and do you harm and consume you, after He has done you good.

In each age God has spoken through his prophets. His revelation of Himself has been continuous and on-going.

God wants to proceed in giving revelation in this very day we live. But, I fear that the great Creator of the Universe desires to be far more intimate with us then we suspect or even desire. Therefore, we, no doubt, miss a great deal that could be ours. Some people have no interest at all in God's opinion, His Way, His Will, His Purpose.
Psalm 82:5 They know not, neither will they understand; they walk on in darkness.

John 3:19 And this is the condemnation, that light is come into the world, and men loved darkness rather than light, because their deeds were evil.

And then there are those upon whom God has just absolutely delighted. Abraham had much favor with God, Who said:
Genesis 18:17 "Shall I hide from Abraham that thing which I do?"

There was something about Abraham that God loved. What does God look for in us? What is it about a man that grabs God's attention? I think it is the attitude we have toward the Almighty. Do we know Him enough to fear Him? To whom will the Almighty God reveal His Promises?
Psalm 25:14 The Secret of the Lord is with them that fear Him; and He will show them His Covenant.

The fourth chapter of *2 Kings* deals with the relationship of the prophet Elisha and a great woman from Shunem, whose son died. Elisha had been very confident that he had always been able to hear from God and to know what to say and to do. But, this day he had not received information from God.
2 Kings 4:27 The Lord has hid it from me, and has not told me.

Elisha seems to have been comfortable with that, too. He trusted God, and he feared God. Prophets of the future ought to keep this event in mind.

To know the awesome power of God will cause one to fear. That is attractive to God. But, many, even most, bumble through life, even some in the Church, having no clue to the majesty, power, and revelation of Christ. They have little regard for Him. Of course, God is not going to reveal His Covenant to them. They wouldn't know what to do with it, if they did have it. They, perhaps, are the weeds growing in the Lord's garden. Oh, the Lord is looking for those with whom He can be intimate! That is just what Jesus was looking for in his disciples.

John 15:15,16 No longer do I call you servants, for a servant does not know what his master is doing; but I have called you friends, for all things that I heard from My Father I have made known to you.

To be called "a servant of God" is great. But greater is he whom the Lord calls "a friend."

In the earliest days of the church in Jerusalem there were many who served God and were called to the ministry. There were five offices of the ministry, apostles, prophets, evangelists, shepherds, and teachers. This is the complete ministry of the church, and we understand that all these offices were and ARE necessary in the Church of God.

However, about fifty years after the Church was inaugurated on the Day of Pentecost, the structure of the House of God, the Church, began to be altered. Gradually, the Judaizers began to have greater influence on the composition and organization of the Church. Regressively, the "synagogic" style began to hold sway. The pastors, who had then-to-for been careful shepherds of the Flock of God, began to take on a rabbinic mode. Rather than being "counselors," they became "preachers." They acted like the rabbis.

At the same time the church gradually eliminated the other four offices. After a while there were no apostles, no prophets, no evangelists, no teachers. The church had only ordained pastors. Eventually, some pastors began to acquire influence in particular geographic areas and achieved the title of "bishop." Then, certain bishops gained considerably more power and became "arch-bishops." Ultimately, the Bishop of Rome became the Pope.

Gone was the simplicity of the early church. Gone was its spiritual power, too. But, the church did gain political power, influence, and wealth. Furthermore, as the church spread to different countries, it amalgamated the pagan customs of those lands into the ritual of the church.

The apostasy, the falling-away, of the church was already beginning in the years of the apostle Paul's ministry. The Light of Christ which had gloriously gleamed, had gradually faded, bringing the whole world into the Dark Ages. Not only was spiritual understanding dissipated, but scientific knowledge languished. The world was plunged into centuries of darkness. There may have been a vestige of the holy church that came out of the upper room, but history records precious little, if nothing of its actual existence.

When the Protestant Reformation began in earnest in sixteenth century Europe, the simplest understandings of truth began to thrill the hearts of men and women who had been suspecting there was something better than what they had been experiencing, something more than the pomp and finery of Rome.

For the last five centuries the God of Heaven has been slowly moving, slowly restoring His Church. It has been happening, not ever by any human power or initiative, but at the direction of the holy spirit. As a sail boat does not move on its own power, but as the wind impels it, so has the Church of Christ been directed in its recovery.

William Sowders was one who saw and appreciated the moves of God taking place in the twentieth century. He saw that the most recent apostasies of the Church were the first ones to be corrected. He reasoned that **the steps of the restoration of the church would take place in the reverse order of their falling away. In other words, the first steps in the apostasy would be the last phases** of the repairing and healing of the Body of Christ.

As we have noted, the first digressions of the early church were Judaization, synagogation, the corruption of the office of the pastor, and the complete eradication of the other four offices. These then, are to be the last restorations of the Church, the last moves of God in bringing the glorious manifestations of Christ on the earth as a last witness and testament to the gentile nations before the end of this age.

Much could be drawn from the *Scriptures* declaring what the true order of the early church was and what the latter church will be, but we would like to confine our remarks herein to the office and ministry of Prophets, because they are the ones who first see divine light and proclaim it.

We get a very good picture of this office from Peter when he was discussing the salvation by Jesus Christ that had been prophesied throughout the *Old Testament*:
*1 Peter 1:10-12 Of this salvation the **prophets** have inquired and searched carefully, who **prophesied** of the grace that would come to you, searching what, or what manner of time, the spirit of Christ...in them was indicating when (the spirit) testified beforehand the sufferings of Christ and the glories that would follow. To (the prophets) it was revealed that, not to themselves, but to us they were ministering the things which now have been reported to you through those who have preached the Gospel to you by the holy spirit sent from heaven -- things which angels desire to look into.*

Those prophets of yore were inspired by the holy ghost to speak of the coming of the Christ, the Messiah. They realized that their message did not apply to the Age in which they were living. They understood that the words they were uttering were meant for the benefit of the congregation that would follow the Christ when He finally appeared.
Psalm 22:30,31 A seed shall serve him; it shall be accounted to the Lord for a generation. They shall come, and shall declare his righteousness unto a people that shall be born...

Peter declared that even the heavenly hosts were supremely interested in these prophetic messages.

Of course, there were many "false" prophets throughout the centuries. They were a dime a dozen, so to speak. No one ever had to contend with the false prophets more than Jeremiah. When God spoke through Jeremiah, he said:
*Jeremiah 23:28 The **prophet** that has a dream, let him tell a dream; and he that has My Word, let him speak My Word faithfully.*

God's *Word* is to be spoken as absolute truth, faithfully spoken. What then would you say would be a good test for the validity of a prophet?
*Jeremiah 28:9 When the word of the **prophet** shall come to pass, then shall the **prophet** be known, that the Lord has truly sent him.*

There is an awe about a prophet of God, a mystique. They see the truth of God in any situation. Therefore, they are to be feared.

False prophets may conjure up some kind of spectacle, but Moses warned in the *Law* that they are not worth considering:

> *Deuteronomy 18:22 When a **prophet** speaks in the Name of the Lord, if the thing does not happen or come to pass, that is the thing which the Lord has NOT spoken; the **prophet** has spoken it presumptuously; you shall not be afraid of him.*

No. A false prophet is not to be feared. But, this implies that true prophets ARE to be feared. Prophecies demand our earnest attention. We should give all heed to them as we would to a lamp in a dark cave. Ezekiel plainly declared the sign of a true prophet:

> *Ezekiel 33:33 And when this comes to pass -- surely it will come -- then they will know that a **prophet** has been among them.*

The prophet whom God has sent speaks the Words of God. It is no small thing which he speaks. His words are God's Words. A prophet says what bears upon his mind by a foreign influence, from another world. His utterances are inspired from Heaven. Thus Peter explained:

> *2 Peter 1:21 For the **prophecy** came not in old time by the will of man: but holy men of God spoke as they were moved by the holy ghost.*

Paul was very particular that what he uttered was absolutely correct.

> *2 Corinthians 2:17 For we are not like many others, who corrupt the Word of God: but as of sincerity, but as of God, in the sight of God we speak in Christ.*

Not only did Paul speak "in Christ," that is, by the inspiration of Christ, but He declared that his utterances were as if they had been spoken by God:

> *1 Thessalonians 2:13 For this cause we also thank God without ceasing, because, when you received the* Word of God *which you heard from me, you received it not as the word of man, but as it is in truth, the Word of God, which effectually works also in you who believe.*

It behooves men of the ministry to choose their words carefully. For that matter, so should every Christian. Thus did Jesus, our example:

> *John 17:8 I have given to them the words which You have given Me.*

In the dark night of this present age God has given us His Word, both Written Word of the *Bible* and present-day prophetic utterance. Their purpose is to shed light on our way. It is the only true light we have respective the future and guiding us to eternity. How blessed we are to have prophecy.

It tells us what is necessary for us to know about God, our duty, the way of salvation. The first prophet mentioned in the Church Age was Barnabas. After the scattering of the saints in the first persecution, the news reached Jerusalem that many saints had relocated in Antioch, Syria, and that they had begun a church there. This assembly was not begun by the work of an apostle, nor was it in order. To help Antioch, Barnabas was sent.

> *Acts 11:22-24 Then news of these things came to the ears of the Church in Jerusalem, and they sent out Barnabas to go as far as Antioch. When he came and had seen the grace of God, he was glad, and **encouraged** them all that with purpose of heart they should continue with the Lord.*

For he was a good man, full of the holy spirit and of faith. And a great many people were added to the Lord.

Eventually, in the Antioch assembly there were five men who were respectively either a prophet or a teacher. At least one other beside Barnabas was a prophet, who was functioning in the local church. Paul was one of the ordained teachers in the assembly.

*Acts 13:1-3 Now in the church that was at Antioch there were certain **prophets** and teachers: Barnabas, Simeon who was called Niger, Lucius of Cyrene, Manaen who had been brought up with Herod the tetrarch, and Saul. As they ministered to the Lord and fasted, the holy spirit said, "Now separate to Me Barnabas and Saul for the work to which I have called them." Then, having fasted and prayed, and laid hands on them, they sent them away.*

Paul and Barnabas were then ordained to be apostles. They had been elders in their assembly, but God changed their ministry. Away there were sent to establish works in other cities as the spirit would lead them.

Another prophet in the Jerusalem assembly was Agabus.

*Acts 11:27,28 And in these days **prophets** came from Jerusalem to Antioch. Then one of them, named Agabus, stood up and showed by the spirit that there was going to be a great famine throughout all the world, which also happened in the days of Claudius Caesar.*

We ought to notice that Agabus functioned locally in Jerusalem, but then he went to another church to minister. Thus, prophets, unlike pastor/shepherds, are not only local, but can be transient. We should note that the church in Antioch actually received his words as though God had spoken them. They quickly received an offering from the saints and sent it to help the church in Jerusalem. They did not hesitate. They set right in and got it together.

Acts 11:29 Then the disciples, each according to his ability, determined to send relief to the brethren dwelling in Judea.

We yet know that Agabus continued mobile in the ministry, for years later, when Paul, Luke, and others were staying for a short season with Philip in Caesarea, Agabus showed up.

*Acts 21:10,11 There came down from Judaea a certain **prophet**, named Agabus. And when he was come unto us, he took Paul's girdle, and bound his own hands and feet, and said, "Thus says the holy ghost, So shall the Jews at Jerusalem bind the man who owns this girdle, and shall deliver him into the hands of the Gentiles."*

This was not the first time that such a warning came to Paul. Most everyone felt that this meant that Paul should surely <u>not</u> continue on to Jerusalem. But, Paul understood that it was God's Will for him to go to Jerusalem and to be arrested. He received Agabus' words as those of guidance and direction. He also took comfort from them, that in obedience to the prophet's message, he would continue to be in the divine Will.

Judas and Silas were yet two more prophets from the Jerusalem assembly. It seems that there arose a very serious problem in the Antioch assembly, when members of the Jerusalem congregation went to Antioch and preached that the gentile members of the church needed to observe the sabbath and to be circumcised. Barnabas and Saul were unable to convince the assembly that this was incorrect, so they took the problem right back where it had originated: Jerusalem.

When we read the account it is difficult to feel the passion and emotion they came forth in this conference in Jerusalem. However, when a decision was finally made, it was determined to put it in the form a letter and send it back the saints in Antioch. To add extra weight to the authority of this letter, they decided to send two prophets from the Jerusalem assembly to lend their strength and influence.
> *Acts 15:22 Then pleased it the apostles and elders, with the whole church, to send chosen men of their own company to Antioch with Paul and Barnabas; namely, Judas surnamed Barsabas, and Silas, **chief men** among the brethren.*

Judas and Silas were introduced to the Antiochans in the letter:
> *Acts 15:27 "We have sent therefore Judas and Silas, who shall also tell you the same things by mouth."*

Judas and Silas were to verify the letter which had been sent by the Council.
> *Acts 15:32-34 Now Judas and Silas, themselves being **prophets** also, **exhorted** and **strengthened** the brethren with many words. And after they had stayed there for a time, they were sent back with greetings from the brethren to the apostles. However, it seemed good to Silas to remain there.*

Obviously Judas returned to Jerusalem, but the spirit bade Silas to remain.

It was not long till Silas teamed up with Paul on his next missionary journey. The apostle and the prophet worked in tandem. Later on, Timothy joined their labor. They had a powerful ministry together in Corinth.

Of course, prophets, as well as teachers, are vital ministers in the local church, though they may be transient from time to time.
> *1 Corinthians 12:27,28 Now you are the Body of Christ, and each one of you is a part of it. And in the Church, God has appointed first of all apostles, second **prophets**, third teachers...*

One of the differences between apostles and prophets is that the apostles, having established an assembly, will move on. They are continuously about the business of starting new works. They only remain with an assembly for so long. **They** are not members of the assemblies which they found. On the other hand, the prophets which are raised up in the apostle's work, are members of the local church. As we have already stated, though they may move about the world at the behest of the holy ghost, their home base is their local church.

The local prophets may or may not be among the ruling elders, those shepherds whose task it is to govern the church. We are saying that the governance of the local assembly is the responsibility of the pastors, and the prophets might or might not be involved in ruling and organizing.

Yet, their role in the assembly is vital. Their role is one of spiritual guidance, exhortation, and warning. Their reputation is fearful, and they are deeply respected by the members. When the local assemblies meet together, the prophets often play a key role. We know a little about this because the prophets in the Corinthian Church abused their responsibility to such an extent that they dominated the meetings. It was necessary to write and correct their error. Paul declared that at most, two or three prophets might speak. The very nature of their ministry, being spiritual, there would be occasions when the spirit revealed something to another prophet. In such a case Paul maintained that they were to actually interrupt the speaker, who, himself, was to cease speaking.

> *1 Corinthians 14:29-32 Let two or three **prophets** speak, and let the others weigh what is said. If a revelation is made to another sitting by, let the first be silent. For you can all **prophesy** one by one, so that all may learn and all be encouraged; and the spirits of **prophets** are subject to **prophets**.*

One can only imagine the awe, the reverence, and the amazement that attached to those meetings when men of such eminence were speaking under the spirit's influence.

There is a great deal of information about the function of the local churches which has not passed down to us in writing. There is much of the order of church meetings that manifested in the early days of the church of which we are ignorant. We function in the church today basically on the customs and traditions handed down to us by our predecessors. If there be Romish or synagogic elements in our church order, in the government, and in our worship, we are ignorant. God has not seen fit that such correct understanding of church order was preserved in writing for our benefit.

Many there are in the church today who believe that the Church of Jesus will be restored to the glory and power that was manifested in its earliest days. But, the information, the directions, will have to be revealed by no other means than the holy spirit. More than likely, it will be the prophets who will be the key recipients of this insight.

It is very likely that the Church will give the prophets a hard time, for they will be advocating changes to customs and traditions that go back centuries. It will not be everyone who will heed the prophets' words. Well, that's what often befalls these men!

In the day of Samuel and later during the ministries of Elijah and Elisha there were Schools of the Prophets. They formed a loose brotherhood and seemed to have held allegiance to the great men of God. Inspired, particularly by Elijah and Elisha, they went up and down the countryside agitating against the King and the Queen. They agitated against the false practice of religion. They were relentless in stirring up the people. They tried to goad them in the right direction.

By contrast, today's Church seems to have few outside its halls who care at all what She says or does or thinks. But, as we come closer and closer to the end of this age, you will begin to see more and more prophetic activity. The new prophets will not be holding their peace. God will instigate them to cry out. They will raise up opposition to those who are standing against God. They will not be like the political rabble of the twentieth and twenty-first centuries, for they will be only concerned with the things of the holy ghost.

They will be detested by the power-seekers in government and in the organized Church. Not only will they be persecuted, beaten, and imprisoned, but they will be the impetus for persecution to come upon the true

Church of Jesus Christ. Today, in the United States the Church is becoming less and less popular. But, there is nothing like the persecution that the early Church had. However, in other countries, especially in China and central Africa, the Church is already suffering much martyrdom.

This is but a hint of what is yet to happen. Two powerful forces, one being God and his prophetic church, and the other being that satanic beast system, are about to collide. Chaos and misery will reign. Unrest and conflict will lead to greater and greater conflagrations.

The prophets will not be silent. The "schools of the prophets" will inflame, exacerbate, and disturb. At the same time they will be proclaiming to the saints the peace of God that cannot be understood. They will exhort to greater endurance, greater holiness, greater consecration, greater piety, greater unction. They will embolden the Church.

This is a part of the ministry of the prophets you will see in the last days.

Of all the offices of the ministry, the only one that functions much in the Church today is that of the pastor/shepherd. And, that office is not functioning in most places as it was designed in the Plan of God.

The other offices are just about absent. The Church has done without them for so many centuries, She seems to feel she can get along with them to the end of the Age.

But, when God said to "build it according to the plan," He was including the ministry, all of it.

It seems out of place at the time of this writing to discuss God-ordained, hands-laid-on teachers. But, the Church will have such men. And, they will be so-needed. It doesn't stir much interest these days to talk about sending out apostles to start new works. I knew one man who went to Haiti, and established hundreds of churches and somewhat set them in sort of order; this man is about as close to a real apostle as I have seen to date.

We've had evangelists going around for a couple of hundred years, but I suspect that when we see the real thing, it won't look anything like what we've seen before. The only evangelist recognized in the *Bible* was Philip.

Acts 8:6-8 And the multitudes with one accord heeded the things spoken by Philip, hearing and seeing the miracles which he did. For unclean spirits, crying with a loud voice, came out of many who were possessed; and many who were paralyzed and lame were healed. And there was great joy in that city.

Does this sound like anything you have heard about these days?

There are men who are pastoring churches who rather have other gifts. As gifted as they are, they have not been real successful in establishing "New-Covenant" assemblies. Why? Because they were out of place. Wait till you see real shepherds at work!

Wait till you see what REAL prophets are like. If the anointing on other kinds of ministers causes them to appear a little odd, it will be more so with the prophets. They will be known in their local assemblies, the general Church, and around the country. They will cause a stir wherever they go. They will NOT be popular, not even in the Church. They will cause a lot of trouble by what they say. They also shall suffer a great deal, like John the Baptist did. But, they will not be deterred.

I do not suppose that I shall live to see the prophets and also the other offices of the ministry in their full-blown completeness. Would you please make sure that they get a copy of this chapter.

I do expect that there will be *coenubias* of schools of prophets around the world, just as there were in Jericho, Jerusalem, and Carmel in olden times. There these men of God will congregate. They will minister to one another, strengthen one another. There they will gain a space of rest from the rigors of their ministries. And then, off they will go again.

Many churches around the world will continue to function as they always have. They will continue in the Babylonious pattern of one pastor per church and no other men serving in the ministry. How can the Church be restored without functioning evangelists, apostles, teachers, and prophets? How well would a maimed hand function with only one finger?

How can the Church support numerous ministers, while it spends huge amounts of money keeping up houses of worship and building new ones?

But, there will be those who will become so radically different as to be unrecognizable from their present form. They will have dared to "step outside the box," away from the calf path. They will have been dedicated to striving to restore the Church to the pattern that came out of the Upper Room.

It will come to pass!

Chapter 20. The Role of the Ministry In "Going on to Perfection"

Is it really possible for human beings to achieve perfection? The very thought of it seems silly and unnecessary. Can every one attain it? Can anyone? Yet, Jesus exhorts us:

Luke 13:24-27 <u>Strive</u> *to enter in at the strait gate.*

Jesus says the way is very narrow, but he says "strive" to attain it. "Strive" means: endeavor, aim, struggle, try, attempt, toil. He is not saying it's easy; he's not saying it's a sure thing. In the *Psalms* he gives us one of the tools a striver might use to attain perfection:

Psalm 119:10,11 With my whole heart I have sought You. Oh, let me not wander from Your Commandments! Your Word I have **hidden** *in my heart, that I might not sin against You.*

Of course! It's the *Word of God*. Assuredly, one cannot become perfect, if he does not devote himself to reading the *Bible*, and not just "reading," but <u>hiding</u> the *Word* in his heart.

Some people will not claim the prize of eternal life, because they have not sought God with a "whole heart." They made a "half-hearted" effort.

Luke 13:24 For many...will seek to enter in, and shall not be able...

What do you mean "half-hearted?" They thought they made a huge effort!

Luke 13:25-27 "Lord, Lord, open for us," and He will answer and say to you, "I do not know you (or) where you are from." Then you will begin to say, "We ate and drank in Your presence [We read the Bible *and felt the holy ghost], and You taught in our streets [we have Bible-teaching in our churches]." But He will say, "I tell you I do not know you, where you are from. Depart from Me, all you workers of iniquity."*

What a shame! Sitting in a church pew for countless hours and years and to not make it! To have thought you were doing it all, and it was naught! To have sung in the quartet, been an usher, labored in the church kitchen, to have given generously in the offering, to have always dressed according to appropriate standards, to have always been in fellowship with the "right people," to have said and done all that religion requires--and to miss it!

Where did we go wrong? We labored, but we missed perfection AND eternity. Jesus exhorts us to work on meaningful things.

John 6:27 Do not labor for the food which perishes, but for the food which endures to everlasting life.

There it is. We were striving for the wrong kind of perfection. Not that what we were doing was sinful or wrong. But, our motive was never holy. Do you mean I spent all that time doing right, and I missed the Son of Man?

1 Corinthians 9:24 Do you not know that those who run in a race all run, but one receives the prize? Run in such a way that you may obtain it.

We're in a race. Against whom? Against our old nature; that's our foe. We're running against our old selfish self. It is possible to run nowhere. It's possible to box against the shadows and to think we're really winning.

We were a flurry of church activity, and went nowhere!

It's sad to think that all of us are not going to achieve eternal life. Now, of course, it's never our place to judge which is which and who is who. But, it is the responsibility of the church and the ministry to promote every saint toward that perfect goal.

> *Colossians 1:28   We proclaim (Jesus), admonishing and teaching everyone with all wisdom, so that we may present everyone perfect in Christ.*

We rest assured that the opportunity has been presented to every saint to come to that eternal home, but knowing that some will stumble.

> *2 Peter 1:10,11 Therefore, brethren, be even more diligent to make your call and election sure, for if you do these things you will never stumble; for so an entrance will be supplied to you abundantly into the everlasting kingdom of our Lord and Savior Jesus Christ.*

You could stumble, but you needn't. Jesus, himself, tells us that we don't just "plop" into eternal life. He says we must travel a narrow way to get there. He tells us that there must be changes that take place in our life. We must be changed and converted and worked on and improved AND perfected.

> *Matthew 7:13,14 Enter in at the strait gate: for wide is the gate, and broad is the way, that leads to destruction, and many there be which go in thereat: Because strait is the gate, and narrow is the way, which leads unto life, and few there be that find it.*

> *Matthew 18:3 Verily I say unto you, "Except you be **converted**, and become as little children, you shall not enter into the kingdom of heaven."*

When he said, "Converted," he didn't mean the way we usually take that word; he meant "converted: to be changed," not the beginning of salvation, but the continuing process of salvation, that is, "going on to perfection." Surely, the lesson must be that we cannot attain this on our own, by our will power, by our own wishes, but only through God.

> *Matthew 19:24-26 And again I say unto you, "It is easier for a camel to go through the eye of a needle, than for a rich man to enter into the kingdom of God." When his disciples heard it, they were exceedingly amazed, saying, "Who then can be saved?" But Jesus beheld them, and said unto them, "With men this is impossible; but with God all things are possible."*

So then, our striving for the mastery cannot be within oneself, but through the power of God, with Whom all things are possible.

Teaching and Teaching

If you're sitting at the feet of a proper ministry, you will be taught about your own personal perfection. But alas, we find in most churches, if they have any teaching at all, an emphasis is on other things; they never get beyond the basics. Paul wants us to go farther than that.

> *Hebrews 6:1,2 Therefore, leaving the discussion of the elementary principles of Christ, let us **go on to perfection**.*

The *Greek* word used here for "perfection" means "completion, consummation." We, of course, need the basic principles, but,

we've got to go beyond them. Here are six basic principles of Christianity:
1. repentance from dead works
2. faith toward God
3. the doctrine of baptisms
4. laying on of hands
5. resurrection of the dead
6. eternal judgment

Articles and volumes have been written on each of the elementary principles, including myself. But,
leaving the principles of the doctrine of Christ, let us go on unto perfection (KJV).

Let us stop going over the basics of Christianity again and again (NLT).

...Let us press on to maturity (NAS).

We would never minimize the importance of the basic Christian teachings. If you've not been instructed nor learned them, you'll have precious little on which your salvation can be built. You may have repented, been baptized in water, and received the baptism of the holy ghost, which are the "keys to the Kingdom" and are requisite for eternal life, but you must also know the basic doctrines. THEN, we are ready to go on to perfection. THEN we are ready to go on to perfection. After we have the three keys and the six basic principles, THEN we are ready to move on to perfection.

Don't take this "perfection" too lightly; Jesus is quite serious about this. He said in the "Sermon on the Mount:"
Matthew 5:48 **Be perfect**, *therefore, as your heavenly Father is perfect.*

Jesus said that. How perfect? Like God.
Be perfect, therefore, as your heavenly Father is perfect.

James tell us that God is
James 1:17 the Father of lights, with whom is no variableness, neither shadow of turning.

And of Jesus it is said that he is
Hebrews 13:8 the same yesterday, and today, and forever.

We're to become that stable, that constant, that dependable, that perfect. To accomplish this, God has given us several tools, among which are the holy spirit, the cross of Christ, the judgments of God, the fellowship of the saints, the *Bible*, prayer, and the work of the ministry. Of this last "device," the ministry, Paul speaks of its purpose:
*Ephesians 4:11-13 (God) gave some, apostles; and some, prophets; and some, evangelists; and some, pastors and teachers for the **perfecting** of the saints, for the work of the ministry, for the edifying of the body of Christ, till we all come in the unity of the faith, and of the knowledge of the Son of God, unto a perfect man, unto the measure of the stature of the fullness of Christ...*

You might ask, "What else needs to be done in our lives once we've gotten the keys to the Kingdom?" What more is there to do or get?

It's not so much something more we're to get; it's the bad things in us that we need to get rid of. They are what block us from perfection.

What things?
1. We were born with character flaws.
2. We have picked up bad habits along life's journey.
3. We have received wounds to the soul.

Of course, these things render us "imperfect," don't they? Flaws, bad habits, wounds. You'd never call someone "perfect" with those, would you? Could you? There'd be no way to give a list of all the character flaws and bad habits one could have. There are limitless ways people can be hurt; they haven't all been thought up, yet. These problems weigh us down; they prevent our flying with the eagles; they block us from bounding upon our high places to which have been destined. We must not be content to live out our Christian walk bogged down. Not only are we to BECOME CHRISTIANS, but we're to BECOME PERFECT, unencumbered, unfettered. So we are exhorted:

> *Hebrews 12:1 Let us lay aside **every weight**, and the sin which doth so easily beset us, and let us run with patience the race that is set before us...*

We're not dealing here just with "sins that so easily beset us;" we're also talking about the "weights" that are hanging on to our lives, that have us obstructed and impeded. We often do not even know what our problems are; that's another reason we need the ministry—to help us recognize those things. They are not sins; they're just nagging problems that keep robbing us and limiting us in having a victorious life. They impede perfection.

"But, you don't know what I've gone through!" "What's normal for Jesus is NOT what's normal for me!" "Well, I'm not going to change; that's just the way I am." "You can't become perfect until there's a perfect church." "You don't know the abuse I've taken." "I've been living this way all my life, and I guess I'll die that way." "As long as I'm saved, that's all I care about." "I can't change; that's just me." "You can't become perfect as long as you're walking around in this flesh and blood body." "No one could go through this ordeal, and keep his right mind." "I felt like cussing!"

You've just heard about ten lies or excuses to not strive to become like the Master. Don't you believe that you can't do it! Don't listen to Satan. Don't listen to the devil. Jesus of Nazareth has walked this way before, and He will give you the victory. Count on it!

"You'd have fears, too, if you'd experienced what I have gone through."

Say, Jesus beat fear.

"I'm afraid of dying, aren't you?"

I'm telling you, Jesus went through that one, too. He experienced everything. Guess what? He got the victory! Through his death on the cross, Christ destroyed the one who had the power of death, the devil.

> *Hebrews 2:14,15 Through death he might destroy him that had the power of death, that is, the devil...*

The devil is destroyed. "Fear" is destroyed! Yes. One of the things he accomplished on the cross is that Jesus delivered us from that fear:

> *v15 And deliver them who through fear of death were all their lifetime subject to bondage.*

When we take stock of our lives we see that we may not only fear bondage, but many imprisonments. We've got these unlawful fondnesses and idiosyncrasies and peculiarities and obsessions and wounds and routines and negative thoughts and tendencies and dispositions and habits. They're not like-Christ, and we're trapped in them. We've each got our own little prisons. We live a good, righteous,

Christian life, but these little things have their stronghold deep inside us.

But, if we're "in Christ," he has already given us weapons, spiritual weapons of our warfare that
> *2 Corinthians 10:4 are not carnal, but mighty through God to the pulling down of strong holds.*

We don't need to put up with strong holds, the nagging, haunting, seductive, little enemies that spoil our life and our testimony.
> *Song of Solomon 2:15 Take us the foxes, the little foxes, that spoil the vines.*

We want the "vine" of our life to be successful and productive. Jesus can get into your life and get rid of those "little foxes." Please note that they are just "LITTLE foxes." They're just little flaws, little quirks, little lusts, a little over-eating, little perversions, little indiscretions, little traits. But, they exercise such domination over us. They don't usually seem like little foxes, but huge beasts. We forget that Jesus has <u>already</u> destroyed the devil. He's already won the victory.
> *2 Corinthians 2:14 But thanks be to God, who always causes us to triumph in Christ.*

How often does He cause us to triumph? ALWAYS.
> *Thanks be to God, who ALWAYS causes us to triumph in Christ.*

> *Psalm 34:19 Many are the afflictions of the righteous, but the Lord delivers him out of them ALL.*

Out of them ALL! Shout this to the saints.

Listen how Jesus began his earthly ministry two thousand years ago: He went to his old home-town synagogue in Nazareth where he was called upon to come to the Bible stand and read. The assigned passage was *Isaiah 61:1-3*. After he had read part of it he closed the book. Turning to the people he said:
> *Luke 4:21 This day is this scripture fulfilled in your ears.*

That passage the congregation knew very well to be prophetic of the coming Christ. When he informed them that he was the fulfillment of those verses, they had no doubt about what he was trying to claim; he was claiming to be the Christ. Here is that passage as quoted by Luke, followed by the entire reference from Isaiah:
> *Luke 4:18,19 The Spirit of the Lord is upon me, because He has anointed me to preach the gospel to the poor. He has sent me to <u>heal the brokenhearted</u>, to proclaim <u>liberty to the captives</u> and recovery of sight to the blind, to set at liberty those who are <u>oppressed</u>; to proclaim the acceptable year of the Lord.*

> *Isaiah 61:1-3 The Spirit of the Lord God is upon me; because the Lord has anointed me to preach good tidings unto the meek; he has sent me to bind up the brokenhearted, to proclaim liberty to the captives, and the opening of the prison to them that are bound;*

> *To proclaim the acceptable year of the Lord, and the day of vengeance of our God; to comfort all that mourn; to appoint unto them that mourn in Zion, to give unto them beauty for ashes, the oil of joy for mourning, the garment of praise for the spirit of heaviness; that they might be called trees of righteousness, the planting of the Lord, that he might be glorified.*

Jesus declares that he has been anointed by the Almighty for a ministry that includes:
- to heal the broken-hearted
- to heal the blind
- to heal the bruised
- to open the prison for the bound
- to replace heaviness with praise
- to comfort mourners
- to liberate the captives
- to free the oppressed
- to give beauty for ashes
- to give joy instead of sadness

Jesus accepted and began that ministry two thousand years ago. By the *aegis* of the holy spirit and by the ordained ministry of his church Jesus continues his priestly ministry to this day. His purpose has not changed. He's still healing; he's still liberating; he's still cleansing; he's still delivering. He's still comforting. He's the same today as he was yesterday.

You don't have to remain crippled by your old problems. You don't have to be mired down with phobias. You don't have to be less than you can be. Jesus wants to make you a "tree of righteousness, the planting of the Lord." He wants to make you a glory to his Father.

We have said that it is by the holy spirit God works on His people. He also does this by and through His judgments, by trials, His Mercy, circumstances, the fellowship of saints, crosses and fiery trials, the *Bible*, spiritual gifts, and life's blessings. But, even more than those is the work of the ministry in raising up the saints of God.
> *Ephesians 4:11,12 (God) gave some (to be) apostles; and some, prophets; and some, evangelists; and some, pastors and teachers,* **for the perfecting of the saints**...

to equip God's people to do his work and build up the church (NLT).

to prepare God's people for works of service (NIV).

What is it the ministers are to do? How are they to do it?

If God has given the oversight, he will also give the anointing. Then, <u>they</u> can
> *2 Timothy 4:2 preach the Word; be instant in season, out of season; reprove, rebuke, exhort with all long-suffering and doctrine.*

The saints must be taught by their shepherds that they have been empowered to overcome their flaws, scars, reversals of fortune. They should be instructed to go to the altar, making their problems living sacrifices. These difficulties, dilemmas, setbacks, snags, addictions, predicaments, crises are to be given to the brazen altar until they are destroyed. They may need to be counseled on how to deal with their situations, which are not occasions for the laying-on of hands; they are opportunities for our high priest to heal us inwardly.

The Work of the Ministry

After the death of Paul, the church began to fall away from apostolic order. An early step of apostatizing was the changing of the roles of pastors from being counselors to that of being rabbinic-type preachers. The synagogue pulpit (*lu-akh*) became the location of authority of Christian ministers. Church members became less and less personally touched by this preaching. Whereas "preaching the *Word*," which had heretofore often been done by example, now became oratory. Going-to-church became a religious rite, rather than a holy-ghost experience. Instead of being discipled, church members became pew-sitters.

But, notice how Paul gave us his example of how to minister:

1 Thessalonians 2:10-12 You are witnesses, and God also, how devoutly and justly and blamelessly we <u>behaved</u> ourselves among you who believe; as you know how we <u>exhorted</u>, and <u>comforted</u>, and <u>charged</u> every one of you, as a father does his own children, that you would walk worthy of God who calls you into His own kingdom and glory.

He preached first of all by his behavior. Paul undertook his task "devoutly." He exhorted, comforted, charged. He gave <u>further</u> instructions on dealing with the saint's problems:

1 Thessalonians 5:14,15 <u>Warn</u> those who are unruly, <u>comfort</u> the fainthearted, <u>uphold</u> the weak, <u>be patient</u> with all. See that no one renders evil for evil to anyone, but always pursue what is good...

Titus 2:15 These things <u>speak</u>, and <u>exhort</u>, and <u>rebuke</u> with all authority.

Warn, comfort, uphold, be patient, exhort, rebuke. He's talking about ministering and "perfecting," not sermonizing.

2 Thessalonians 3:14,15 And if anyone does not obey our word in this epistle, note that person and do not keep company with him, that he may be ashamed. Yet do not count him as an enemy, but <u>admonish</u> him as a brother.

Feminization of the Church

Since the industrial revolution in the nineteenth century, fathers have left the home to work in the factory and to start business enterprises. Child-rearing became the domain of the mothers. Then, the mothers left the home to help the family bring in even more money. Schools and day-care centers became responsible for tending to children during their formative years. The family unit has become greatly altered from previous eras. The most glaring deficiency of this format has been the disappearance of solid, male role-models. This has led the entire society toward feminization. Both boys and girls have less stable personalities. People have become so very sensitive. They find it difficult to forgive and forbear. The high rate of divorce is evidence of that. People just do not appreciate being corrected, confronted, or assisted.

This attitude has consumed the Church, as well. Ministers find it difficult, if not impossible to meet personal problems head-on or to challenge their parishioners because of some fault or improper life-style or attitude. Any allusion or suggestion becomes regarded as an offensive insinuation. Often, ministers shy away from correcting and resolving conflicts for fear of offending a church member. But, Brother Minister, that is what you are getting paid to do. If, for fear of offending a big giver or a member who has lots of kinfolks in the congregation, you do not call a spade a spade, so to speak, you will be, by your negligence, participating in the saints' sins; you will not help them to perfection; they will miss eternal life; and so will you!

The ministers are told to do, "correcting." They are helping the saints come to perfection by admonition. Sometimes one's flaws make him seem to be an enemy of the church, the ministers, even of God. Be patient, love, admonish.

When Jesus spoke to Peter, he said:
John 21:15 "Simon, son of Jonas, do you love me more than these?" He said to him, "Yes, Lord; you know that I love you." He said to him, "Feed my lambs."

Feeding. This mode of the ministry of Jesus was prophesied:
*Isaiah 35:3; 40:11 Strengthen the weak hands, and confirm the feeble knees...He shall **feed** his flock like a shepherd: he shall gather the lambs with his arm, and carry them in his bosom, and shall gently lead those that are with young.*

How did Jesus declare God's Faithfulness? He did the best kind of teaching there is-- BY EXAMPLE. Same today for pastors (shepherds).

It is God's intention that the ministers portray to the people the nature of Jesus; they are to be taught to become like Christ, to behave like that man Jesus. There is no other perfect goal for the saint of God, than to become like the Lord. God, Himself, has prepared a distinct plan for each of His saints which, if followed, will lead him to perfection. It is the minister's job to assist in this divine weeding effort.
Romans 8:29 For whom He did foreknow, He also did predestinate to be conformed to the image of His Son...

***

Before time began, God knew His people. He laid out a course for their lives that would make them become like Jesus (*Hebrews* 12:1). He incorporated into each plan every uprising and down-falling each of us individually would need. He included every blessing and every cursing, every promotion and every demotion, every victory and every defeat, every birth and every death, every cross and every healing needed to makes us like God's son. This means that all those awful traits and discouraging problems are to become eliminated.

One way to do this is to give your dilemmas and doubts to Jesus. I mean, just let Him have them. "Lord, I give them to you." "I put them on Your altar, and I give them to you. I'm not going to worry about them any more. They're Yours."

And then, Jesus Christ is going to give you
Isaiah 61:3 beauty for ashes.

Some years ago several girls murdered another teen, mutilated, and burned her body. It was a sensational case. I saw one of the girls after she was convicted and sentenced. The deputy was leading her across a parking lot, and she screamed. She let out another long scream and crumbled to the ground. Such anguish, such torment, such agony! They helped her to her feet and led her away.

I thought that here she was, and that her life was going to rot away in a correctional facility. What happened in her past that brought her to a place of such debauchery? Why had she gone astray? I wasn't thinking at that moment of the victim in the case, just this one tormented, guilty child.

Would one day someone reach out to this incarcerated girl? Would there be some compassionate prison ministry that would find her and help restore her? Would there be someone who could tell her that in spite of all her debasement there was hope?

Would they tell her that Jesus of Nazareth had seen everything that she had done, as well as everything that happened in her young life, and though He did not approve, He understood it all? Would they explain that she might not get out of this prison, Jesus had come to set her free from her guilt and torment and anguish? Would there be someone to lead her into right paths, who would show her the way to peace and joy and sabbath rest?

I have visited prisons several times, but frankly, this is not a ministry for which I was called. However, there are those ministerss who have such generous hearts whom the Lord has equipped for such service.

I have chosen this most extreme example to point out that, if God could redeem this girl from all the guilt and damage in her soul, He could so easily restore and perfect you.

Whatever it is, lay your load on the Altar of Sacrifice and let him burn it up. Pretty soon, your rotten trait and your troublesome situations are gone. You gave them to Jesus. He burned them up. He made ashes out of that deep wound caused by treachery. He gives you a beautiful spirit, a smiling face, an understanding, sympathetic heart. Beauty for ashes. What an exchange! All of the sudden you're resilient! It is the role of the ministry to explain God's solutions over and over to the saints.

Don't believe that it can't happen for you. You're His. He heals and perfects. But, churches and ministers, who do not believe the saints can overcome in this day and age, will never bring about perfection in them.

What a tremendous work and responsibility the Ministry has!

1 Thessalonians 2:13 For this cause also thank we God without ceasing, because, when you received the Word of God *which you heard from us, you received it not as the word of men, but as it is in truth, the* Word of God, *which effectually works also in you that believe.*

It's a joyous reward a shepherd has! Listen to Jesus speaking here:

Revelation 3:18-21 I counsel you to buy of me gold tried in the fire, that you may be rich; and white raiment, that you may be clothed, and that the shame of your nakedness do not appear; and anoint your eyes with eye salve, that you may see. As many as I love, **I rebuke and chasten**: *be zealous therefore, and repent.*

Behold, I stand at the door, and knock: if any man hear my voice, and open the door, I will come in to him, and will sup with him, and he with me. To him that **overcomes** *will I grant to sit with me in my throne, even as I also overcame, and am set down with my Father in his throne.*

Jesus says to buy fire-tried gold and white raiment (which is "righteousness"). That's what we want to wear. Get your eyes salved so you can see like God sees, not as man sees. Jesus rebukes and chastens. To those who have a passionate desire to receive these loving blows, he heals. They overcome all their old fetishes, perverted tendencies, and sore dispositions. Having become perfect, they will sit down with Jesus upon the throne of God.

Jeremiah 17:7-10 Blessed is the man that trusts in the Lord, and whose hope the Lord is. For he shall be as a tree planted by the waters, and that spreads out her roots by the river, and shall not see when heat comes but her leaf shall be green; and shall not worry in the year of drought, neither shall cease from yielding fruit.

The heart is deceitful above all things, and desperately wicked: who can know it? I the Lord search the heart, I try the reins, even to give every man according to his ways, and according to the fruit of his doings.

Beloved, Jesus is examining you right this minute.
Psalms 139:23,24 Search me, O God, and know my heart: try me, and know my thoughts: And see if there be any wicked way in me, and lead me in the way everlasting.

That's what we want: to let God search our hearts. Brother Shepherd, help your flock to search their hearts. Help them to see that as long as they live in this world they'll be exposed to turmoil. But, if they have laid aside every weight, they've entered into Christ's triumph. This is so tremendous what he says:
*John 16:33 In the world you shall have tribulation: but be of good cheer; I have **overcome** the world.*

"Overcoming" is mentioned in the *Bible* twenty four more times, and "being perfect" nineteen times. It is our goal.

God's people carry so many problems that hinder them. Some have had childhood problems; some feel insecure; some were abused, physically or verbally; some feel unworthy; some are overcome with guilt. The saints should be encouraged to put all of those things on the altar, to ask Jesus to burn them up, and to give them beauty for ashes.

Some have been belittled and insulted; some have doubts about God; some have been **gossiped about;** some are very protective; some are control people; some are always fretting; some have been deeply involved in **immorality.**

Remember that Jesus was sent
Luke 4:18 to heal the broken-hearted, to preach deliverance to the captives, and recovering of sight to the blind, to set at liberty them that are bruised...

The saints unnecessarily carry wounds, character flaws, and bad habits that keep them from perfection. Pastoral counselors must get down to the nitty-gritty, to comfort the broken-hearted, to help free those who are bound, to open the eyes to the *Good News* those who are blind to God's truth, to liberate those who are imprisoned in false religion and wrong doctrine. I'm persuaded that those ministers who do will build triumphant assemblies and raise up more ministers for Jesus Christ.
*2 Corinthians 13:11 Finally, brethren, farewell. **Be perfect**, be of good comfort, be of one mind, live in peace; and the God of love and peace shall be with you.*

It's not: "Can you do it?" It's: "Can He do it?" Or, moreso: "Will you let Him do it?"

Brother Minister: How are conducting the equipping of sheep?

Is it really possible for human beings to achieve perfection? Can every one attain it? Can anyone? The apostle concluded:

Finally,.........be perfect!

Chapter 21. Saviors

Surely our fathers have inherited lies! Jeremiah 16:19

> *Obadiah 21 And **saviors** shall come up on Mount Zion to judge the Mount of Esau; and the Kingdom shall be the Lord's.*

The *Greek* word for "savior" is *Christos*, which anglicized is "Christ." It is translated from the *Hebrew* word *mo-shee'-ya*, and is from the same root as the word for "anointed: "*mo-shee-akh'*, that is, "to be anointed with oil," (or with the spirit of God). The title of "Messiah" or "Savior" was familiar to those of old. Here are two examples where this word was translated as "deliverer."

> *Judges 3:9,15 And when the children of Israel cried unto the Lord, the Lord raised up a **deliverer** (mo-shee'-ya) to the children of Israel, who delivered them, even Othniel the son of Kenaz, Caleb's younger brother...*
>
> *v15 When the children of Israel cried unto the Lord, the Lord raised them up a **deliverer**, Ehud the son of Gera, a Benjamite, a man left-handed...*

God raised up a "deliverer," that is, an anointed one, a Christ, a savior, a messiah. He did this many times. In the times of the kings of Israel:

> *2 Kings 13:4,5 Jehoahaz besought the Lord, and the Lord hearkened unto him: for he saw the oppression of Israel, because the king of Syria oppressed them. And the Lord gave Israel a **savior** (mo-shee'-ya).*

Speaking of King David:
> *1 Samuel 2:10 The adversaries of the Lord shall be broken to pieces; out of heaven shall He thunder upon them: the Lord shall judge the ends of the earth; and He shall give strength unto his king, and exalt the horn of his **anointed** (mo-shee'-akh) (David).*

Nehemiah said to God:
> *Nehemiah 9:27 According to Your manifold Mercies, You gave them (Israel) **saviors**, who should save them from the hands of their enemies.*

The Jews have long believed in "saviors" from God. They have understood God's anointing on these "deliverers." They have a song they sing every winter during the Festival of Lights (Feast of Dedication) which says:

> In every age,
> A Hero or Sage,
> Who can count them?
> In every age,
> A hero or Sage,
> Came to our aid.

The list of Israel's saviors is lengthy including Moses, all the judges, many of the Kings and Prophets, Mordecai and Queen Esther, Ezra, Nehemiah, Joshua, Zerubbabel, and Judas Maccabeus. Many others thought that they were "messiahs," but they were not, among whom we might list:

> *Acts 5:36,37 For before these days rose up Theudas, boasting himself to be somebody; to whom a number of men, about four hundred, joined themselves: who was slain; and all, as many as obeyed him, were scattered, and brought to nought. After this man rose up, Judas of Galilee, in the days of the taxing, and drew away much people after him: he also perished;*

and all, even as many as obeyed him, were dispersed.

In 135 A.D. Simon bar Kochba raised up rebellion against Rome. In the Middle Ages in Poland, a Jew, who took the name, Baal Shem Tov, thought he was the messiah. Also did Shabbetai Zevi, a Turkish Jew, imagine himself to be the messiah. In 1665 one Nathan of Gaza prophecied the imminent restoration of the Jews via the bloodless victory of this Shabbetai Zevi, riding upon a lion. The thrill of the coming Christ sped throughout the Jewish communities of Europe, Asia, Africa. However, the next year Zevi was arrested in Constantinople, where the Sultan gave him the choice of death or converting to Islam. Zevi's apostasy hit world Jewry with the force of a thunderclap, many converting to Islam themselves. Shabbateanism continued in the Jewish world community for over a hundred years. Even today in Turkey there are still Jews who believe Zevi to be the christ.

Of course, the Jews missed the true Savior, Jesus. And, they also continue to miss the saviors who keep on coming out of the Christ's Church as the prophet Obadiah concluded in his inspired message:

*Obadiah 21 And **saviors** shall come up on mount Zion to judge the **Mount** of Esau.*

What does this "mount" represent? The whole of *Obadiah* deals with God's judgment of the descendants of Israel's brother, Esau. God says they are to be destroyed:

v18 There shall not be any remaining of the house of Esau; for the Lord has spoken it.

Mount Esau represents deceptive "human pride."

v3 The pride of your heart has deceived you.

Of all the descendents of Esau, the most famous was King Herod. There cannot be a more consummate example of pride than Herod. When he heard from the Magi that a king had been born, he feared this child to be a threat to his reign. He killed all the baby boys in the Bethlehem area. When he was at one time called to Rome, he gave orders that if he did not return that his wife was to be executed; he didn't want anyone else to ever have her. He did not intend to execute John the Baptist, but he had promised Herodias' daughter that he would grant her wish. Herod and the people of Esau truly exemplified "pride."

On the other hand, "Zion" speaks of God's order and His government. I think when that word, "Zion," appears in the *Old Testament*, it is often speaking prophetically of the Church of Jesus Christ.

*Psalm 2:6 Yet have I set my king upon my holy hill of **Zion** (that is, the Church).*

*Psalm 68:16 This is the **Hill** (the Church of Christ) which God desires to dwell in; yea, the Lord will dwell in It for ever.*

*Micah 4:2 And many nations shall come, and say, "Come, and let us go up to the Mountain of the Lord, and to the house of the God of Jacob; and he will teach us of His Ways, and we will walk in His Paths:" for the Law shall go forth of **Zion**, and the Word of the Lord from Jerusalem.*

The church is God's holy hill; it is His dwelling place. Mount Zion stands over against Mount Esau; God's holy mount stands against the mountains of deceptive human pride; the Church resists the world.

The people of God have always been persecuted by the proud heathen. But, God promises that a remnant of His people will escape to Zion. God hates human pride; He will judge it in the End Time.

> *Isaiah 37:31,32 And the remnant that is escaped of the house of Judah shall again take root downward, and bear fruit upward. For out of Jerusalem shall go forth a remnant, and they that escape out of Mount **Zion**: the Zeal of the Lord of hosts shall do this.*

> *Obadiah 14-16 You should not have stood at the crossroads to cut off those among them who escaped. Nor should you have delivered up those among them who remained in the day of distress. For the Day of the Lord upon all the nations is near. As you have done, it shall be done to you. Your reprisal shall return upon your own head. For as you drank on My holy **mountain**, so shall all the nations drink continually. Yes, they shall drink, and swallow. And they shall be **as though they had never been**.*

The proud and the ungodly will be "as though they had not been." But, in Mount Zion shall be an escaped remnant. And, the prophet concludes:

> *Obadiah 17,21 But upon Mount **Zion** shall be deliverance, and there shall be holiness...**Saviors** shall ascend on Mount Zion to judge the mount of Esau; and the kingdom shall be the Lord's.*

Obadiah began, "it shall be holiness;" he closes, "and the kingdom shall be the Lord's to judge the mount of Esau." There shall be judges, divinely appointed, to judge the people; they are the saviors, raised up by God, to deliver.

The word "saviors" includes those who, before and afterward, were the instruments of God in saving His Church and people. Yet, all saviors shadowed the one Savior, who alone has the office of Judge, in whose kingdom, and associated by Him and with Him,

> *1 Corinthians 6:2 the saints shall judge the world.*

Do you see, then, that the saints of the church are anointed ones? They are saviors under the leadership of Christ for all the ages. Jesus said to His Apostles:

> *Matthew 19:28 You who have followed Me, in the regeneration when the Son of Man shall sit in the throne of His Glory, you also shall sit upon twelve thrones, judging the twelve tribes of Israel.*

These last words must at all times have recalled that great prophecy of Jesus' Passion, and of its fruits in the conversion of the Pagan, from which it is taken,

> *Psalm 22:16-20 For dogs have compassed me: the assembly of the wicked have enclosed me: they pierced my hands and my feet. I may tell all my bones: they look and stare upon me. They part my garments among them, and cast lots upon my vesture. But be not Thou far from me, O Lord: O My Strength, haste Thee to help me. Deliver my soul from the sword...*

> *vv25-29 My praise shall be of Thee in the great congregation: I will pay my vows before them that fear Him. The meek shall eat and be satisfied: they shall praise the Lord that seek Him:*

your heart shall live forever. All the ends of the world shall remember and turn unto the Lord: and all the kindreds of the nations shall worship before Thee. For the kingdom is the Lord's: and He is the Governor among the nations. All they that be fat upon earth shall eat and worship: all they that go down to the dust shall bow before him: and none can keep alive his own soul.

Indeed, Jesus did suffer according to the Scriptures. But, look at the benefit bestowed upon those who seek Him. And look at the adversaries of the Lord as represented by Edom, estranged aliens and enemies to God, to whom His kingdom is not revealed. In those who seek Him, He reigns and will reign, glorified forever in His saints, whom He has redeemed with His most precious Blood.

And the kingdom shall be the Lord's.

Majestic, comprehensive simplicity of prophecy! All time and eternity, the struggles of time and the peace and the rest of eternity, are summed up in those words. Zion and Edom retire from sight; all that will be left is the Kingdom of God, and God is "all in all."

*1 Corinthians 15:28 And when all things shall be subdued unto him, then shall the Son also himself be subject unto Him (God, the Father) that put all things under him, that God may be **all in all**.*

All pride and ungodliness will have been disposed. The strife is ended; not that ancient strife only between the evil and the good, the oppressor and the oppressed, the subduer and the subdued; but the whole strife and disobedience of the creature toward the Creator, man against his God.

Outward prosperity will have passed away, as David had said the great words:

Psalm 22:28 The kingdom is the Lord's.

Dark days had come. Obadiah saw on and beyond to darker yet, but knits up all his prophecy in this; "the kingdom shall be the Lord's." Obadiah foresaw the kingdom of Judah broken by Nebuchad-nezzar, "the hammer of the whole earth." So did Jeremiah:

*Jeremiah 50:23 How is the **hammer of the whole earth** cut asunder and broken! how is Babylon become a desolation among the nations.*

The petty kingdom of Judah had become hammered into pieces, and carried captive, all its people, including Daniel. But, Daniel saw beyond the present distress. He saw the consummation of the ages. He also saw the triumphant Kingdom of God, the Church of Jesus Christ.

Daniel 2:44 And in the days of these kings shall the God of heaven set up a Kingdom, which shall never be destroyed: and the Kingdom (the church) shall not be left to other people, but It shall break in pieces and consume all these kingdoms, and It shall stand for ever.

Daniel 7:14,27 And there was given Him (Christ, the savior) dominion, and glory, and a kingdom, that all people, nations, and languages, should serve him: His dominion is an everlasting dominion, which shall not pass away, and His kingdom (the church) that which shall not be destroyed...And the Kingdom and Dominion, and the greatness of the Kingdom under the whole heaven, shall be given to the people of the saints of the most High, whose

Kingdom is an everlasting kingdom, and all dominions shall serve and obey him.

Zechariah, too, saw the poor fragments which returned from the Babylonian captivity and their destitute estate, yet said the same:
Zechariah 14:9 And the Lord shall be king over all the earth: in that day shall there be one Lord, and His Name one.

All at once that kingdom came by Jesus of Nazareth; the fisherman, the tax gatherer, and the tentmaker were its workers; the whip, the cross, rack, sword, fire, torture, the wild-beast, these were endured; the dungeon and the quarry; and from these humble saints came fiery words of truth, which were the
Psalm 45:5,6 sharp arrows in the hearts of the King's enemies: Thy throne, O God, is for ever and ever; the scepter of Thy kingdom is a right scepter.

Luke 4:32 They were astonished at (Jesus') doctrine: for his Word was with power.

God spoke by His saviors, whose word "is with power." The strong and wise of the world shall be converted and joined together in that one song:
*Revelation 19:6 And I heard, as it were, the voice of a great multitude, and as the voice of many **waters**, and as the voice of mighty thunderings, saying, "Alleluia: for the Lord God omnipotent (all-powerful) reigneth."*

The "waters" are the great sea of saved humanity who shall ever sing God's praises. The deception of the world, at the end, shall be forced to resign to the worship of the One God. When the prophets had spoken, it had seemed to be the God of the Jews only. Great mystery it was that the kingdom was to be composed of representatives of
Revelation 5:9,10 every kindred, and tongue, and people, and nation, and has made us unto our God kings and priests: and we shall reign on the earth.

Who could foretell such a kingdom, but He Who alone could found it? Who alone has for these twenty centuries preserved, and now is anew enlarging it? It is God Omnipotent and Omniscient, Who wakened the hearts which He had made, to believe in Him and to love Him. Down with Edom's pride! It is the humble who shall inherit the Kingdom.

Such a glorious vision of the eternal Kingdom of God! And by what means shall the Lord effect it in these last days? What shall be His mighty instruments of war against the pride of Edom and the conversion of our sinful race?
*Obadiah 21 And **saviors** shall come up on mount Zion to judge the mount of Esau (Edom); and the kingdom shall be the Lord's.*

The saviors are the members of the Church of God. They have an obligation to reach out to one another with a helping hand; they have a responsibility to reach out to the unsaved and also to the back-slidden. Not only is the unseen Hand of God running through the earth today, and not only is the holy spirit moving, but God is also working through human agency. They are Christian Workers, and they are to be very active in the promotion of the *Gospel*. God will not be satisfied with them just attending Babylonious church services every week or singing in the choir, and so forth; they must be reaching out to help others. Our lights must shine!

It is not enough to be saved yourself; it is requisite that your fountain bubble over for the benefit of others.

> *Proverbs 10:11 The mouth of a righteous man is a well of life.*

> *Song of Solomon 4:12,15 A garden enclosed is my sister, my spouse; a spring shut up, a fountain sealed...A fountain of gardens, a well of living waters...*

> *Proverbs 11:30 The fruit of the righteous is a tree of life. And he who wins souls is wise.*

What a wonderful thing it is to spread around the life of Jesus and to win souls.

> *James 5:20 Let him know that he who turns a sinner from the error of his way will save a soul from death and cover a multitude of sins.*

No work which man can perform is more acceptable to God; none will be followed with higher rewards. God approves and loves the Christian Worker's aims and efforts, though the success is ultimately to be traced to God, Himself. The prophets expressed the great importance of God's people being saviors.

> *Jeremiah 23:4 "I will also raise up shepherds over them and they will tend them; and they will not be afraid any longer, nor be terrified, nor will any be missing," declares the Lord.*

> *Daniel 12:3 And they that be wise shall shine as the brightness of the firmament; and they that turn many to righteousness as the stars forever and ever.*

I believe the *Bible* teaches the absolute requirement to reach out to the lost and the sinner. It is, if you please, an obligation and a duty of Christians. By reaching out to others we release ourselves of this divine requirement. The prophet Ezekiel said it like this:

> *Ezekiel 3:21 If you have warned the righteous man that the righteous should not sin, and he does not sin, he shall surely live because he took warning; and you have delivered yourself.*

Jesus and all the apostles instruct us to be teachers, good examples to others.

> *Matthew 5:16 Let your light so shine before men, that they may see your good works, and glorify your Father which is in heaven.*

This means that wherever we are and whatever we're doing, we are to function as children of God. His Light is to shine through us. We are even taught in the *Word* to not grumble and complain demonstrating that we are

> *Philippians 2:14,15 blameless and harmless, children of God without fault in the midst of a crooked and perverse generation, among whom you shine as lights in the world.*

When we are pressed upon, and yet do not murmur nor complain, God's Light shines, and we can be effective saviors.

> *Psalm 51:13 Then I will teach transgressors Your Ways, and sinners shall be converted to You.*

Our evangelism is two-fold: 1) we are to reach out the dying world; and 2) we are to serve our brethren in the church. Thus said Jesus:

> *Luke 22:32 But I have prayed for you, that your faith fail not: and when*

you are converted, strengthen your brethren.

He told Peter (and us) that when we get straightened out in this or that, that we need to turn right around and strengthen others. In all of our activities, in all of our attitudes, we should always be aware we are saviors representing the King.

2 Corinthians 5:20 We are ambassadors for Christ.

Paul gives such marvelous instructions to the ministry. Listen how he taught Timothy how to reach out to others:

1 Timothy 4:14-16 Neglect not the gift that is in you, which was given you by prophecy, with the laying on of the hands of the presbytery. Meditate upon these things; give yourself wholly to them; that your profiting may appear to all. Take heed to yourself, and unto the doctrine; continue in them: for in doing this you shall both save yourself, and them that hear you.

That's right. Those who hear you, and those who observe, will know your godly ways are to be emulated. Although the church's ordained ministers have enormous responsibilities, we are all Christian Workers, good examples.

Notice how Paul adjusted himself to fit into his circumstances. He did not want to appear as a critic. He did not want to appear exalted, proud, or conceited. He wanted quietly and simply to be a savior.

1 Corinthians 9:22 To the weak I became weak, that I might gain the weak: I am made all things to all men, that I might by all means save some.

Serving God will usually not permit you to do your own thing. But, gradually the Christian Worker's heart is directed in such a way that it is bent upon one thing: pleasing the Father. We may need to squelch our opinion or our feelings sometimes and wait for God's moment. We may need to endure hardships in our role as a savior. Paul wrote:

2 Timothy 2:10 I am more than willing to suffer, if that will bring salvation and eternal glory in Christ Jesus to those God has chosen.

1 Corinthians 9:19 I made myself servant unto all, that I might gain the more.

He also instructed the ministry that there are times they will need to demonstrate tough love. They may have to get on someone quite severely, remembering all the while that they may be that person's savior.

*Galatians 6:1 Brethren, if a man is overtaken in any trespass, you who are spiritual **restore** such a one in a spirit of gentleness, considering yourself lest you also be tempted.*

*2 Thessalonians 3:14,15 if any man obey not our word by this epistle, note that man, and have no company with him, that he may be ashamed. Yet count him not as an enemy, but **admonish** him as a brother.*

Of course, we are not God, but only a fellow human being. We are never permitted to "lord" it over someone else. But, sometimes we may in a gentle way need to be quite frank.

Let us say, for example, that a sister in the church has been back-slidden for some years, in particular, sexually. Lately she has been under conviction of the holy spirit, and come back to church. But, the flesh has risen back up. She has decided to quit resisting evil, and return to her wickedness. Be careful here, and be very prayerful. It may be God's Will for you to speak out very boldly right now. This may be her last chance. God has equipped you for this occasion. You are a savior. You won't even have to think very hard what you will say. You are ready to go into action right now.

Proverbs 31:6 Give strong drink unto him that is ready to perish.

The "strong drink" may be a strong message. When the holy spirit is with you, you'll have all the equipment you'll need. Remember, "they that turn many to righteousness will be as the stars forever and ever."

God knows that He has not given us an easy and simple responsibility as saviors. But, I am reminded in the early chapters of *Acts* how the saints where constantly in fellowship with one another, building up one another, encouraging one another, confirming one another. This fellowship is a requirement for Christian Workers.

Malachi 3:16 Then they that feared the Lord spoke often one to another.

Acts 4:31 And when they had prayed, the place was shaken where they were assembled together; and they were all filled with the holy ghost, and they spoke the Word of God with boldness.

We are empowered to reach out. We must never have the attitude of Cain:

Genesis 4:9 Am I my brother's keeper?

Not only are we to reach out to strangers and to the brethren of the church, but we have a responsibility to bring salvation to our families. Our holy example may be the thing that will draw our kin to Christ.

Following are instructions toward ungodly or back-slidden spouses:

1 Peter 3:1 Wives, likewise, be submissive to your own husbands, that even if some do not obey the Word, they, without a word, may be won by the conduct of their wives.

*1 Corinthians 7:16 For how do you know, O wife, whether you will **save** your husband? Or how do you know, O husband, whether you will save your wife?*

Saviors shall come out of Mount Zion, the church. You could be a savior to someone in your own family. You could be a savior to your your spouse; to a brother or sister in the church.

Matthew 18:15 If your brother sins against you, go and tell him his fault between you and him alone. If he hears you, you have gained your brother.

I used to think that when I was offended, I needed to go to the offender and tell him, so I could get it off my chest. But, this is contrary to Jesus' doctrine. He refers to these offenses as "oughts."

*Matthew 5:23-25 Therefore if you bring your gift to the altar, and there remember that your brother has **ought** against you, leave your gift there before the altar, and go your way. First be reconciled to your brother, and then come and offer your gift.*

I had always regarded these "oughts" as some great big offenses. But, actually, "oughts" are the same as "naughts," as "zero," "nothing." What do you mean "zero?" Do you know how so-and-so hurt me? That is not a "zero." But, oh yes it is, IF you are in Christ. Offenses are "nothings" when we are Christians, for we've given them to Jesus. "Somethings" become "nothings."

Well then, if they're "nothings," why even bother to "go and tell him his fault?" The answer is that they are "zeros" to us, because we've given them to the Lord, BUT the benefit is to your brother; he needs to deal with this offense; he needs to ask forgiveness; he needs to get this off his record. When we go to our brother with an "ought," we are giving him the chance to clear himself. In this way, we are saviors.

On the other hand, we may need to get our own record cleared. We do not need to be burdened by "oughts."
*Mark 11:25 And when you stand praying, forgive, if you have **ought** against any: that your Father also which is in heaven may forgive you your trespasses.*

It is often the Christian Worker is a savior, not by what he says, but by his good deeds and the holy life he lives.
1 Peter 2:12 Live such good lives among the gentiles that, though they accuse you of doing wrong, they may see your good deeds and glorify God on the day He visits.

We may be accused all day long by the world. But, we bring salvation to them by our righteous behavior. We will often need to stop our tongue from expressing the wrong thing.
Ephesians 4:29 Let no corrupt communication proceed out of your mouth, but that which is good to the use of edifying, that it may minister grace unto the hearers.

That is what saviors do: they minister grace. It also takes a great deal of love, I mean deliberate, purposeful, pre-meditated love, to win others to Christ. When we love, we bring salvation to those who witness it. They become convinced that Jesus Christ, the savior of the world, has indeed come.
John 13:34,35 A new commandment I give to you: That you love one another; as I have loved you, that you also love one another. By this shall all men know that you are my disciples, if you have love one to another.

And, by this shall we be deliverers. By this shall we be saviors. It is nothing less than our duty as disciples of Christ to win or restore others to Jesus.
Isaiah 58:11 You shall be like a watered garden, and like a spring of water, whose waters fail not.

Hebrews 12:22-24 But you are come unto Mount Sion, and unto the city of the living God, the heavenly Jerusalem, and to an innumerable company of angels, to the general assembly and church of the firstborn, which are written in heaven, and to God the Judge of all, and to the spirits of just men made perfect, and to Jesus the mediator of the new covenant, and to the blood of sprinkling, that speaks better things than that of Abel.

Obadiah 17,21 Upon Mount Zion shall be deliverance, and there shall be holiness...And saviors shall come up on Mount Zion to judge the mount of Esau; and the Kingdom shall be the Lord's.

For a long time now Christians have felt they were appropriately serving God by going to Sunday services, giving to charity, and going to the church picnic. We've arrived at the end of the age, and I believe that God is calling on His saints to work in the fields for the up-coming harvest. He is wanting us to be saviors, and, you shall see that the anointing of the spirit is present for the job at hand!

The calf path upon which the Church wanders has no thought other than the saints sitting upon their pews and watching sermonic, Babylonious, theatrical shows.

Chapter 22. Doing the Lord's Work

It is always presented to us that if we, as Christians, can become good enough, we can eventually go to heaven. After all, it is clear to us that immortality is the end-result of walking with Jesus. Paul declared:

> *2 Corinthians 5:4,5 For we who are in this tent groan, being burdened, not because we want to be unclothed, but further clothed, that mortality may be swallowed up by life. Now He who has prepared us for this very thing (i.e. eternal life) is God, who also has given us the spirit as a guarantee* (NKJV).

It is that breath of heaven that enters us by baptism, the earnest, that is, God's pledge, that eternity awaits us.

But, living in this earthly tent of a body, we experience sickness and injuries. It is a mortal body, and, as we age, it becomes more and more a burden to us.

> *Ecclesiastes 12:1 Remember now your Creator in the days of your youth, before the evil days come, and the years draw near when you say, "I have no pleasure in them."*

It is not that we seek being rid of our decrepit bodies, but that we look forward to that glorious day when we obtain a new one,

> *2 Corinthians 5:1 an house not made with hands, eternal in the heavens.*

Paul has stated that God is preparing us for eternal life. God

> *2 Corinthians 5:5 has prepared us for this very thing.*

All who are being designed for eternal life are being prepared for heaven while they are here; the stones of that spiritual house are to be fashioned now. And He Who has fashioned us for eternal life is God. Nothing less than a divine power can make a human soul "partaker of a divine nature;" no hand less than the Hand of God can work us for this thing. A great deal is to be done to prepare our souls for heaven, and that preparation of the heart is from the Lord. Paul told us:

> *Galatians 3:26-29 For you are all sons of God through faith in Christ Jesus. For as many of you as were baptized into Christ <u>have put on Christ</u>. There is neither Jew nor Greek, there is neither slave nor free, there is neither male nor female; for you are all one in Christ Jesus. And if you are Christ's, then you are Abraham's seed, and heirs according to the promise.*

What he said would seem to be an obvious contradiction to reality. After all, people are, in fact, either Jews or gentiles; they are either slaves or free; they are either males or females. But, he was not speaking of us in the natural, but rather, in the spiritual; he was speaking of our soul, our true self, our inner man. God is not so concerned with the "outer man," with its beauties, and uglinesses, its strengths and frailties; but He is most concerned with our inner person. God, you may have noticed, has not saved your body; He has, however, saved your soul. It is therefore, our soul that God has planned for eternal life; and it is to be housed in a new body, one eternal in the heavens.

The tools to accomplish eternal life for us go beyond the shed blood of our savior and his resurrection from the dead, but include his suffering, the Word of God, the fellowship of the saints, and the ministry of the church. Further, His giving us the holy spirit empowers us to obey God and to hear and to perform His Will.

> *Philippians 2:13 For it is God who works in you both to will and to do for **His good pleasure**.*

> *Hebrews 13:21 Working in you what is well pleasing in His Sight, through Jesus Christ,*

> *Romans 8:29 For whom He foreknew, He also predestined to be conformed to the image of His Son, that He might be the firstborn among many brethren.*

Paul declared that, even though we are yet living upon this old earth and inhabiting these earthly bodies, we have

> *Ephesians 4:24 put on the new man which was created according to God, in true righteousness and holiness.*

Although, we still have our old bodies, yet we have a redeemed new man within.

> *Colossians 3:9,10 You have put off the old man with his deeds, and have put on the new man who is renewed in knowledge according to the image of Him who created him.*

God has given great, new power to the "new man" to learn to live like Jesus Christ, our example. All the necessary circumstances and events needed for each one of our individual lives to accomplish this have been planned out by God BEFORE the world even began.

> *Ephesians 1:4,5 God chose us in Him (Christ) **before the foundation of the world**, that we should be holy and without blame before Him in love, having predestined us to adoption as sons by Jesus Christ to Himself,* *according to the good pleasure of His will.*

It is NOT that each of us has been pre-selected to eternal life regardless of what we do in our life-times, but that a Plan has been set in motion to accomplish that end.

> *Ephesians 2:10 We are His workmanship, created in Christ Jesus unto good works, which God has **before ordained** that we should walk in them (KJV).*

> *Ephesians 2:10 For we are His workmanship, created in Christ Jesus for good works, which God **prepared beforehand** that we should walk in them (NKJV).*

It is not that eternal life is our guaranteed destiny, but that eternal life is God's objective for us. Paul has told us that in our journey that there are certain "good works" that He has scheduled for us to accomplish. These "good works" are, therefore, God's immediate objectives for us to achieve, execute, complete, and to fulfill while in this present life.

This involves the idea of a previous, divine determination, an arrangement beforehand for securing a certain result. This previous preparation here referred to was: the Divine Intention. The meaning is that God had pre-determined that we should lead holy lives. It accords, therefore, with the declaration in *Ephesians* 1:4, that He had chosen His people before the foundation of the world that they should be holy. Whether we achieve this or not will be determined by our individual walks with God.

This salvation is far from being our own work, or granted for our own works' sake. We, ourselves, are not only the creatures of God, spirit, soul, and body, but our "new creation" was produced by His Power; and the "new creation" is created in Christ Jesus for good works. He has saved us that we may

> *1 Peter 2:9 proclaim the praises of Him Who called (us) out of darkness into His marvelous light.*

For though we are not saved BY our good works, yet we are saved that we MAY DO good works, to the glory of God and the benefit of man.

The before-ordaining, or rather preparing, refers to the time when God began the new creation in their hearts; for from the first inspiration of God upon us, the soul begins to love holiness; and obedience to the Will of God is the very element in which a holy or regenerated soul lives.

God has marked out for each in His Purposes-beforehand the particular good works, the time, and way, which He sees best. God both makes ready by His Providence the opportunities for the works, AND makes us ready for their performance. Jesus once said:

> *John 15:16 I chose you and appointed you that you should go and bear fruit, and that your fruit should remain.*

Yet, it is not that "good fruit" is guaranteed by merely "being saved," but that by our new divine possession, the holy ghost within, we begin first to be cleansed from our old manner of living.

> *2 Timothy 2:21 If anyone cleanses himself from (dishonorable thoughts and actions), he will be a vessel for honor, sanctified and useful for the Master, prepared for every good work.*

This inner cleansing begins to make us fit to do good work. It appears that all is of grace, because all our spiritual advantages are from God. We are His workmanship in respect to the new creation, not only as human beings, but as saints. The new man is a new creature; and God is its new Creator. It is a new beginning, and we are begotten of His Will, in Christ Jesus, that is, on the account of what He has done and suffered, and by the influence and operation of his holy spirit, to do good works.

Paul, having previously attributed this change to divine grace in exclusion of works, lest he should seem thereby to discourage good works, he here observed that though the change is to be ascribed to nothing of that nature (for we are the workmanship of God), yet God, in his new creation, has designed and prepared us FOR good works. We are created to do good works, with a design that we should be fruitful in them. Wherever God by his grace implants good principles, they are intended to be for good works. God has before-ordained, that is, decreed and appointed and prepared us, that is, by blessing us with the knowledge of His Will, and with the assistance of his holy spirit, and by producing such a change in us, that we should walk in them, or glorify God by an exemplary behavior, by our works, and by our perseverance in holiness.

As we stated at the beginning of this chapter, the notion has been fostered that, if we get good enough, we get to go to heaven. But, that is not what all the scriptures quoted above are saying. We have zeroed in on passages that declare God's Intention that there are things, "works," for us to do while we are yet here. It is to a large extent, therefore, that the accomplishment of these "works" will determine our eternal destiny.

Here is the question: Do I suppose that, if I get saved, that I shall automatically enter eternity?

Or better yet: Do I suppose that, if I quit doing the nasty things I once did, that I shall have eternal life?

Or, more specifically: Do I suppose that, if I don't smoke, don't chew, don't cuss, don't lie, don't commit adultery, and go to church, pay my tithes, sing in the choir, and listen to a lot of sermons that I shall go to heaven?

My answer to these questions has probably been, "Yes. What more could the Almighty expect of me?"

Just as I was feeling smugly secure, I see a seasoned veteran, no less than the apostle Paul very late in his walk with Jesus, exclaiming:
> *Philippians 3:12,13 Not as though I had already attained, either were already perfect: but I follow after, if that I may apprehend that for which also I am apprehended of Christ Jesus. Brethren, I count not myself to have apprehended.*

What? At this late date, he'd not fully grasped that which had been God's Plan for him? Was it only his personal resurrection from the dead that yet lacked? Or were there yet unattained missions or life-changes he still needed to fulfill? Or were there not-yet-experienced deaths he still must experience.

This is a distinct assertion of the apostle Paul that he did not regard himself as a perfect man. Had he not reached that state where he was free from sin? It is not indeed a declaration that no one was perfect, or that no one could be in this life, but it is a declaration that he did not regard himself as having attained to it. Yet, who can urge better claims to having attained perfection than Paul could have done? Who has surpassed him in love, and zeal, and self-denial, and true devotedness to the service of the Redeemer? Who has more elevated views of God, and of the plan of salvation? Who prays more, or lives nearer to God than he did? That must be an extraordinary piety which surpasses that of the apostle Paul. One who lays claim to a degree of holiness which even Paul did not pretend to, must surely NOT have it.

Was the apostle claiming that all that he yet lacked in his personal race was the Olympic victory wreath, which, in his case, symbolically represented eternal life? Or was he acknowledging that there were yet chores, perhaps even not yet known to him, that he was still to accomplish?

I think Paul knew that the end of his race was approaching, yet it had been foretold of more suffering yet to unfold. The last we know of him is:
> *Acts 28:30,31 And Paul dwelt two whole years in his own hired house (in Rome), and received all that came in to him, preaching the kingdom of God, and teaching those things which concern the Lord Jesus Christ.*

Both history and the *scriptures* tell us no more. One thing we must observe, however, is that Paul displays no anxiety that he might be leaving something yet undone. He was utterly confident that his heart was open to what might be his next duty for his Lord.
> *Philippians 3:14-16 I press on toward the goal for the prize of the upward call of God in Christ Jesus. Let us therefore, as many as are perfect (mature), have this attitude; and if in anything you have a different attitude, God will reveal that also to you. (And what we have already attained, let us be faithful to it.)*

Paul was even confident that so much as an out-of-place-attitude would God reveal to him in due time. Thus he encourages us

Philippians 1:6 being confident of this, that He Who began a good work in you will carry it on to completion until the day of Christ Jesus.

We, also, have this supreme certainty that when all of our focus is on pleasing our Jesus and our fulfilling the ordained work He has planned for us, we will.

But, this I fear for myself and for the many: that I might be lulled into a sense of complacency, that I have already done my all, and am entitled to sit back and watch the show play on before me, that I've already got it locked up, that I've already attained, accomplished, apprehended that which Jesus has intended for me.

But, Paul kept pressing on, did he not? And so near the end! Oh, Lord, what labor have you yet ordained for me to perform? What is my Master's Will for today? Oh, Lord, let me not sit in my pew and blithely hear the choir sing on, the preacher drone on, and me think I've already done my all! Let me not drop the ball so close to the goal! Let me not ease up the race I'm running!

Ephesians 2:10 For we are His workmanship, created in Christ Jesus for good works, which God prepared beforehand that we should walk in them.

The Lord's good pleasure for us includes doing the "good works" for which we have been grabbed by the Lord out of our "old life" to do in His Kingdom. How remiss I would be to think that there is not a thing for me to do but be faithful in attending church services! I suspect most Christians fall in that category.

But, the truth is that we are the hand-made product of God's good work in our lives; we have received Jesus into our beings and become new creatures. The Master has prepared in advance "good works" for us to do. As a matter of fact, he prepared them for us before we were born, even before the world existed.

I do not want to rest on my laurels; I want to keep on doing the good works that I have been contracted and obligated to do; it is important for my eternal salvation that I find out what I'm to do, and then to do it.

Jesus said:
Matthew 20:16; 22:14 Many are called, but few are chosen.

Why do "few" make it? Some become entangled with the affairs of this present world; some have not the heart to make a total commitment to Jesus; some succumb to opposition. But, I suppose there are many who do not complete or even know the labors for which they have been predestined.

Ephesians 2:10 For we are God's masterpiece. He has created us anew in Christ Jesus, so that we can do the good things He planned for us long ago (NLT).

Let us suppose that you have hired me to work for your company. You tell me what my wages are to be and how I am to get started and how I am to be instructed and informed for the future tasks I am to perform. At pay-day I come to collect my salary, although I have not done my assignments. You may inquire why I had not done the job. I will tell you I didn't know what more you wanted me to do. You may then inquire that since I had not tried to find out what my duties were, just what had I been doing? I will tell you that I stayed out of everybody else's way, that I behaved myself, that all the other workers liked me a lot, and that I often lent a helping hand.

But, the fact remains: I didn't do that for which I had been hired. Are you about to pay me?

Most Christians never think to ask God what He would have them to do. We just go to Babylonish church services. Have you ever noticed that in most churches there is that handful which does all the work, and the rest just go to church? You might think that the really busy members are faithfully doing the Lord's intended work. And you might be amazed they've never gotten any divine direction; they're just busy being busy; they're NOT doing what God had planned for them.

And, what about the rest? Well, they just go to church. They're also missing out on what God has for them to do. That is why

Matthew 22:14 many be called, but few chosen.

So many are deceived thinking that going to church, giving in the offering, and helping in the church kitchen is their calling. But, have they fulfilled all the "good pleasure" of the Master? We need to ask that question of ourselves often. Have I done what I'm supposed to have done? Have I tried to hear that "still, small voice" secretly and privately giving me my orders? Have I asked my minister to help me to know my special works? Have I prayed and asked the Lord: "Lord, how may I bring glory to You today?"

2 Thessalonians 1:11-12 Therefore we also pray always for you that our God would count you worthy of this calling, and FULFILL all the good pleasure of His Goodness and the WORK of faith with power, that the Name of our Lord Jesus Christ may be glorified in you, and you in Him, according to the grace of our God and the Lord Jesus Christ.

***

Yet more, in addition to works, God has placed in each one certain gifts:

Romans 12:1-3,6-8 God has allotted to each a measure of faith...We have differing gifts according to the grace given to us: ...prophesying,... serving,... teaching,... exhorting,... organizing,... giving,... showing mercy.

Why do most Christians never even discover their gift? Firstly, having not made themselves a sufficient "living sacrifice" (v1), they are unable to detect God's good, acceptable, and perfect will (v2). In other words, too-much-flesh hides our gift from ourselves. Secondly, our shepherd has not helped us to identify our gift. I think this is one of the greatest weaknesses of the modern church: the saints hear lots of preaching, but there is never enough close personal contact between a shepherd and his sheep for him to get a handle on their problems OR their gifts. Spiritual maladies go undetected and therefore undealt with; graces are wasted; the Church is impoverished. Mines go un-quarried; rich ore never un-earthed.

If we do not discover what God's graces are for us in this life, do we reckon that we will do differently in eternity? (Many are called; few are chosen.)

"It is God Himself who has made us what we are and given us new lives from Christ Jesus; and long ages ago He planned that we should spend these lives" (*TLB*) doing the projects He has laid out for us to do.

***

If it is correct that the <u>manner</u> of the early church will be exhibited again in the last days of this age, it would seem to me there is precious little time left to accomplish it. If God's Light was revealed to the Jewish people before His wrath fell upon them, will it not be the same grace for the gentiles before the judgment of the last day befalls them?

If it is not correct that power of the early church will be exhibited again in the last days, oughtn't it be a worthy bench-mark by which we measure ourselves? Ought not there be, at least, some standard, some goal for which we might aim?

If we are close to being right about the nearness of the time of the end, there is but a short season to get the church restored to the glorious order it once enjoyed. This makes sense to me that we cannot continue to do and teach and believe and behave as we have traditionally done; there's not time to continue to trod the same old, erroneous calf path. While it is still light, good men ought to be fervently seeking the Almighty for new insight. They must bravely give it out, not being at all concerned for the consequences. Of course, they will be opposed, but there will be enough who will hear the clear sound from Heaven and act on it.

Although it often seems that the world and everything in it is going to hell, I am staunch in the fact that God will have His Way, that His Will be done, and that He will accomplish exactly what was His
>   Acts 2:23 *determinate counsel and foreknowledge.*

have planned.

>   Acts 15:18 *Known to God from eternity are all His Work.*

That, however, does not let us off the hook. Those who are devoted must still pray, fast, and study the *Word*. All the way out of Babylon, they will see the glorious conclusion of the Day.

But, there is much that we do not know all about what *Elohim* wants us to know. It is proffered that we emulate the Church as she was in her early days, that we might see the awesome divine manifestations that she experienced. But, the truth is, bulk of what we know about those days comes to us from Paul's epistles, which mostly dealt with problems in the local assemblies that needed to be corrected. Thus, we know somewhat about those things. For example, we might not know that they spoke in tongues had not there been a problem with that in Corinth.

But, what of the things that did not to be corrected? What about the things they were doing right? We do not know! How many people were there to one shepherd? How many shepherds were there in a local church? How did they relate to one another? How did evangelists, prophets, teachers, and apostles relate to the shepherds? What was their place in the local assembly? Were they universally recognized for their gift outside their city by all other assemblies? Where did the assemblies meet? What were their meetings like? Were they entirely spiritual?

How will we discover the answers? I say, they will only be revealed to us by concerted prayer and fasting. Let us not be content to keep circling the same mountain! Lets quit trodding the same old calf-path. "Pray" and "fast." That is the message of the hour. Amen.

<><><>

Made in the USA
San Bernardino, CA
03 June 2014